Baseball
IN PENSACOLA

AMERICA'S PASTIME & THE CITY OF FIVE FLAGS

SCOTT BROWN

Charleston · London

THE
History
PRESS

Published by The History Press
Charleston, SC 29403
www.historypress.net

Copyright © 2013 by Scott Brown
All rights reserved

Front cover, top: Pensacola Fliers. *Courtesy of Pensacola Historical Society*.
Back cover, top right: Didi Gregorious. *Courtesy of Pensacola Blue Wahoos*.

First published 2013

Manufactured in the United States

ISBN 978.1.60949.782.8

Library of Congress CIP data applied for.

For the people of Pensacola who have always loved the game, and to those that have held baseball dear to their hearts, even when bats fell silent.

In special memory of Wally Dashiell, Ted Williams and Fred Waters. We still hear your voices.

CONTENTS

Acknowledgements   7
Introduction   9

1. The Nineteenth-Century Era: 1869–1900   13
2. The Dead-Ball Era: 1901–1919   22
3. The Live-Ball Era: 1920–1941   39
4. The Integration Era: 1942–1960   67
5. The Expansion Era: 1961–1976   120
6. The Free Agency Era: 1977–1993   152
7. The Long-Ball Era: 1994–Forward   196

Index   249
About the Author   256

ACKNOWLEDGEMENTS

E ach name and organization mentioned represents valued support, resources, encouragement and inspiration enlisted during the research and writing of *Baseball in Pensacola*. Without any one of them, the completion of this work may have never been realized. My gratitude goes beyond words, and my hope is that together we have brought honor to the diamond heroes of the past and secured an enduring legacy for the future.

Many organizations supplied assistance for this project through archival materials, personnel and use of facilities, including Ames, Iowa Historical Society, Heroes of the Diamond, Blue Angel Recreation Park (Bronson Field), Cincinnati Reds, Gulf Islands National Seashore, Garth's Antiques, National Baseball Hall of Fame, Pensacola Naval Air Station MWR, Pensacola Pelicans (Amarillo Sox), Pensacola Bay Brewery, Pensacola Blue Wahoos, Pensacola Sports Association, Pensacola Historical Society, Pensacola State College, Seattle Mariners, Toronto Blue Jays, University of West Florida, USS *Abraham Lincoln* and WSRE.

Special mention must be made of the numerous individuals and families who have shared their comments, experiences and memories to help weave together the story of baseball in the City of Five Flags. These are Terry Allvord, John Appleyard, Bruce Baldwin, Bill Bavasi, Mrs. Pit Bell, Bob Bishop (deceased), Bill Bond, Earle Bowden, Bernie Carbo, Rusty Bizzell, Mrs. Tom Cheek, Ed and Gloria Coleman, Diane Crona, Mark Downey, Jeff English, Brooke Fleming, Hal Gordon, Brodie Greene, Bill Hamilton, Frank Hardy Jr., Leila Hattaway, Phil Hiatt, David Ivey, Mike Jacobs, Ryan

LaMarre, Dennis and Kathy Lewallyn, Jason Libbert, Steve Lipe, Keith Little, Greg Litton, Mike McCormick, John Mugarian, Wes Mugarian, Tim Mulroy, Peter Ezra Murphy, Talmadge Nunnari, Joe Panaccione, P.J. Phillips, Hosken Powell, Jack Reed, Warren Reilly, Dalton Renfroe, Terry Reynolds, Jim Riggleman, Billy Sadler, Brad Salmon, Jack Sanchez, Kevin Saucier, Russ Scarritt III, Tim Spooneybarger, Buck Showalter, Dan Shugart, Chip Simmons, Dottie Sims, Mike Veeck, Jerry Waldrop and Ken Wright.

Additionally, there were those who made access to information and interviews as easy as a Billy Hamilton stolen base. I am grateful for support from Richard Brosnaham, Jay Clune, Wendy Davis, Andrew Demsky, Jonathan Griffith, Bill Harrell, Ted King, Mike Rowan, Tim Schnoor, Ray Sayre, Mike Sidebottom, Quint Studer, Jackie Wilson and Harry White.

And then there is my bullpen. They have cheered me on with every pitch and were always ready to come in for a few innings in relief. My deepest gratitude is for Dawn, Zac, Katie and Aaron, along with Tony Ferguson, Jill Hubbs (St. Jill), Sean LaGasse, Dave Stafford, Cindy Thomson and Chris Woods.

INTRODUCTION

On July 12, 2012, thousands of local residents and out-of-town visitors converged on Pensacola Beach to celebrate the annual Blue Angels Air Show. The U.S. Navy's Pensacola-based flight demonstration squadron draws spectators each year for a frolic on the beach and an aeronautic introduction into the history of the City of Five Flags. While the oldest American aerobatic team was the focal point of the mid-July weekend, Pensacola's visitors were treated to other activities that reflected the city's historic past.

Walking tours featuring the homes and haunts of Pensacola's Historic District ushered weekend vacationers past the unmarked memorials of baseball's earliest imprint on Northwest Florida. Taphophiles making a pilgrimage to St. Michael's Cemetery observed the headstone of one Thomas Lewis Gittinger. Few viewing the grave of the former city employee knew that Tom played twenty seasons professionally and spelled his name "Gettinger" during his days as a ballplayer. Gittinger has the distinction of being one of Pensacola's first Major League players.

Other headstone hunters browsed the rows of silent citizens inside St. Johns Cemetery, unaware that a legendary ball diamond once stood just a block away. The site of old Maxent Park, later called Legion Field, harkens memories of Major League spring training games, Negro League exhibitions and revered Minor League players. Fans once shouted the names of Babe Ruth, Lou Gehrig, Bill Terry and Jackie Robinson from the wooden stands of the venerable stadium. If one listens closely enough

A rolling billboard for tourism in Pensacola, the Fliers' travel bus beckoned both would-be vacationers and visiting challengers to the City of Five Flags. *Courtesy of Pensacola Historical Society.*

in the fading light of a summer day, the crack of big "Hack" Wilson's bat may still be heard.

Those taking the opportunity to see the "Wall South" Vietnam Memorial probably don't picture Admiral Mason Ballpark looming above where they stand. Cal Ripken Sr., Bo Belinsky and Fred Waters ran the base paths just yards from where Pensacola's weekend guests now peer into the pond at the Veterans Memorial.

On that July afternoon in 2012, just around the shoreline from the memorial, a group of people gathered in Historic Pensacola Village. Those individuals were not in town to see the Blue Angels even though they were focused on the significance of the city. The Buck O'Neil Chapter of the Society for American Baseball Research (SABR) came together to commemorate over 140 years of baseball as a unifying element in Pensacola. They purposely congregated inside the Pensacola Bay Brewery because it sits a few feet away from Seville Square, where the city's first baseball diamond was plotted.

Inside the brewery, chapter members listened to reports by local historians concerning teams such as the Seminoles, Bay City, Hope, Dudes and an all-female team that played as early as 1867. Joining the assembly was World Series pitcher Kevin Saucier, who shared his experiences of growing up in

Pensacola's youth leagues and memories of playing for the Philadelphia Phillies and the Detroit Tigers. SABR members and brewery patrons alike hung on every word describing Pensacola's baseball legacy.

Beginning with the 2012 season, baseball rekindled the sporting passion of the Pensacola citizenry. A brand-new stadium was constructed on the waterfront and a new Double-A affiliated team had taken up residence at the park. Baseball was on the tip of most everyone's tongues in Pensacola. Not since the 1962 Pensacola Senators had a professional team with a Major League benefactor called the city its home. Now the Pensacola Blue Wahoos were headline news and dinner table conversation.

The Wahoos' parent club, the Cincinnati Reds, understood the significance of having a presence in a town with a deep history of the game, not unlike their Ohio city. A four-year affiliate extension between Pensacola and Cincinnati came one month later in August, further validating the City of Five Flags as a professional baseball community.

Pensacola has been known for its sugar-white beaches, moderate temperatures, exceptional seafood and hospitable residents. As a town that has historically birthed Major League-level players, Pensacola was the perfect setting for a Reds Minor League club. Terry Reynolds, Cincinnati's senior director of professional and global scouting, made his appraisal when he said:

> From ownership to the unparalleled setting of the stadium to the playing surface and the clubhouse, Pensacola has hit a home run. Very seldom do all these aspects come together in a way that is fan and player friendly, and this facility does that and more. The Reds are excited to be partnered with the Blue Wahoos. We believe this partnership is a win-win for the Reds and Pensacola. We have felt like we are a part of the family since the day of our first meeting and could not be more thrilled with our affiliation in Pensacola!

During the Wahoos' first season, Pensacola fans saw members of their team move up to Triple-A and even to the Reds Major League roster. Shortstop Billy Hamilton broke the all-time Minor League stolen base record. Sell-out crowds packed the stands at Bayfront Stadium. Fan attendance reached 300,000 before the end of the season. Pitcher Daniel Corcino combined with reliever Wilkin De La Rosa for a 6–0 no-hitter against rival Mobile, Alabama. And the Wahoos' home field was named "Ballpark of the Year 2012" in a contest that pitted Major and Minor League stadiums in an annual best-of-the-best selection.

Self-proclaimed "Wahooligans" cheered on every player by name, knew their stats and hometowns and wore Pensacola "Fish" t-shirts with pride. But like the out-of-town beach guests, many were unaware of the foundation that their award-winning stadium had been built upon. The Wahoos were not the first team to be aligned with a Major League franchise in Pensacola. Before the Reds, there was the Brooklyn Dodgers, Philadelphia Phillies, Chicago White Sox, Baltimore Orioles and Washington Senators. Pensacola-area high schools helped develop the early careers of Don Sutton, Travis Fryman, Jay Bell and Mark Whiten, among others.

On any given game night at the Wahoos' Bayfront Stadium, few of the new fans could have named the Pensacola teams that are now mere shadows of an age gone by. Minor League teams with names like the Fliers and Dons, Negro League clubs identifying themselves as the Giants, Seagulls and Pepsi-Cola Stars and even an independent franchise commissioned as the Pelicans pounded their way along the base paths and annals of Pensacola's baseball history.

Despite any individual's knowledge of past diamond heroes, the people of Pensacola have held fast to the game of baseball as they have since the end of the Civil War. For almost a century and a half, Pensacola has hospitably extended this offer: "Come play!"

CHAPTER 1

THE NINETEENTH-CENTURY ERA: 1869–1900

PENSACOLA'S SEVILLE SQUARE SPORTS A DIAMOND

Pensacola, Florida, originally settled as Santa María de Ochuse in 1559 by Spanish explorer Don Tristan de Luna de y Arellano, has been adorned with multiple nicknames during the course of the city's over-450-year history. "America's First Settlement," "City of Five Flags," "Florida's First Place City," "The Cradle of Naval Aviation," "Western Gate to the Sunshine State," "The Port City" and "Red Snapper Capital of the World" are a few of the more commonly used monikers. And according to the old sign leading to Pensacola Beach, the fifty-two miles of sugar white sand are the "World's Most Beautiful Beaches," a fact made known to all who encountered former Pensacola resident and Toronto Blue Jays announcer Tom Cheek.

Regardless of the name by which one would know this Florida Emerald Coast beach community, Pensacola has for decades been a destination for those seeking a warm-weather haven and a temperate playground. Native Americans historically wintered and lived near the fish-filled waters surrounding Pensacola and brought with them their own style of athletic competition and ballgames. The local Panzacola Indians, as they were referred to by the Spanish, were well familiar with the "ball play" engaged in by most Southeastern tribes, as recorded by anthropologist James Mooney.

Beyond Native Americans and Spanish settlers, the region has also played host to French conquerors and British soldiers. General Andrew Jackson accepted U.S. ownership of Florida from the Spanish in the central plaza of Pensacola in 1819, and during America's Civil War, both the Union and Confederate forces occupied the city's four bayside fortresses.

Baseball became a psychological diversion and team builder among northern and southern forces throughout the theaters of battle during the War Between the States. Both Union and Confederate officers endorsed the game, seeing it as a morale builder and physical conditioning exercise. Private Alpheris Parker of the Tenth Massachusetts Regiment described his experience with the game with these words: "The parade ground has been a busy place for a week or so past, ball-playing having become a mania in camp. Officer and men forget, for a time, the differences of rank and indulge in the invigorating sport with a schoolboy's ardor."

During the aftermath of the Civil War, Pensacola residents, along with the rest of those living throughout the southeastern United States, began to rebuild their lives. Although Pensacola's homes and businesses had not fallen as a casualty of battle, unlike those in Atlanta and Savannah, community morale and normality had been most certainly wounded. New merchants, the timber shipping industry and a population boom all helped Pensacola's economy and overall well-being. Leisure time activities and sporting events were on the rise as well, with one in particular that would unify cities, regions and eventually a nation. That sport was baseball.

Prior to the outbreak of the War Between the States, an early form of baseball had already taken hold in pockets along the Atlantic Seaboard, throughout the Midwest and even in corners of the Deep South. But the look and feel of the game was markedly different from the shape of what was to come. Americans now playing "base-ball" were molding and shaping the game to fit their new way of life, transitioning the sport further and further from its English influences of town ball and rounders.

Formerly accepted rules of the game fluctuated to meet the changing times. Foul balls were not initially counted as strikes, and reaching the first bag on a base on balls rule varied from three balls to nine before settling on today's rule of four. The distance to the plate from the pitcher moved from forty-five feet to fifty feet to sixty feet and six inches, while batters originally had the ability to call their own pitches. Home plate initially took the shape of an actual diamond, and 90 percent of pitchers starting a game finished it.

As baseball became more centralized in the larger towns east of the Mississippi, organized leagues were formed and participants began to take their involvement more seriously. In 1869, Cincinnati, Ohio, became the first city to pay an entire squad of players to perform their duties on the diamond, thus establishing the first professional baseball club. Even as professional leagues, such as the Union Association and Players League, set the tone for organization on a regional scale, city leagues sprouted throughout the country, offering anyone wishing to test their skills on the field an opportunity to engage in the popularly growing sport.

Pensacola boasts a long and rich history of the game, even preceding the introduction of the first professional team in Cincinnati. Almost a century and a half after Cincinnati's employed ballplayers took to the field of play, Ohio and Pensacola would be drawn together through the game itself. And when the citizens of Pensacola formed their own relationship with the game, a love affair between the City of Five Flags and baseball began that would last well past the next one hundred years.

John Muller sits front right as a member of the Pensacola Hope, one of the earliest organized clubs in the City of Five Flags. The 1881 Hope team donned a fitting nickname for the future of baseball in a community that had already made the game its sport of choice. *Courtesy of Warren Reilly.*

Henry Chadwick's *Ball Players' Chronicle* reported on July 25, 1867, that the "base-ball disease has attacked the women, the young ladies of Pensacola, Florida, having organized a base-ball club." One of the rules of the girls' league, according to Chadwick, was that if a young lady became entangled in the steel wire of her hoop skirt while running the bases, she was immediately expelled from the league. The date of this report suggests that this was one of the earliest organized teams in Pensacola—and certainly one of the strictest.

An article from the July 4, 1868 edition of the *Pensacola Tri-Weekly Observer* covered a matchup between the Seminole and Bay City baseball clubs in a game that took place on Pensacola's Seville Square. A Pensacola team carrying the club name Mallorys formed during the early 1880s, and the Hope team was an established city squad by 1881.

The March 3, 1886 edition of *Sporting Life* magazine stated that the Pensacola Baseball Park Association had organized cash capital in the amount of $1,100, earmarked for the construction of a centralized ball field in the city. The proposed field was to be located on a plot of land near the residential portion of the town and was to be built by a locally contracted fencing company with an accompanying grandstand. The reporter referenced that the officers of the park association proclaimed that they, with the new field, would be "putting as good a team on the diamond as any Southern city."

THE SPEED OF SUNDAY

Whether or not the Pensacola Baseball Park Association had the original intent of promoting baseball beyond the local or regional level is not known. However, by 1888, the busy fishing port and its newly constructed showcase diamond drew the attention of national baseball organizations. In an April editorial of *Sporting Life*, Pensacola winter resident and Chicago baseball reporter Harry Palmer noted "Pensacola's unequaled advantages as a place for spring training."

Palmer, in his editorial, beckoned to Major League clubs in Chicago, New York and Detroit to take note of Pensacola's good weather, fine soil, welcoming residents, proximity to other training locations, ample local resources and other activities for players. Palmer even suggested to sporting goods magnate, publisher and baseball promoter Albert Spalding that if he would but view the area it would be "dollars to cents" that he would play his all-star traveling teams here.

Billy Sunday, best known for his wild and energetic style behind the pulpit, also demonstrated the same charisma on the diamond before a career shift into evangelical ministry. Sunday was a formidable adversary on the base paths and in the outfield when he joined the Pittsburgh Alleghenys in their 1890 spring training exercises in Pensacola. *Courtesy of Ames, Iowa, Historical Society.*

While Spalding did not follow Harry Palmer's advice, the Pittsburgh National League club did. Negotiations between the City of Pensacola and the Alleghenys (later Pirates) to utilize the Florida city as the base for their spring exercises began in mid-1889. By the time the preseason operations started in earnest, the Alleghenys were in town, thus opening the door for Pensacola to become a warm-weather proving ground for young players and seasoned veterans looking to get back in shape. Pensacola offered the Pittsburgh club southern hospitality, along with many amenities. The Alleghenys provided Pensacolans top-level baseball entertainment, which featured a speedy base runner and outfielder by the name of Billy Sunday.

Sunday played eight seasons as an outfielder for the Chicago, Pittsburgh and Philadelphia National League clubs. He broke into the majors under the tutelage of Chicago's legendary player/manager Adrian "Cap" Anson and quickly gained a reputation as a threat on the base paths. With the Alleghenys, Sunday became one of the league leaders in stolen bases. Billy Sunday retired from professional baseball with a .248 batting average and enjoyed a second successful career as a nationally known fire and brimstone evangelist.

DUDES, GIANTS AND PETS

"Baseball is all the rage here now," reads a dispatch from Pensacola to the *Spirit of the South* newspaper. While regionally and nationally ranked teams were finding their way to the Gulf Coast, Pensacola offered its own organized ball clubs as worthy opponents. The City of Five Flags fielded clubs such as the Pastimes, Harwells and Dudes with enough talent to put forth a bid for inclusion in the Southern League circuit. Although the newly formed Southern League opted to include Memphis, due to its location, rather than Pensacola to round out the league in 1890, the Dudes continued to compete regionally with above-average talent.

Beyond local players, the Dudes added journeymen professionals from time to time. On October 12, 1890, over six hundred spectators watched the Pensacola club compete against the Mobile, Alabama team, with catcher Jake Wells of the St. Louis Browns on the Dudes' roster. Relationships and teamwork generated by the Dudes helped form legacies that would influence Pensacola for generations to come. John Merritt, founding member of the Pensacola Area Chamber of Commerce and Rotary Club

The Pensacola Dudes prided themselves in their appearance on and off the field but took their activity in the game quite serious. Journeymen players with professional backgrounds found the Dudes organization a comfortable place to lend their skills. *Front row, left to right*: J.S. McGaughey, Joe LeBaron. *Middle row, left to right*: Knowles Hyer, John Merritt and John Maxwell. *Back row, left to right*: Charlie Turner, Charlie Simpson, Jim Blount, J.S. Reese, Bob Hyer and Chipley Jones. *Courtesy of Pensacola Historical Society*.

of Pensacola and shareholder in numerous Pensacola businesses and enterprises, played for the Dudes baseball club in the 1890s.

Merritt later spoke with fondness about his days playing for the Dudes:

> *As to sports, I have always been more or less a baseball fan. I played myself, up to the year I was married. I played second base on the Dudes team, which considered themselves the socialites of Pensacola at the time. Simpson Reese, Knowles Hyer, Bob Hyer, and various others were on the team, while Charlie Turner was the typical "Dude," and when we had our picture taken, Charlie was on the front row in a silk hat and striped trousers and all the rest of the regalia to prove we deserved our name.*

Kupfrian's Park, located east of modern-day North Pace Boulevard on the site now occupied by Pensacola Retirement Village, offered several recreational activities and diversions for citizens in the late nineteenth century. The park featured a beautiful pond, picnic area, horse racing track and a fairground. Along with the formation of several fully outfitted African American baseball clubs, Mayor William D. Chipley's family provided for the construction of a suitable baseball field with a five-hundred-seat grandstand on the park property.

With an article titled "Two Crack Afro-American Base Ball Teams," the *Freeman Illustrated Colored Newspaper* delivered a glowing report on the most illustrious teams using Kupfrian's Park in August 1890. It was noted that each team was neatly uniformed, splendid in appearance and possessing all the necessary equipment to be used during a game. "Pensacola colored people are justly proud of their several base-ball clubs. Prominent among them are the Onwards and the Giants," exclaimed the *Freeman*.

The Onwards were managed by John Boyle, a locally celebrated chef. Onwards pitcher and vice-president P. Barrios was said to have been comparable in his duties on the mound "with any white pitcher in the game." With ushers seating fans at Kupfrian's, "good order was maintained, and a gratifying result in the permanency of the fact that the whole affair is controlled entirely by colored gentlemen," continued the *Freeman's* reporter.

While on a training jaunt through the Gulf Coast during the first month of 1892, John McGraw and a small reserve squad from the Baltimore Orioles came into town to take in a little winter practice. Under the managerial direction of Mobile resident "Honest John" Kelly, the Baltimore team worked out with the Pensacola city club. Kelly managed the Acid Iron Earth club of the Gulf Baseball League, and McGraw, after an illustrious career as a player, would become one of Major League Baseball's most legendary managers.

John "Little Napoleon" McGraw spent sixteen seasons as a player with the Baltimore Orioles, St. Louis Cardinals and New York Giants. After his playing career, McGraw managed the New York Giants for thirty-one years, taking them to ten National League pennants and three World Series championships. John McGraw was elected to the National Baseball Hall of Fame in 1937. Pensacola's effort against the 1892 Orioles was dismal, losing to Baltimore 47–0 in the first contest.

The Class-B Southern League circuit replaced the Birmingham Grays with the Pensacola Pets in its twelve-team lineup in 1893. The league and Pets manager Jake Wells had great hopes for Pensacola's first fully paid professional team. Although Pensacola finished 34 and 58—in eleventh place—the city's passion for the game was not dampened. Pensacola craved more.

In a September 9, 1893 article titled, "Want More in '94," the *Sporting Life* magazine wrote:

> *Jake Wells had a good team at Pensacola, Fla this year and drew well. There was not a Southern League club that tackled the Florida team this year that did not leave at least one scalp. Pensacola's hunger for good ball is not appeased, and the city wants a berth in the organization of '94. If that is not possible, an independent club will again be organized, and the teams of the South will be booked coming and going.*

Jake Wells, who had played professionally in Detroit and St. Louis, went on to manage in Mobile, Atlanta and Richmond, Virginia, all the while keeping a home in Pensacola.

A need for more ball fields became evident by the end of the 1890s as the rising number of local recreational clubs clamored for space. Palmetto Beach, near the present-day Star Lake subdivision in Warrington, presented a very nice venue for a field with a view of the bay. The field was important enough to appear on an 1896 merchant map of the city, just on the outskirts of town. Palmetto Park would later become the home of Pensacola's Cotton States League team.

CHAPTER 2

THE DEAD-BALL ERA: 1901–1919

PENSACOLA BASEBALL COMES OF AGE

During the early years of the 1900s, the Wright Brothers powered and sustained heavier-than-air human flight for the first time in history. The flight was to have a dramatic effect on the development and growth of Pensacola as the future Cradle of Naval Aviation. Henry Ford's Model T was available for the general public, making travel to the whole of Florida readily accessible from the north. Pensacola would see a population boom from 1900 to 1903, with over four thousand new residents. Those residents living near Pensacola's shorelines would be challenged during the back-to-back devastating hurricane seasons of 1906 and 1907.

The period from 1901 to 1919 is traditionally referred to as baseball's Deadball Era, which is derived from the less-than-lively action of the early 1900s baseball when struck by a bat. This is not to say that a hit ball never traveled over the outfield fence, just not as frequently as in later years. This ball was softer in construction, making it harder to drive. A more "active" ball was secretly introduced during the 1910 World Series, and while it was used in the seasons following, the sphere still did not have the "pop" enjoyed by batters of today.

Home runs may not have been the name of the game during the Deadball Era, but strategy certainly was. Playing the positions on the diamond strategically, much as a general would devise a battle plan, became the legacy

As two of the first Pensacola clubs, the Flyers and Orioles teams were closely linked with their counterparts in the City League. Ensuring the continued growth and development of baseball in Pensacola, the Flyers, Orioles, Warringtons and other local teams frequently crossed rivalry lines as players often filled the rosters of their opposing club's short-staffed squads. *Courtesy of Pensacola Historical Society.*

of many baseball heroes of the day. Managers such as John McGraw and Connie Mack, pitchers "Big Six" Mathewson and "Three Finger" Brown and fleet-of-foot base runners like Ty Cobb and "Shoeless Joe" Jackson made the strategy of the game as important as preseason conditioning. And it would be the game's preseason exercises that would forever intertwine several of baseball's legendary figures with the city of Pensacola.

At the end of the 1901 season, a group of professional baseball owners met in Chicago to form the National Association of Professional Baseball Leagues. This organization, later called Minor League Baseball, was instituted to protect the player development interests of the Major League clubs. Prior to the regular season of that year, the American League was officially formed with franchises in Baltimore; Philadelphia; Boston; Washington, D.C.; Cleveland; Detroit; Milwaukee; and Chicago.

In a secret attempt to integrate Major League Baseball, or moreover to acquire good talent for his new American League club, in 1901, John

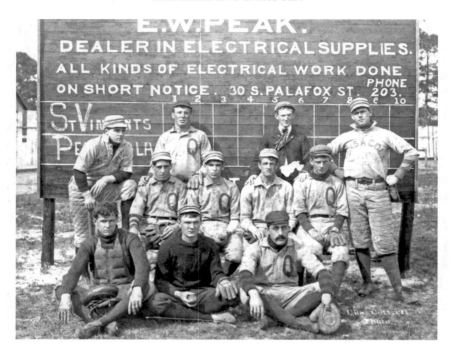

Baseball quickly became a community affair in Pensacola after the birth of the twentieth century. Pensacola entrepreneurs and merchants realized that the draw of the game also meant strategically focused advertising and awareness. Benefiting from the Pensacola Baseball Park Association's desire to see high-level teams play in their town, Pensacola's City League clubs played on three of the best diamonds in the Deep South. *Front row, left to right*: Emmet Touart, Sam Lever and John Oliver. *Middle row, left to right*: Phil Sanchez, Buddie Bricker, Fred Moore and Joe Villar. *Back row, left to right*: Tom Cummings, Tom Harris, Sam Flynn and Willie Wells. *Courtesy of Pensacola Historical Society.*

McGraw tried to pass off African American second baseman Charlie Grant as a Native American named Tokohoma. Although the ruse did not achieve the desired outcome, Negro Leaguer Grant had made a noteworthy attempt at crossing baseball's color line several decades before Jackie Robinson. All of these seemingly unrelated events throughout the world of baseball would have a direct impact on the history of baseball in Pensacola.

City Teams and Military Squads

Pensacola made advancement toward expanding its competitive borders in 1903 by entering a team in the short- lived Southern Interstate League. The league included Mobile, Brewton, Troy, Selma and Montgomery, Alabama. Although the Interstate experiment gave Pensacola fans much to look forward to on a professional level, the established City League and military clubs from Pensacola's Navy Yard did not disappoint either.

The *New York Times* presented an article on April 9, 1905, reporting on the U.S. Navy's heightened involvement with the game of baseball: "Never before in the history of the American Navy has the baseball fever been so prevalent among the crews of the ships from battleship to gunboat as it is at the present time." The story continued by stating that almost every fleet vessel had a team, and it further touted the accomplishments of the sailors-turned-ballplayers competing against their fellow mariners.

During a ship-to-ship pennant race, which included the battleships *Kearsarge, Missouri, Massachusetts, Iowa, Illinois, Kentucky, Alabama* and *Maine*, most of the vessels were positioned off the Pensacola Navy Yard. Over twenty smaller craft had teams involved as well, and all were reported to be using the bulk of their off hours training for competition. Pensacola's stationed sailors, marines and army personnel added their own organized squads to the mix.

Pensacola's military teams bore names reflecting their duty involvement. The Marines, Barrancas, Seventy-seventh Company, Twenty-second Company and others were somewhat better prepared for the navy's organized competition due to regular matchups against Pensacola City League teams. Among Pensacola's locally fielded clubs were the East Ends, Eddys, Rounders, Warringtons and Orioles, all giving the enlisted boys a run for their money. As the men stationed at the navy yard sharpened their fundamental skills playing Pensacola's finest, the town clubs grew stronger by squaring off against the professional Southern Association organizations.

New Orleans, Birmingham, Montgomery, Atlanta and others comprised the lineup for a Class-A Southern Association Minor League circuit. While Pensacola competed in its own league against regional cities, the exhibition games with Southern Association teams gave Pensacola players and fans alike the opportunity to see future Major Leaguers such as Tris Speaker, Jack Ryan and Zack Wheat. Pensacola's 1908 Orioles fielded men of above-amateur level with the fortitude to match professional clubs. Orioles pitcher Earl Gordon competed at such a high level of play that opposing managers continually hounded him to sign on with their bullpens.

The Pensacola Baseball Park Association made certain that the City League, Southern Association and professional clubs using the City of Five Flags as a headquarters for spring training were availed with fields worthy of their skill. Various diamonds dotted the town, but three wooden stadiums offered over-the-top amenities for spectators and athletes. Palmetto Beach Park in Warrington; Maxent Park, located strategically off Gregory and G Streets; and Magnolia Bluff Park, positioned above Pensacola Bay on present-day Scenic Highway, opened the door for a level of baseball that easily rivaled cities double in population to Pensacola.

An early 1900s U.S. Department of State report detailing the resources available in Pensacola described the Magnolia Bluff amusement area as a "beautiful suburban pleasure resort" with picnic grounds, concert accommodations, a dance pavilion, a restaurant and a baseball grandstand seating one thousand people. The government agent collecting information to be included in the state report made mention that the "baseball grounds have also been laid out and votaries of our national game repair here frequently and in large numbers to witness the playing of the home clubs, or as is often the case, a home club pitted against professional talent from abroad."

Transportation to Palmetto Park and Magnolia Bluff was served by Pensacola's standard gauge railroad, called a "Dummy Line." Electricity and

By 1907 and 1908, stalwart Pensacola teams were drawing competition from regional clubs, including those from the Southern League. Pensacola's three premier parks offered pristine fields and top-quality competition. Pensacola had risen in development of venues to attract the highest rung of visiting teams and offered imposing adversaries in their City League teams. *From left to right*: Jack Bergin, Ernie Roach, Dillon Touart, Charles Van Meter, Earl Gordon, William Lurton, Peters, B. Griffin, Jim Laird and Jim Burke. *Courtesy of Hal Gordon.*

steam powered the small engines pulling passenger cars for the convenience of Pensacola's citizenry. A round-trip token from Fort Barrancas, Old Warrington and Woolsey cost thirty-five cents, and trains left Pensacola and Fort Barrancas on the hour, meeting at Palmetto Park. James Nix, a Warrington resident living in the community during the early 1900s, later remembered the wooden outfield fence of Palmetto Park and the adjacent dance hall with refreshment stand that sat just a short distance from Big Bayou (Village) Road.

The Pensacola Orioles utilized Palmetto Beach for their home grounds in 1907 and 1908, defending this position against all comers. In a mid-season battle, an exceptionally large crowd witnessed the Orioles defeat the Union Springs, Alabama team in a 3–1 victory. The local newspaper described the game as "fast and snappy," which is what fans came to expect from their O's. Pitcher Earl Gordon and catcher William Lurton found that one of their best defenses was to speed up the game against an unprepared opponent.

EARL GORDON AND PENSACOLA'S TALENTED ATHLETES

Russiaville, Indiana, native and Pensacola transplant Earl Gordon quickly became a valuable asset to the local city clubs. Gordon, a pitcher by trade, was not only versatile as an off-the-bench infielder but was also doubly willing to assist his team by throwing from the rubber in one game of a double-header and taking the second base position in the next. As if his defensive flexibility were not enough to endear him to the Pensacola baseball culture, Gordon made himself a presence at the plate as well.

The Pensacola newspapers loved Earl Gordon, recounting his daily performances with enthusiasm. Earl's meticulous diaries prove that the accolades did not go to his head but instead kept him focused on his game. They reveal a student of the game, as Gordon listed his achievements, blunders, specifics about opponents, attendance, weather, field condition and a myriad of other details, helping him to plan ahead for his next outing.

As a fixture in Pensacola baseball by 1908, Earl Gordon had been listed on the rosters of several city clubs. Predominantly, however, Gordon worked for the Orioles and at the beginning of the 1908 season had become one of their regular starters. Gordon's notoriety was not limited to his new hometown.

Offers to sign with other organizations became almost commonplace after Shreveport, Louisiana, of the Texas League, made an overture toward the young pitcher to move west.

Gordon began the 1908 season at home and then signed with Chipley, Florida, after Pensacola's City League season closed. In 1909, Earl accepted an offer from Columbus, Georgia, in the South Atlantic League but was released early in the season due to an overage of pitchers. Columbus had utilized Gordon as a second baseman, and upon his return to his old team in Florida, he remained at his post as an infielder. Second base was his position when Pensacola defeated the much stronger Southern Association Nashville Volunteers in a July 28 ten-inning affair that ended in a 3–2 score at Magnolia Bluff Park.

The Bluff's diamond hosted out-of-town teams, as did its crosstown sister fields. In one 1910 preseason exhibition, a barnstorming Bloomer Girls club dropped in for a quick series. Bloomer Girls teams, although taking their name from their all-girl beginnings, were anything but dainty in their challenge. Many females still filled roster positions after the first decade of the new century, but more often than not, budding male sluggers looking to break into professional baseball signed on for extra practice and much-needed pay. Future power hitter Rogers Hornsby received his start with a Bloomer Girls club. Pensacola took on the semipro mixed-gender traveling show and set them down 8–4 in short order. The Bloomer Girls' manager saw a potential add-on for their lineup and offered a contract to Gordon. But not wishing to hoof it around the countryside playing for his supper, Gordon respectfully declined.

BIRTH OF THE FLYERS

On August 2, 1909, the U.S. Army accepted its first airplane from Orville and Wilber Wright. Lieutenant Frederick Humphreys became the first army pilot to solo in the new Wright Military Flyer during October of that same year. Eight days after Humphrey's flight, Lieutenant George Sweet became the first navy officer to ride in the Wright Flyer.

Donning a club nickname that was an apparent nod to the military's newest defense acquisition, the 1909 Pensacola Flyers were one of what were now numerous city teams bringing good athletic entertainment and fueling neighborhood rivalries. The Flyers' team name may have waxed somewhat prophetic, as the relationship between Pensacola, naval aviation and baseball would strengthen and become intertwined during the years to come. The U.S Navy secured an appropriation from Congress in 1911 to create the first permanent Naval Air Station in Pensacola.

The Flyers proved to be a powerful force during the lion's share of their games against other City League teams throughout the 1909 and 1910 seasons. Meridian, Mississippi, and Greenville, Alabama, had evolved into the Flyers' greatest opponents, with Greenville and Pensacola facing each other during the 1910 playoffs, which resulted in a Pensacola upset. Although a final deciding double-header was split between the two clubs, the September 6 *Evening News* proclaimed in front-page fanfare, "Pensacola, Undisputed Champions Of The Season."

Pensacola's premier teams and professional playing fields persisted in drawing the Southern Association clubs through the bayside town. The circuit, also referred to as the Southern League somewhat interchangeably for a time, placed those that Earl Gordon called "the best players in the South" right at the front doorstep of Pensacola's baseball faithful. One Southern Association player who left his mark as a visiting challenger was the Montgomery Rebels' twenty-two-year-old outfielder, Casey Stengel.

Baseball Digest chronicled an incident with Stengel in one of the odder moments surrounding the prankster:

> *Casey Stengel once pulled a ruse in a Southern League game in 1912 while playing with the Montgomery, Alabama, club in a game at Pensacola, Florida. Casey noticed that in left field the groundskeeper had a sunken box containing the water pipe extension for sprinkling the field. In the seventh inning, with his team several runs ahead, Stengel removed the lid and crawled down into the box. However, nobody in the park noticed Montgomery was minus one left fielder while the first two batters were being put out. But when the next hitter stroked a fly to left field, the startled crowd began to howl when they could not see a left fielder. To the surprise of many, Ol' Case popped out of the box and caught the ball for the third out. The question is, did Montgomery have all nine players on the field at the time the Pensacola batter swatted the fly to left field? After all, Casey was under the field and not on it.*

Regardless of the call, Casey Stengel went on to become one of the game's most beloved heroes, playing twenty-three seasons between the Minor and Major Leagues. Stengel is most remembered and revered for his twenty-five years as manger with the Brooklyn Dodgers, Boston Braves, New York Yankees and New York Mets. The fun-loving, witticism-speaking "Old Professor" logged ten league pennants and seven World Series titles as skipper. Stengel was inducted into Cooperstown in 1966 as a manager.

THE SNAPPERS COME ASHORE ON PALMETTO BEACH

Pensacola joined the ranks of the professional baseball arena with the formation of the Snappers and the team's inclusion into the Class-D Cotton States League. The Snappers, named for the abundant locally harvested fish, began their inaugural season as residents at the Palmetto Beach ball field. Six regional teams comprised the Cotton States League in 1913. Along with Pensacola, the Jackson (Mississippi) Lawmakers, Columbus (Mississippi) Joy Riders, Clarksdale (Mississippi) Swamp Angels, Meridian (Mississippi) Metropolitans and the Selma (Alabama) Centralities rounded out the league lineup.

The 1913 Pensacola Snappers of the Cotton States League played their home games at Palmetto Beach Park in Warrington. The Snappers fielded able-bodied players who kept pace with their Cotton States rivals and the Major and Minor League teams utilizing Pensacola during spring training. *Front row, left to right*: E. Long, Charles Miller, William McGill, Rabbit Jewell, Jimmy Hamilton and M. Hains. *Back row, left to right*: Beim, James Gudger, LaRue Kirby, Michael Hauser, Clarence Burmeister, Leo Townsend and E. Berger. *Courtesy of the author.*

Two of the Snappers' 1913 roster players, LaRue Kirby and Leo Townsend, would see play at the Major League level. Kirby and fellow Snappers outfielder Albert Winkleman would later play under the managerial direction of future Hall of Fame pitcher Mordecai "Three Finger" Brown. Pensacola's skill level shown during 1913 impressed at least one out of town tourist, as she wrote back to her husband in Pittston, Pennsylvania. "This sure is some baseball town, but no wonder, their team is playing great ball, they are now leading the league," penned Mrs. Harriet Fullager.

The season prior to joining the Snappers, LaRue Kirby was a brief write-in on the National League champion New York Giants lineup. The 1913 Snappers finished sixty-seven and twenty-nine, four and a half games behind the Jackson Lawmakers, which landed Pensacola in second place. After 1913, the Cotton States League folded due to insufficient income, leaving Pensacola unorganized as a league club for the following year.

PENSACOLA BECOMES A SPRING TRAINING DESTINATION

Although Minor League Baseball was struggling to get a consistent foothold in Pensacola, the Major Leagues had not forgotten about the inviting surroundings of the bayside town. The owner of the Cincinnati Reds, Garry Herrmann, attempted to bid for training in Pensacola in 1912 but was unable to get a release from his Hot Springs, Arkansas contract. The Cleveland Naps (later Indians) also made a bid during 1912 to train their club in Pensacola for the following preseason. After securing a contract with Pensacola officials, the Naps, along with a sparring team, were scheduled to arrive in Florida with enough time to condition and soak in the warm sunshine before starting regular season play.

Cleveland's player/manager, Joe Birmingham, dispatched scout Bob Gilks late in the year to "superintend the laying out and grading of the practice diamond," according to an October 7, 1912 release of *Sporting Life*. Gilks, a veteran of the professional diamond himself, was now overseeing player development for the Cleveland squad. Birmingham requested that the infield "be sodded, so that the Naps will have a practice diamond in keeping with those in Major League parks." As early as the fall of 1912, Cleveland rolled into Pensacola for an exhibition game and to try out their new Florida diamond and then returned at the end of February 1913 for spring training.

The scheduled plan was for the Cleveland Naps to arrive in Pensacola for spring exercises on February 28. A lead group of twenty-five players, along with Birmingham, would come one week ahead of the rest of the team. The Toledo Mud Hens of the American Association were to follow. By mid-March, Cleveland fielded an entire team in Pensacola, as well as a full practice squad in the form of the Minor League Toledo Mud Hens. The fine people of Pensacola were given quite an exhibition of talented ball play. Players such as Doc Johnson, Steve O'Neill, Nap Lajoie and "Shoeless Joe" Jackson pulled out the stops while getting in shape for the coming Major League season.

Another factor in the Naps' choice of Pensacola as their 1913 training venue was that team secretary William Blackwood resided there. Blackwood must have wielded a good amount of influence in the spring training location decision since Pensacola was soon thereafter discussed as a permanent spring venue. When Cleveland left for the regular season, Toledo remained behind for additional practice. The Minor Leaguers' season schedule would start a short time after that of their Major League brothers.

Joseph Jefferson Jackson, more commonly referred to as "Shoeless Joe," is one of the most widely recognized names in twentieth-century baseball. Jackson spent thirteen seasons in the Major Leagues with the Philadelphia Athletics, Cleveland Naps and Chicago White Sox. Jackson was an incredible threat at the plate and in the outfield, with a lifetime batting average of .356 and a .964 fielding percentage. Babe Ruth claimed to have modeled his hitting technique after Shoeless Joe's.

Jackson later met with devastating allegations during the "Black Sox" scandal surrounding the questionable events occurring during the 1919 World Series. After the Cincinnati Reds defeated the Chicago White Sox, surprising some folks, Jackson and other Chicago players were accused of taking money from bookmakers to throw the series.

Six years before the scandal, however, Shoeless Joe Jackson was in top form, endearing himself to the people of Pensacola and disappointing no fan. "Joe Jackson…clout the first ball pitched to him on Friday [so] far over the fence they stared in wide-eyed wonderment. Joe, just to prove that the smash was not a fluke, repeated the trick two more times in the morning practice," reported *Sporting Life* on March 15, 1913. Later that afternoon, during the next practice game, Shoeless Joe belted out a triple during his first at-bat.

Another enormously popular player was Cleveland mainstay Napoleon Lajoie, considered by many baseball historians to be one of the greatest

Shoeless Joe Jackson thrilled Pensacola fans with his hard-hitting plate appearances during the 1913 preseason exercises for the Cleveland Naps. Six years prior to his assumed participation in the "Black Sox" World Series scandal, Jackson demonstrated dominance with his bat and glove. Shoeless Joe became one of many legends of the game who would leave their spike marks on the base paths of Pensacola. *Courtesy of National Baseball Hall of Fame Library.*

players during the early days of the American League. Nap Lajoie was so highly revered in northern Ohio that for over ten years the Cleveland team adopted Lajoie's nickname and called themselves the Naps. In 1909, he became the highest paid player in Major League Baseball.

Lajoie, an accomplished second bagger by trade, consistently frustrated opposing pitchers with his bat. "Jumpin' Jahosophat, how does he sock 'em! Infielders frequently are bowled over like ten-pins by his terrific liners, and even the outfielders have difficulty handling them," exclaimed the *Sporting News*. Winning three batting titles, Nap Lajoie became one of Ty Cobb's biggest rivals in the American League.

Lajoie brought this same top-performance play to Pensacola during the 1913 spring training practices. The *Sporting Life* reported that while Nap Lajoie conditioned in Pensacola, he and other veterans truly showed up the younger members of the Cleveland and Toledo squads. Further, Lajoie had a hand in helping to shape up the new recruits. During Lajoie's stay in Pensacola, he took special interest in working with Pete Shields, a new catcher recently picked up from the University of Mississippi. Napoleon Lajoie was inducted into the National Baseball Hall of Fame in 1937.

PLAYER DEVELOPMENT ON THE EMERALD COAST

Having Major League stars pound out the base paths under Pensacola's sunny skies seemed to have caused more than one professional franchise office to take notice of untapped player and geographic location resources afforded by the Emerald Coast. By the beginning of the 1914 season, the two Major League divisions reluctantly had to acknowledge the existence of what some would refer to as the "Third Major League." Others would curse the newcomer league as a renegade faction. Regardless of individual opinions, many National and American League heavyweights were throwing caution to the wind and opting for individual contracts with the newly formed Federal League. The Federal League offered higher salaries and the promise of no reserve clause. Under a Federal League contract, an individual player had the right to direct his own future, an option not available with the other two Major League organizations.

Not only was the Federal League in need of high-level talent to fill the rosters of its eight-team league, but quality spring training sites also had to be secured. The Cleveland Naps ultimately chose Athens, Georgia, for their 1914 exercises. Meanwhile, Pensacola's groomed baseball diamond, prepared the previous year, was an appealing draw. By February 28, 1914, the Brooklyn Tip Tops of the Federal League made a bid and won the privilege of using Pensacola's pristine field.

During the first days of March, however, the Brooklyn Feds had some reservations and attempted to breach their contract with Pensacola. But the still-intact and strongly organized Pensacola Baseball Park Association knew its field lease agreement rights. The organization had recently turned down an offer from the Indianapolis Federal club in favor of the Brooklyn franchise. With judgment still pending into the spring months, the Brooklyn Tip Tops traveled only as far as Columbia, South Carolina, to get into shape.

Robert Gilks, the man responsible for the maintenance of the Cleveland practice field in Pensacola, doubled up scouting duties with managing the Montgomery club during the 1914 Southern Association season. When the league did not renew Montgomery for the 1915 season, Gilks returned to Pensacola with the intention of founding a "School of Baseball." With Gilks having such strong relationships with Major League owners and managers, he was positioned for success from the inception of the school.

Bob Gilks further dangled Pensacola's diamond carrot in front of Major League front offices, which were in search of preseason operation sites. The December 12, 1914 edition of the *Sporting Life* let it be known that the St. Louis Cardinals, New York Yankees and the Indianapolis Indians of the American Association were all in tentative negotiations to come to Pensacola for 1915 preseason conditioning. Although Gilks was ultimately unable to draw a nationally ranked team back to town in 1915, he was successful in sending several players from his Pensacola school to professionally organized baseball clubs. Most notable were Julian Osborne to the Detroit Tigers, Johnnie Gibson to the Chicago Cubs and in 1917, Julian Olson to the New York Yankees.

Pensacola kept its enthusiasm for baseball alive with or without Major League representation. The residents of the city enjoyed their sport so much that the Pensacola Carnival Association included locally staffed baseball exhibitions to draw crowds to its July 5, 1915 citywide event. The Carnival Association's baseball extravaganza drew nearly five thousand spectators and led to the association becoming the Pensacola Interstate Fair, founded by John Frenkel Sr. in 1935.

AVIATOR TY COBB

One of the most competitive ballplayers of all time, Tyrus Raymond Cobb, lived and played with unparalleled intensity. Ty Cobb's induction into the Hall of Fame during the first round of voting in 1936 came as no surprise to him. Not that Cobb thought of himself as a great athlete; in fact, he stated just the opposite for the better part of his career. But it was an inner drive to be first that compelled him to be a fierce competitor.

Thus, it is no surprise that Ty Cobb would take advantage of an opportunity to be one of the first civilians to take a flight at Pensacola's newly established Naval Aeronautic Station. The Detroit Tigers were headquartered in Gulfport, Mississippi, for 1915 spring training. During Detroit's preseason trek around the southern states, the "Georgia Peach," as Cobb was known, dropped by for a look at the navy's new endeavor and to take a ride in one of the airplanes. *Baseball Magazine* reported on Cobb's adventure in the air, stating, "Ty is always in the forefront of progress and anxious to try out a new thing." Ty Cobb commented of his outing, "It was quite an experience. I can't say that I would like a steady diet of it, but one voyage was interesting. I noticed that every once in a while the machine would seem to skid a bit, if I may use that word, though there wasn't anything to skid upon air."

Pensacola's Government Flying School drew more than just the attention of Ty Cobb. The Cincinnati Reds' venerable manager, Buck Herzog, also showed interest in the navy's flight program, opting for the Pensacola experience over the Wright Brothers' school in Dayton, Ohio.

During the summer, ball teams made up of sailors and soldiers from the navy yard continued to battle it out with local clubs. However, they were not the only game in town. Pensacola's Negro League teams were up and running at full barrel.

One of the unique benefits for the Negro League in Pensacola during 1915 and the years to come was the ability to play on professionally designed ball fields used by white players. In other cities across the South, Negro League teams of all levels more often than not were restricted to makeshift parks and less-than-desirable playing conditions. In Pensacola, however, teams like the Giants, Nine Devils, Pirates, Light Crust Dough Boys and Clowns played in high-end style.

"The Pensacola Giants and the Pensacola Pirates crossed bats last Friday night at Maxent Ball Park, one of the finest ball parks in the south, formally used by the white boys. A large number of fans were in attendance, including many white people. The game was called at 4 o'clock by umpire Fred R. Preer," came a report from the August 7, 1915 edition of the *Freeman*, which further listed the Giants' battery to consist of Wright and Cotlett, while the Pirates sent Turner and Gillins to lead their defense. The Pirates bested the Giants 3–2 before a jubilant crowd.

COASTAL DEFENDERS

In the decades following the Civil War, President Grover Cleveland's secretary of war, William Endicott, initiated a program to retool America's coastal defenses. A series of large concrete batteries were built along twenty-nine of the nation's most vulnerable shorelines and outfitted with an array of weaponry. Breach-loading cannons, mortars, floating batteries and anti-submarine mines all combined to make the U.S. coastline impenetrable.

Fort Pickens, on Santa Rosa Island, south of Pensacola, was completely refitted with new twelve-inch rifles mounted on disappearing carriages, which were capable of firing shells approximately eight miles. Manning several batteries making up the Santa Rosa Island defense system were artillery units, mine specialists and infantry, all living among the sugar white sand dunes of Pensacola's beachside fort. The men serving in and around Fort Pickens had access to diversions such as fishing and swimming to boost leisure time morale. In addition, baseball became a means of healthy recreation between units and other troops stationed across the bay at Fort Barrancas.

Games between the men were most assuredly friendly competition, but the level of play among Pensacola's military installations might have surprised those who had only participated in amateur matches back home. Peppered in among Fort Pickens' regular team in 1917 and 1918 were a few who knew their way around a professional diamond. Joining the roster of the Fort Pickens team were John Joseph "Jack" Smith, who listed with the 1912 Detroit Tigers; Frederick "Mysterious" Walker, who spent five seasons in the majors playing for the National League, American League and Federal League before coming to Pickens; and Harry Golden, who had a brief stint with Atlantic City in the B-Class Tri-State League.

Across the bay, the members of Pensacola High School's 1918 baseball team were outfitting for their playing season. The school's newspaper, the *Tattler*, exclaimed in the May edition, "They've come at last! The baseball

Off-duty hours were filled with good exercise and elevated morale, as the 1917 Fort Pickens Army personnel baseball team competed against Fort Barrancas and the Navy Yard clubs. Locally based military squads also faced the City League teams from Pensacola and Warrington. The biggest winners of the matchups were most certainly the fans and spectators. *Front row, left to right*: Harry Golden, Sam Bailey, Frank Nabor, Flem Brittain and Frank Mikels. *Back row, left to right*: Roy Stillion (mascot), James Deegan, John Smith, Richard Lavender (manager), Roy Simmons, Frank Plum and Fred Walker. *Courtesy of Gulf Islands National Seashore Archives*.

uniforms of course. The team needed suits very much, so the dance committee very generously donated them and the boys are very proud of their spick and span appearance." Apparently, the boys had worn out their old jerseys and pants, but the tattered uniforms had not dampened the boys' motivation in giving their best on the field. The report went on to say that the PHS squad had played Walton High, DuFuniack, Palmer College, a YMCA team and the Forty-third Infantry team stationed at the Pensacola Armory. All games, except for the match with Walton, were won by the Pensacola High School squad.

CHAPTER 3
THE LIVE-BALL ERA: 1920–1941

THE ROBINS NEST IN PENSACOLA

Mark Twain called baseball the great unifier—a game that brought neighborhood and nation alike under a common rallying banner. While baseball's color barrier still separated the races at the professional level, it did not stop raw talent of every color from exhibiting a passion for the game. A passage from W.C. Kinsella's book *Shoeless Joe* conceptualizes the sentiment of Americans toward their beloved game:

> *The one constant through the years has been baseball. America has rolled by like an army of steamrollers. It's been erased like a blackboard, rebuilt, and erased again. But baseball has marked the time. This field, this game, is a part of our past. It reminds us of all that once was good and it could be again.*

After World War I, and with America heading unknowingly toward involvement in a second global engagement, baseball brought a much-needed escape for the citizens of Pensacola. As a town growing up around a coastal defense system and a naval air station, military personnel were part of the greater Pensacola community and economy. Baseball on the national scale was going through changes of its own, which would trickle down and affect even the Minor Leagues in America's small-town markets, including Pensacola.

Pensacola's population was growing, and thus, so was its fan base. The 1920s opened its doors to a new generation of wealthy Pensacola residents, and the growth of luxury homes in the fifty-block North Hill district was indicative of the citizens' prosperity. As a part of the "New South," the City of Five Flags rose from a provincial town of a little over seventeen thousand people just after 1900 to around eighty thousand in the surrounding area by 1945. Even after a devastating hurricane in September 1926, Pensacola rebounded to continue its rise.

This period of growth in Pensacola fostered business opportunities, more accessible transportation routes, quality entertainment, social organizations, tourism and, of course, a growing relationship between the city and the United States Navy. The Sanger Theater opened in 1925, bridges spanning both Pensacola Bay and the Santa Rosa Sound opened to traffic in 1931, the Casino Beach Resort opened that same year and Sicilian-born snapper fisherman Giuseppe Patti established Joe Patti's Fish Market on DeVillers Street in 1935. From 1920 to 1941, the influence of such local growth created a perfect backdrop for baseball's success in Pensacola. For Pensacola, baseball has marked the time as Kinsella described.

On December 15, 1921, the *Miami News* foretold the coming of the Brooklyn National League club to Pensacola the following spring. The Brooklyn Robins had made inquiries with the Pensacola Baseball Association for the use of the grounds at Maxent Park in March 1922, which was to include games against the Louisville Colonels Minor League team and matches with local baseball squads. The Robins began their 1922 spring training operations in Jacksonville and then moved to Pensacola, beginning with a three-day exhibition series facing the Colonels.

The reason for the trek to Pensacola was a strategic calculation by the Robins' manager and future Hall of Fame member Wilbert Robinson. According to the *New York Times*, Robinson wanted to use Pensacola as an experimental proving ground for his batting order and to work with his pitching staff. Pensacola offered competitive local opponents and a place to get away from the prying eyes of other clubs' scouts scouring Florida's eastern coast. Robinson reflected on his unique perspective of staffing his bullpen by stating, "There's only one theory on pitching. Get the biggest guy you can find who can throw a ball through a two-inch plank and you got yourself a pitcher." The legendary manager, affectionately known as "Uncle Robbie," had already been to Pensacola while catching for the 1892 Baltimore Orioles and was reminded of the "big guys" he had seen there.

Besides Brooklyn's manager, the 1922 club featured three other players who would see enshrinement in Cooperstown: pitchers Burleigh Grimes and Dazzy Vance and outfielder Zack Wheat. Wheat was the bane of pitchers. His hard-hitting tactics at the plate made short work of most. Zack's lifetime batting average was .317 in nineteen seasons of Major League play. Casey Stengel lauded Wheat as one of the finest hitting instructors he had ever seen.

The Robins' Minor League counterparts in Pensacola fielded their own powerhouses and future legends. Joe McCarthy managed the Louisville Colonels from 1919 to 1925 and then became the manager of the Chicago Cubs in 1926. McCarthy applied his managerial skills to the Cubs, Yankees and Red Sox, spanning twenty-four seasons in the Major Leagues. Joe's diverse coaching style helped earn him nine league championships and seven World Series titles. McCarthy received three *Sporting News* Manager of the Year awards and was inducted into the National Baseball Hall of Fame as a manager in 1957. Joe McCarthy stands as the Yankees all-time leader in wins by a manager with 1,460.

McCarthy brought his Louisville team to Pensacola ahead of the Brooklyn squad, staying on afterward to engage the city clubs for preseason workouts. Louisville outfielder Earle Combs, tuning up his famous throwing arm at Maxent Park, would play for McCarthy again with the 1925 Yankees. The two men would be permanent companions as inductees to the Hall of Fame after their baseball careers. The Colonels also fielded somewhat of a tourist draw in pitcher/outfielder Ben Tincup. Tincup was a full-blooded Cherokee from Adair, Oklahoma, whose playing abilities and later, coaching prowess, earned him an induction to the Oklahoma Baseball Hall of Fame.

Negro Leagues and New York Yankees

Before the official incorporation of the Negro National League, the Negro Southern League harbored many of the most talented players and competitive clubs that the nation had to offer. Several Negro baseball federations organized throughout the country in answer to the exclusion of blacks from white professional baseball. As early as 1885, with the formation of Cuban Giants, black teams had made their mark on the game as strong as any white counterpart. Influenced by proximity to the Negro Southern League franchises, Pensacola African Americans formed their own organizations, sending Emerald Coast players to professional-level ball.

Elander Victor Harris was born in Pensacola, Florida, on June 10, 1905. Although Vic Harris and his family moved to Pittsburgh in 1914, "Vicious" Vic's tie to Pensacola was more than just a birthplace. Harris began his professional career in 1923 with the Cleveland Tate Stars of the Negro National League. African Americans would not break the color barrier until after Jackie Robinson signed with the Brooklyn Dodgers organization, but Vic Harris gave boys growing up in Pensacola's black neighborhoods a hometown hero to emulate and be proud of.

Vic joined the Homestead Grays in 1925 for what would become a twenty-three-season relationship as player and manager. During his tenure with the Grays, he played alongside and managed future Negro League Hall of Fame notables, including Cool Papa Bell, Oscar Charleston, Josh Gibson, Buck Leonard and Smokey Joe Williams. Vic managed the Grays to nine consecutive pennants and two Black World Series titles. Harris later managed and coached with the Baltimore Elite Giants and Birmingham Black Barons. While managing the Barons in 1950, Vic Harris helped the development of a young up-and-coming player by the name of Willie Mayes.

Bobby Robinson, another nationally acclaimed Negro Leaguer with ties to Pensacola, earned the nickname the "Human Vacuum Cleaner" for his all-star abilities as a third baseman. Robinson began his career with organized ball playing for the Mobile Tigers and honed his skills alongside fellow rookie teammate Satchel Paige. In 1924, Robinson covered third base for the Pensacola Giants and doubled as a team scout.

During a road trip against Birmingham, a scout for the Indianapolis ABC's took note of Bobby's vacuum-like abilities as a third baseman. The ABC's scout offered Robinson the opportunity to play at a more competitive level with Indianapolis. Choosing to remain with Pensacola for the rest of 1924, Bobby Robison played the following year for the ABC's. The 1925 season would mark the beginning of a prosperous professional career launched from Robinson's foundational days in Pensacola. He played eighteen seasons as a professional with eleven different teams.

During Robinson's season in Pensacola, the New York Yankees made a one-game stop at Maxent Park on April 1, 1924, near the end of their spring training excursion. Traveling by train with the Yankees was the Rochester Tribe of the Minor League American Association. The two teams faced each other on several stops across the South under the direction of New York's manager, Miller Huggins. Yankee pitchers Waite Hoyt and

The New York Yankees first utilized Pensacola's hospitality and well-maintained baseball fields during their 1924 Florida spring exhibition tour. As the Yanks took on the Rochester Minor League team at Maxent Park, the citizenry of Pensacola were treated to a game filled with all-stars normally only read about in the newspaper. Babe Ruth, ever the friend of the young fan, patiently greeted the throngs of children waiting to speak to their hero of the diamond. Fortunately for Pensacola's "Knot-Hole Gang," it would not be the only time they would see the Bambino on their home turf. *Courtesy of Pensacola Historical Society.*

Bob Shawkey held Rochester to only two hits in a 4–0 victory at Maxent. Over four thousand Pensacola fans crammed into the wooden stadium and overflow bleachers, with nearly one thousand children sitting on the outfield perimeter in hopes of catching a glimpse of Babe Ruth in action. One newspaper reporter stated that the Babe tried so hard to please the crowd with a home run that he broke his big bat in the process.

New York's bullpen contained right-hander George Pipgras. George's brother Ed would later pitch for Pensacola on the same field in 1927. Among the players working out for the Yankees was twenty-one-year-old Lou Gehrig, beginning only his second season on the New York roster. Gehrig made certain that his turn at bat would not be forgotten, as he drove the ball hard and legged out each base. Military personnel were honored at each exhibition game. But the pageantry at Maxent Park was not the only game in town for the sailors and soldiers stationed in Pensacola.

The Fort Barrancas senior command made a formal proclamation at the beginning of the 1925 cadet training camp, stating that athletics on the base were of the utmost importance for the physical development of their personnel. Camp athletic officer, Lieutenant Berliner, organized a committee to oversee the development of various sports that would bring the "maximum good to the greatest number." Baseball and basketball were

The warm breezes blowing in from Pensacola Bay agreed with Yankees first baseman Lou Gehrig as he reconditioned during a spring training exercise. Gehrig's bat came alive at Maxent Park, as fans had the opportunity to see one of New York's rising stars just as he was ascending the ladder of what would become a Hall of Fame career. *Courtesy of the author.*

already heavily sought after as recreation at Fort Barrancas. Additionally, competitive volleyball, boxing, tennis and bowling contests were carried out between companies stationed at Barrancas. But it was baseball that won out as the dominant sport, enough so that an end-of-season league series was mandated, with the student officers of Battery C winning the championship in an 8–4 final playoff score.

Across town from the fort, Pensacola High School had been without an organized baseball team since 1921, and when the school opened tryouts for a 1925 squad, the response was exuberant. Most of the eighteen young men who made the team had little to no baseball experience, but their passion and enthusiasm carried them far. The school's newspaper stated that "the first string men were on their toes at all times, for fear of losing their uniforms to understudies."

Not to be outdone by their male counterparts, the Pensacola High females took advantage of the reorganization of the sport on their campus. Playing in white cotton shirts and long shorts, the PHS Varsity Girls Baseball team came out swinging in 1925. Mary Graham, Sheila White, Hilda Burleson, Lucille Briggs, Eva Mae Pittman, Doris Wells, Mae Boig, Alberta Maxwell and Estelle Smith comprised the determined girls club.

1927 Pilots

Originally designated as a Class-D Major League affiliated association, the Southeastern League moved up to a Class-B circuit in 1926. Pensacola joined the 1927 Southeastern League team lineup, which was comprised of eight teams from three states. Along with Pensacola, the Alabama-, Georgia- and Florida-based teams included Albany, Columbus, Jacksonville, Montgomery, Savannah, Selma and St. Augustine.

Baseball's growth and establishment in Pensacola has always been a community effort. As capital was needed to ensure Pensacola's place in the reestablished Southeastern League, team owners gave patrons the opportunity to purchase shares. The 1927 Pensacola Pilots were a franchise built on the faith of their city and personal support from their fans. *Courtesy of Garth's Antiques.*

To solidify a spot in the Southeastern League, the Pensacola Baseball Association raised $10,000 to defray team costs and league expenditures. Immediately upon announcement of acceptance into the league, interested parties raised $6,000. For the remaining portion, Pensacola realtor and soon-to-be team vice-president Don Oppenheimer gave the community opportunity to purchase interests in the team in increments of $10 per share when they stopped by his office at 206 South Palafox Street.

Pensacola resident Frank Goodman received a prize for suggesting "Pilots" as the most practical nickname for the team. Sportswriters and fans would interchange the name Pilots and Fliers over the coming years, and the team interchanged the spelling of the nickname between Flyers and Fliers. As if these team appellations were not enough, local reporters began affectionately tagging Pensacola's club the Aviators. The team uniforms were designated as white home game jerseys and road gray with both trimmed in black. A large letter "P" appeared on the home jerseys, and the team's secondary name, Fliers, was emblazoned across the road shirts. The stands at Maxent Park were structured to seat four thousand—not including overflow—and the league set a 142-game schedule to begin on April 10, 1927.

During March, just before the opening of the new season, the Newark Bears of the American Association trained in Pensacola. The Bears were loosely affiliated with the Philadelphia Phillies, but with no formal agreement the club was able to call their own shots. To build their own farm system, Newark made a promise to Pensacola to leave several of their men behind to continue training as part of the new "Deep Water City Team." Newark made good on its promise, and the workout in Pensacola was apparently beneficial, as the team returned home to take on the Phillies in an exhibition match in which they beat their benefactor club 5–2.

The Southeastern League and its Pensacola representation proved to be a good staging ground for a higher level of play. The '27 Pensacola Pilots roster held nine names that had or would experience Major League competition: Bill Clowers, Bruce Connatser, Bill Holden, Doc Johnston, Johnny Pasek, Parson Perryman, Ed Pipgras, Pete Susko and Wally Dashiell. Many more from the Pilots club would see successful careers in the Minor Leagues. At season's end, the Pilots finished fourth in the division at seventy-nine and seventy-three.

BILL HOLDEN'S 1927 ROSTER

Bill Holden managed Pensacola's 1927 club and took a position in the outfield as well. Holden had bounced around in the minors for thirteen seasons, and he spent two seasons in the majors with the New York Yankees and the Cincinnati Reds, making Pensacola his last port of call. Bill had received his first taste of managing professional ball with the Knoxville Smokies in 1925. Holden made Pensacola his home until his death in 1971. He was buried in Pfeiffer's Mill Cemetery on Marlane Drive.

Broadus Milburn "Bruce" Connatser began the 1927 season with the Jackson Senators of the Cotton States League, coming over to Pensacola and playing first base. Connatser made limited errors, finishing the season with

Former Major League outfielder Bill Holden was called upon to manage the 1927 Pensacola club. The City of Five Flags became Holden's adopted hometown after his retirement from baseball. Bill also helped oversee the reconstruction and expansion of Pensacola's downtown park, which hosted Major and Minor League play and allowed cooperative usage by black and white teams. *Courtesy of the author.*

a .985 fielding average. Bruce signed on for two seasons with the Cleveland Indians in 1931 and 1932 and later became a professional baseball scout for the Detroit Tigers and the Philadelphia Phillies. During his career with the Phillies, Connatser worked alongside famed scout Tony Lucadello.

Pete Susko spent the beginning of 1927 with Pensacola before being traded to Montgomery. While with Pensacola, Susko played the outfield and batted .324. He made his Major League debut with Washington in 1934, where he transitioned to the infield and became the Senators' second-string first baseman. Susko managed the Borger Gassers of the West Texas-New Mexico League in 1940.

Pensacola signed veteran Wheeler "Doc" Johnston to a one-season contract in 1927. Johnston began his Major League career with the Reds in 1909. His main role with Pensacola was covering first base; however, having a good arm, Doc was called on as an outfielder when needed. During his eleven seasons in the majors, Johnston lent his talents to Cincinnati, Cleveland, Pittsburgh and the Philadelphia Americans. While with Cleveland in 1920, he batted for a .273 average during the Indians' 5–2 World Series victory over the Brooklyn Robins. After 1927, Doc stayed with Pensacola for the following one and a half seasons as manager.

Niagara Falls, New York native Johnny Pasek began his professional playing career as a catcher with Pensacola in 1927. Pasek perfected his craft as a battery mate during sixteen seasons in the Minor Leagues before being brought up by Detroit in 1933 and later traded to the Chicago White Sox in 1934.

Emmett Key "Parson" Perryman was another of the veterans hired by Pensacola. Perryman's nickname is alleged to have come from his college days at Emory University, where he studied religion. Parson spent twelve seasons in the minors, including two years in Pensacola. The right-handed pitcher threw for a lifetime 2.22 ERA in the Minor Leagues. Perryman took the mound for the St. Louis Browns in 1915, and the October 1915 edition of *Baseball Magazine* called Perryman a "valuable adjunct" to the Browns' club along with fellow rookie George Sisler.

Pensacola became the launching pad for twenty-two-year-old right-handed pitcher Edward Pipgras. Pipgras posted thirteen wins and twelve losses and compiled a .205 batting average in his rookie season. In 1932, Ed had a "cup of coffee" with the Brooklyn National League club, while his brother George played across town for the New York Yankees.

Elmer Strange Tutwiler made his two-game Major League appearance as a relief pitcher for the Pittsburgh Pirates in 1928. Born in Carbon Hill,

Alabama, in 1904, Tutwiler spent the greatest portion of his professional career in the Minor Leagues. While playing in the Southeastern League, Elmer pitched for the 1927 Pensacola Pilots, compiling a 5–7 record in sixteen games. Elmer Tutwiler served in the U.S. Marine Corps during World War II, returning to Pensacola much later in life. At age seventy-one, Tutwiler died at the Navy Hospital in Pensacola and was buried at Barrancas National Cemetery. Elmer Tutwiler, as part of the 1927 Pensacola Pilots, helped usher in a new era of professional baseball on the Gulf Coast.

Pensacola High School had placed its baseball program in mothballs for the 1927 season. However, as the uniforms were put on for 1928, the young men filling them were much more experienced. While their high school offered them no playing schedule during 1927, many of the varsity squad had joined Pensacola's well-established Twilight League, and a couple of the boys even played well enough to work out with the Fliers. The Twilight League fielded teams reflecting its benefactors, such as the Gulf Lifes, Girdlestones, Crystal Icers and Woodmen of the World. While still other teams in the hard-hitting, highly competitive league donned the designation of their area of origin; the New Warringtons, Sevilles, Fort Barrancas and Bayliss Go-Getters stood in for their neighborhoods. Numerous additional teams rounded out the league throughout the 1920s and '30s, making Pensacola a platform for quality play.

The Brooklyn Robins made another visit to the Emerald Shore for a game in March as part of the dedication month for the new field at the Bayliss Park Complex. On May 17, 1928, the City of Pensacola, the Frank Marston Post of the American Legion and the Pensacola Baseball Association dedicated the newly named Legion Field on the site of the former Maxent Park. Maxent had steadfastly served the city for many years, but with rising spectator interest and greater use of the facility, field and seating upgrades were a must.

Seating was expanded to accommodate five thousand in the new grandstands and overflow areas. The name change came at the request of the newly chartered American Legion Post located a short distance from the park's property. The field itself became a part of a larger dedication of the surrounding community park named in honor of Pensacola's mayor, J.H. Bayliss. However, not all of the town's citizens were happy about the field's name change. The Pensacola Women's Club opposed the discontinuation of a name that had given a nod to Don Gilberto Antonio de St. Maxent, the Spanish regional governor in 1782. To quiet the ladies' protest, Mayor Bayliss put forth a formal proclamation keeping existing Spanish names on all other city parks.

Doc Johnston was named manager for the Fliers' 1928 season, overseeing many of the fan favorites from the previous year. Clowers, Dashiell, Pasek and Perryman topped the list of all-stars as Pensacola turned out to see the freshly renovated stadium. When the gates opened for the first time at Legion Field, Pensacolans spilled out en masse with the stands overflowing. As would prove true in coming decades, Pensacola citizens not only cheered on their team with passion, but they also extended Gulf Coast hospitality to the players. Texas-born pitcher John Clowers loved the town and citizenry so much that he said, "I think I would like to call Pensacola home." Carlos Moore, a rookie hurler, stated, "I'm new in baseball, but I've got the Fliers spirit…and I want to produce a winner for a fine bunch of people like there are in Pensacola."

PENSACOLA FLIERS VERSUS NEW YORK YANKEES

The 1928 Pensacola Fliers played with effectiveness in the Southeastern League's split-season format. And while Pensacola finished with the league's best record of 92–54, the Montgomery Lions bested the Fliers four games to two in the playoffs. Pensacola's 1929 team could not repeat the previous year's showing, and Johnston was fired midway through the season and replaced by Tom Pyle.

However, 1929 began as a baseball lover's dream, and all that followed was just icing on the cake. Pensacola's solid foundation as a good location for spring training had netted another visit from the New York American League club. The Yankees had begun to use sites in Florida to get their players into shape as early as 1919. After a couple of preseason headquarters in other various locations, the Yankees returned to Florida in the mid-1920s. Based out of St. Petersburg for 1929 spring conditioning, the New York Americans traveled to several Florida cities, engaging the local Minor League teams in exhibition games. Pensacola welcomed the back-to-back World Series champions with open arms and a parade down Palafox Street to honor the team.

Fans rolled out in droves to see all the diamond heroes from New York, but none brought more interest than George Herman "Babe" Ruth. The Yankees played a practice game against the Pensacola Fliers on March 31 at Legion Field, with thousands of fans coming out to witness the 12–2 Yankee victory. Ruth, ever the chum of the young onlooker, signed an

The Pensacola Police Department was established by General Andrew Jackson in 1821 as keepers of the law and ambassadors of goodwill in the new town. In 1929, Chief Johnny Humphries fulfilled his role established over a century prior by welcoming Babe Ruth and the New York Yankees back to Pensacola for another spring training venue. Ruth signed an estimated one hundred baseballs for young fans during New York's visit. *Courtesy of WSRE.*

estimated one hundred baseballs and also posed for pictures with the children. During the pregame festivities, Ruth signed several more balls and tossed them into the stands.

The 1929 New York Yankees fielded eight future Hall of Fame inductees: Bill Dickey, Lou Gehrig, Tony Lazzeri, Leo Durocher, Earle Combs, Waite Hoyt, Herb Pennock and Babe Ruth. In his first appearance at the plate during the exhibition match, Ruth hit a triple to score Mark Koenig, ungluing the crowd from their seats. Gehrig was next up and reached first after being hit by a pitch. Yankees outfielder Bob Meusel brought Ruth home on a sacrifice fly, and Lazzeri's double scored Gehrig. The score at the end of the end of the second inning was 6–0 Yankees.

The score stayed put until the ninth, when the Yanks tallied six more, with the Fliers making a grand effort by putting two on the board themselves. At the end of the day, the crowd seemed happy to have hosted such an elite game in their own backyard. The adolescent members of Legion Field's "Knothole Gang," which included a young Bill Bond, secured memories of their hero Babe Ruth that would be shared for decades to come.

Four days later, the Brooklyn Robins steamed into town once more for a spring match with the Fliers. Although Pensacola succumbed to the National League club, they did fare better than with the Yankees, losing only 5–2.

The following season, Pensacola-born Bill Henderson pitched a few games for the 1930 Yankees. Henderson spent a total of fourteen seasons in the Minor Leagues, with his last game coming in 1936. Bill Henderson died in Pensacola on October 6, 1966, and is buried at Bayview Memorial Park.

By the 1930s, regardless of amateur or professional, baseball was now permanently woven into Pensacola's cultural fabric. The ball field had become the epicenter for business networking, social advancement and engaging recreation. The businesses of downtown Pensacola, as well as the city's fraternal organizations, found the ball diamond as important a gathering place for their members as the lodge or boardroom. At Pensacola Naval Air Station, officiating personnel took great pride in their well-groomed playing field situated behind Building 45. The supply office and the welfare department provided for meticulous clubhouse accommodations and comfortable grandstands.

Pensacola's navy team made a name for themselves by offering strong competition to the best aggressors the military dished out during the late 1920s. The station's 1930 all-star squad, some of whom had been instrumental in winning an earlier U.S. Navy championship, awaited their "friendly enemies" in the form of the Pensacola Fliers and the latest Major League spring guests.

RUSS SCARRITT AND THE BOSTON RED SOX

Beginning in 1925, the Boston Americans spent three consecutive preseason warm-ups in New Orleans, Louisiana, and then moved to Bradenton, Florida, for two more. A 1930 spring engagement with

Pensacola became the gateway for the Red Sox long-term training future in Florida. The 1930 preseason exercises brought Pensacola continued big-league entertainment and world-class talent for Gulf Coast fans to cheer and support. In a mid-March 1930 exhibition game, the Red Sox jumped right into the fan culture of Pensacola, overtaking the air station's squad 15–3. But the *Air Station News* exclaimed that the day could not have been more beautiful and that each team had enjoyed the other's on-field antics. Just a few days later, the navy boys were able to perform better with a win against the Fliers in a 6–2 affair.

Boston worked out at Legion Field against the Louisville Colonels and the Fliers. Due in part to the Fliers rough season start, Ray Kennedy was handed the managerial duties midway through the 1930 regular schedule. Before coming to Pensacola, Kennedy bounced around the minors for twelve seasons. He skippered in the Southeastern League from 1924 to 1931 as a player/manager, with a very brief appearance in the majors with the Browns in 1916. Ray Kennedy's baseball knowledge was underappreciated until he became a scout for the New York Mets in 1963 at age sixty-eight.

The 1930 Pensacola season eventually became a dark stroke on the Minor League canvas of the Florida Gulf Coast. After two consecutive last-place standings, the Fliers folded their wings and closed their offices. The team's ownership did attempt another run in 1932, but after only five weeks into the season, the circuit in which Pensacola participated discontinued operations because of poor finances and low game attendance. The City of Five Flags representation in the Southeastern League fell quiet until 1937.

While Pensacola's contribution as a viable Minor League town was going through a period of restructuring, the city's appeal to Major League front offices as a spring training site had not waned. The Boston Red Sox were well aware of the exceptional surroundings and facilities offered by Northwest Florida's premier town, thus it became a win-win decision for Boston to make Pensacola their conditioning headquarters for both 1930 and 1931.

Among the players on the roster for the 1930 and 1931 Red Sox franchise were future Hall of Fame pitcher Red Ruffing and Major League doubles leader Earl Webb. Legendary catcher and manager Muddy Ruel was also on hand for Boston, but none could have been more celebrated at Legion Field than Pensacola-born Russ Scarritt. Scarritt's return to Pensacola in a Major League uniform was not just the "local boy made good" story. Russ Scarritt's family was as ingrained in the Pensacola community as snapper fishing and beach vacations.

Born in 1903, Stephen Russell Mallory Scarritt had deep Pensacola roots, with his mother's family being one of the earliest to settle in the area and his uncle having served in the U.S. Senate. Russ played sandlot ball for a few local Pensacola company teams but admitted he did not try out for baseball in high school or for the military prep school he attended. Nor was baseball on his mind during the year he was enrolled at the University of Florida. Even so, Russ Scarritt was a natural at the game. In 1923, former Major Leaguer Jack Ryan, managing the Johnson City, Tennessee team of the Appalachian League, coaxed Scarritt into playing for him.

Russ quickly moved up to Class-A with Greenville, South Carolina, where he hit .377 in 1926 and led the league in RBI standings. In 1927, he began his climb to the majors with St. Paul of the American Association, and by 1929, Scarritt had signed his first big-league contract with the Boston Red Sox. Russ said the Boston fans treated him well as he learned to maneuver "Duffy's Cliff" while playing the outfield. Duffy's Cliff was a ten-foot incline in Fenway's outfield, which transitioned from street level to field level. Later removed from Fenway Park, Duffy's Cliff was a cumbersome obstacle for some outfielders, as they actually had to run up the incline toward the wall to field fly balls. Russ Scarritt stated later in his life that his speed and ability to adjust to the "cliff" could probably be attributed to his chasing "John Henry crabs" down on Escambia Bay.

Scarritt's grandson, Russell Scarritt III, relates the story of his grandfather's first encounter with Babe Ruth:

> *Granddaddy had just come up with Boston and was playing the outfield. The Red Sox were home at Fenway, and the Yankees were in town. Babe Ruth was up to bat with two outs in the inning when Ruth slugged one to left field far enough for a trip around the bases. Granddaddy started back up that ledge they had out in left, and he got up enough to rob Ruth of his hit. As it was three out, Ruth waited on Granddaddy coming into the dugout. Ruth said, "Hey Kid, next time watch the game from the stands."*

A higher compliment could not have been paid to the rookie from Pensacola.

After three seasons with the Red Sox and one with the Phillies, Scarritt returned to the minors for a few years, but not before he left his mark in the majors by leading the league in triples his rookie year. Russ Scarritt returned to his beloved Pensacola in 1937, playing one season with the Fliers. Scarritt took a job with the Ford Motor Company in Pensacola, where he stayed for forty years, and continued to talk to fans and sign autographs until his death in 1994 at age ninety-one. He is buried at St. John's Cemetery in Pensacola. "I really enjoyed playing baseball. I had a good time and have no regrets. I would do it again without thinking about it," stated Scarritt during his last interview.

New York Giants Warm Up in Pensacola

A new Class-D baseball league, featuring cities from southeast Alabama and northern Florida, began to take shape for the 1935 season. Pensacola, Fort Walton and Panama City all showed interest in joining the new Alabama-Florida League. While Pensacola's bid to join the league fell short, the stirring cry for organized baseball to return to the Emerald Coast was increasing.

Although the city did not reacquire a permanent team for 1935, Major League Baseball once again found its way back to Northwest Florida in 1936. The New York Giants, under manager Bill Terry, opted for Pensacola as their spring headquarters. However, it was not just spring training business as usual with the Giants in town. Terry had looked ahead to the talent that Pensacola had to offer and, as a catalyst, opened one of the largest temporary training schools known at the time in organized baseball.

The hope was that while the Giants trained, he and his staff could browse through the regional players and sign a few prospects for the Giants club. Altogether, 165 young men turned out for the month-long instruction. The tuition was only twenty-five dollars, but players had to bring their own equipment and find their own room and board if they were not from Pensacola. From Minor Leaguers with a few seasons of experience to amateurs with a dream of making the big leagues, each hoped to demonstrate their talents in front of the grand old men of the game. The *Sporting News* praised Terry and his instructors for their endeavor, stating that no other institution could have offered these young men a better opportunity. By the start of the 1936 Minor League spring training exercises, Pensacola's Dan Nee, Lefty Lybrand, Paul Bonner and Bert Maxwell represented their city as rookie hopefuls. Bonner and Maxwell played together in the Senators farm system, while Nee began development with the Yankees and Lybrand pitched for the Cubs instructional team. Bill Terry was determined that a larger list of players from Pensacola would sign contracts the following year.

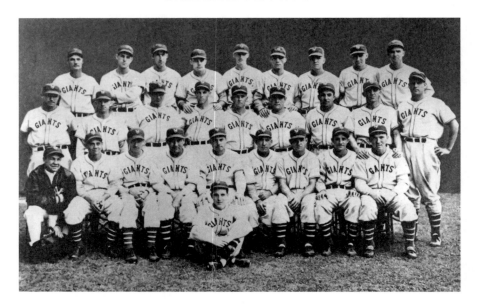

Ever the entrepreneur, New York Giants manager Bill Terry maneuvered to utilize Pensacola as the team's 1936 spring training base of operations. Inasmuch as the Port City offered an overabundance of quality player recruits, Terry's intent was to train prospects for the Giants while getting his New York boys in shape. Bill Terry's proposal of a regional baseball school in Pensacola was repeated on a larger scale years later by Brooklyn Dodgers' general manager, Branch Rickey. *Courtesy of the author.*

Along with Terry, the Giants fielded several additional future Hall of Fame players in 1936. Playing before the Pensacola fans and helping to take the hometown prospects through their paces were Mel Ott, Travis Jackson and Carl Hubbell. Pensacola proved to be the foundation for a successful 1936 season for the New York Giants, as they took the full head of steam built during spring training and rode it to a National League pennant. The San Carlos Hotel on North Palafox was the Giants' Florida headquarters and accommodations during their stay.

MAX MACON

In 1937, Pensacola joined the ranks of the refurbished Southeastern League, once again donning the Fliers nickname. The new operation, managed under Frank Kitchens, brought Minor League baseball back to Pensacola along with local hero Russ Scarritt for his final season in professional ball.

Pitching for the second half of Pensacola's 1937 season was Clem "Steamboat" Dreisewerd, who would later spend a short time in the majors with the Red Sox, St. Louis Browns and the New York Giants. Steamboat spent a total of fifteen years in the minors, becoming a voice for fairness in player contracts by gaining his own free agency in 1938 directly from Major League Baseball commissioner Kenesaw Mountain Landis.

Under Kitchens, the Fliers played a successful season, winning their division with a record of 83–52. The Fliers lost in the championship finals but gave a roaring start for Pensacola's return to regular-season Minor League play.

Pensacola-born Max Macon broke into Major League Baseball in 1938. Macon had signed with the St. Louis Cardinals in 1934 and pitched his way through the minors to reach the big leagues at age twenty-two. The Brooklyn Dodgers purchased his contract in 1939 and split his time between the Brooklyn team and their Minor League affiliate in Montreal.

Primarily an outfielder and sometimes a first baseman, Macon joined the Boston Braves in 1944, and immediately after the season concluded, he entered the United States Army in service to his country. During Macon's military service, he sustained injuries from a dynamite explosion and due to the aftereffects was unable to return to professional baseball until the 1947 season.

After playing in just one game with the Boston Braves in April 1947, Max was sent back to the minors with mixed success. He soon found a new niche by sharing his knowledge of the game with young players. By managing and scouting from 1949 to 1963, Macon developed players' skills and gave them an understanding of life in the game. While managing the 1954 Montreal Royals, Macon helped to develop the playing proficiency of Roberto Clemente and the future managerial abilities of Tommy Lasorda.

BROOKLYN'S CLASS-B AFFILIATE

Pensacola's 1938 team literally brought a whole new ballgame to the field. The Fliers became the Class-B affiliate of the Brooklyn Dodgers, and as an affiliated team, Pensacola had a little more influence over players, uniforms and improvements. Pensacolans fell in love with their favorite sport all over again, as well as their new Major League suitor. With the National League affiliation came some great on-field talent and a seasoned Minor League player/manager/owner in John Wallace Dashiell.

Under the ownership and guidance of Wally Dashiell, Pensacola's Class-B Dodgers affiliate club stepped up their game in experience and expertise. Dashiell's 1938 club featured hard-hitting shortstop Bobby Bragan and carried as many nicknames as it did rising stars. The Fliers, locally dubbed the Pilots and the Aviators, gave Pensacola fans the excitement they demanded and a divisional pennant to brag about. *Courtesy of Pensacola Historical Society.*

Wally Dashiell purchased the Fliers in "bag and baggage," according to the 1938 *Spaulding Guide*. The team formally owned by J.M. Barbee finished first in their division, led the league in hitting and defeated the all-star team formed from the other seven league clubs in a 3–1 victory. The 1938 Fliers fielded several of their own stars who would see Major League play during their careers. Despite a barrage of injuries to the '38 team, the Fliers seemed to always have an ace up their uniform sleeves with the ability to shift players off the bench to fill disabled list vacancies.

Charlie "Sherriff" Gassaway was a fifteen-year veteran of the Minor League system from 1937 to 1952. Gassaway spent the 1938 season with Pensacola before being traded to Binghamton, New York, of the Eastern League during the second half of 1939. In 1938, however, the "Sherriff" handcuffed opposing batters. On the mound for the Fliers, he completed the season with a 2.75 ERA, with eighteen wins and eight losses. At age nineteen, the left-handed pitcher took part in forty-one games and pitched a total of 249 innings with the Fliers.

Charlie took the mound for a total of thirty-nine Major League games between 1944 and 1946 with the Cubs, Athletics and Indians, respectively. Under the guidance of legendary managers Charlie Grimm, Connie Mack and Lou Boudreau, Gassaway gained knowledge for the second half of his career. In 1952, Charlie Gassaway underwent a successful transition from pitcher to field manager. During his nine years managing in the Minor Leagues with the Phillies and Indians organizations, Gassaway won four Minor League division championships and two league championships.

Johnny Hutchings came to Pensacola by way of the Southern Association's Birmingham club in 1938. The twenty-two-year-old already had three seasons with three teams in three different leagues. His varied experience gave him an advantage over most pitchers his age. Hutching notched a 1.97 ERA in forty-eight games for Pensacola during the 1938 and 1939 seasons.

By 1940, Johnny Hutchings made it to the Major Leagues with the Cincinnati Reds. Possibly by chance but more likely due to good scouting, Hutchings wound up smack in the middle of a team running toward a pennant. Johnny Hutchings took the experience gained while playing in Pensacola and other cities and posted a season 3.50 ERA for Cincinnati. The Reds won the World Series over the Tigers, four games to three, with Hutchings pitching in relief during Game 5.

WALLY DASHIELL ADOPTS A CITY

Wally Dashiell began his professional career with Marshall (Texas) of the East Texas League in 1923. Dashiell spent a total of sixteen seasons in the minors with above-average success. Wally had a peek at a Major League dugout with the Chicago White Sox for three games in 1924 before injuring his arm and shortening his time as a player. He again was listed on a big-league roster with the Red Sox for a brief period in 1932. Dashiell spent ten of his sixteen years in the Minor Leagues as a manager or player/manager. Wally's managing skill spoke for itself with six first-place finishes, one second-place finish and three league championships during his managerial tenure.

Although Wally Dashiell hailed originally from Jewett, Texas, Pensacola became his adopted home after he spent time in town as a player prior to 1938. Wally said the first time he came to Pensacola was in 1927 at the request of scout Pop Kitchens, who had organized a group to try out for the Fliers. After getting a good look at the town and the bay, Dashiell called Pensacola home.

Wally, an accomplished entrepreneur, had acquired a percentage ownership in most of the teams he managed during his career. Coming to

Due to his love of the game and love for his adopted hometown, Wally Dashiell served as the Pensacola Fliers' benefactor extraordinaire. Dashiell's experience in both the athletic end of the sport and the business end gave Pensacola an advantage for attracting big-league franchise affiliations and national awareness. Wally first arrived in Pensacola as a player at the age of twenty-five but stayed a lifetime as an integral member of the community. *Courtesy of Diane Crona.*

Pensacola was no different, and after he arrived, he made a move to purchase the Fliers from then owner Barbee. Dashiell gambled most of his personal worth on the young club, but his faith in the town and the talent that it was able to attract gave Wally confidence in his investment.

Dashiell almost immediately became a favorite of Pensacola's fans, as he reflected the city's love of the game and close community ties. Wally's players tended to speak well of him and commented on his strategic prowess on the ball field. Dashiell's Pensacola franchise overcame one obstacle after another, and the players performed well for their skipper. And although Pensacola was a small baseball market in comparison to larger metropolitan areas, the Fliers made a big noise.

The *Sporting News* likened Dashiell's player relations to the deeds of Mack, McGraw and McCarthy when it placed him on the nomination ticker for the 1938 Minor League Manager of the Year. Wally Dashiell stayed as Pensacola's manager for the following two seasons and would return to manage again briefly in 1948. Wally Dashiell continued to hold a percentage ownership in Pensacola's team, even after retiring from active involvement. He later sold insurance in Pensacola and always enjoyed reminiscing about his days on the field with the Fliers. Dashiell died in Pensacola on May 20, 1972, and is buried in Bayview Memorial Park.

BIGHEARTED BOBBY BRAGAN

Robert Randall Bragan is one of the more colorful characters from baseball's rich history. Growing up in Birmingham, Alabama, Bobby was a true son of the South. Bragan was known for his keen sense of humor, innovative

Although Bobby Bragan's stay in Pensacola lasted just two seasons as a Flier, his endearment to the city's fan base was long lasting. Bobby's sentiment equaled that of the city in regard to their mutual admiration. "Those two seasons I spent in Pensacola, '38 and '39—both championships seasons, were memorable from a lot of standpoints. I have fond memories of Pensacola. The ball club and the fans were the best in the world. I shall never forget Pensacola," Bragan said in a 1963 interview. *Courtesy of Pensacola Historical Society.*

contribution to the game and a lifelong passion for baseball. Breaking into the game professionally with Panama City, of the Alabama-Florida League, in 1937, he stayed involved with baseball in some form for almost eight decades.

Pensacola picked up Bobby for 1938 and 1939, and he played 137 games at shortstop for the Fliers in 1938. Above average for a second-year player, Bobby endeared himself to Pensacola fans. He switched to third base in 1939, played another 137 games and belted twelve home runs, leading the team.

Beginning in 1940, Bobby bounced back and forth between the Minor and Major Leagues for a number of seasons. In the minors, he played for the Fort Worth Cats of the Texas League and the Hollywood Stars of the Pacific Coast League.

Bragan started his managerial career in 1948 as a player/manager. Bobby managed at the Major League level with Pittsburgh, Cleveland, Milwaukee and Atlanta. While with the Braves in 1966, Hank Aaron credits Bragan with encouraging him to steal bases. Bobby coached, filled front office and executive roles and continued to manage almost until his death at age ninety-two. Bobby Bragan's achievements and honors in the game of baseball are extensive and legendary. His legacy and character is continued through the Bobby Bragan Youth Foundation.

During a 1963 interview, Bragan reminisced about his time in Pensacola, stating that the "[Fliers'] fans were the best in the world." Bobby remembered the B&B Restaurant and its fine orchestra, staying at Ma Folker's home and the warmth of fans young and old alike. "I will never forget Pensacola," stated Bragan.

For the 1939 season, the Fliers contracted with the Philadelphia Phillies as their Southeastern League affiliate. In celebration, a reported six thousand fans turned out for preseason festivities, which included a grand parade downtown culminating in a "Meet the Fliers" gathering at the San Carlos Hotel. WCOA radio and the president of the Pensacola Baseball Club, Mayor L.C. Hagler, hosted the grand gala, along with the first official meeting of the year for the Knot Hole Club team booster organization. The 1939 Fliers fielded no less than six players who would be written into Major League rosters during their careers: Bobby Bragan, Johnny Hutchings, Garth Mann, Alex Pitko, Harry Walker and Bubba Floyd.

Leslie Roe Floyd had the odd distinction of being the first man in Major League history with the nickname "Bubba." Bubba stayed with Pensacola through 1940 and played shortstop for the Detroit Tigers in 1944. With the Tigers, he batted .444. While in Pensacola, Floyd hit for a .272 batting average in 1939 and .284 in 1940.

Harry "Dixie" Walker, aka "Harry the Hat," made his way into Pensacola for just one season in 1939. Walker was marked as Harry the Hat after he entered the majors due to his habit of adjusting his hat between pitches—in an era that predated the batting helmet. Harry played outfield for the Dashiell dynasty, batting .322 in his 479 appearances at the plate.

By the time Walker rolled into Pensacola, the jovial, on-the-field singing twenty-two-year-old had two full Minor League seasons under his belt in three separate leagues. Walker accumulated a substantial amount of experience in a short amount of time.

Harry Walker hailed from a dyed-in-the-wool baseball family. His father, Ewart, his brother Fred (also nicknamed "Dixie") and nephew Ernie all played in the ranks of Major League Baseball. After eleven years in the big leagues, leading the National League in batting in 1947, Harry Walker managed eighteen years in both the Minor and Major Leagues. A legendary figure in player development, Harry was the first baseball coach at the University of Alabama–Birmingham. Walker, considered by many to be a hitting guru, was credited with turning Matty Alou from a failed prospect into a batting champion. This type of feat was repeated many times during his managerial career.

The 1939 season stood as the third straight year Pensacola finished in first place in the division. But that particular year, the Fliers, behind Dashiell's guidance, took it all the way and won the league championship. Wally Dashiell's boys melded well together. Pensacola's game attendance also took home honors, rivaling the rest of the league's cities that were double the population.

FIBBER MCGHEE AND COMPANY

The Phillies remained as the Major League franchise affiliate of Pensacola's ball club for 1940. Dashiell and Philadelphia farm directors revamped the team with new players as former heroes moved up through the ranks. Yet Pensacola was still a proven breeding ground for budding talent. During the off-season, the Fliers added two new rising stars and one special veteran to the 1940 lineup. Lefty Hoerst and Gene Lambert set to work on the mound for Pensacola, while venerable Bill McGhee covered first base.

Right-handed pitcher Gene Lambert from Crenshaw, Mississippi, played the 1939 season with the Mayodan (North Carolina) Millers of the Bi-State League. Lambert went thirteen and two for Mayodan before being sent to

Pensacola, where his arm proved equally proficient. Gene threw for a season ERA of 3.10 with thirteen wins and eight losses.

Philadelphia was serious about Pensacola and the prospects that could be supplied from the Gulf Coast member of their farm system. Gene Lambert was taken from the Pensacola B-Class team to Double-A and then on to the

Pensacola enlisted Bill "Fibber" McGhee as the starting first baseman on its 1940 roster. The contract with Wally Dashiell's franchise would have been to anyone else a brief stopover on their rise to the Major Leagues. However, McGhee "got sand in his shoes" and returned to make Pensacola his home as a player, manager and businessman. After his retirement, Bill McGhee became the first name in sporting goods for Florida's "Western Gate to the Sunshine State." *Courtesy of the author.*

Phillies Major League bullpen in 1941. Lambert saw a little work with the National League club through 1942, but he continued his baseball career in the minors through 1946. Gene gave up a slice of his ball-playing days to his country, serving in the U.S. Army from 1943 to 1945.

Bill "Fibber" McGhee was already an eleven-year veteran of the Minor League system when he arrived to play first base for Pensacola midway through the 1940 season. McGhee did not begin his career in baseball until he was twenty-three years of age. The thirty-four-year-old first baseman sat atop the Pensacola player's age scale, with only Dashiell his senior by a mere four years.

McGhee preformed well for the Fliers, batting .322 in 1940 along with fielding 1,245 putouts. He returned to Pensacola for the 1941 season and again five years later as a player/manager at age forty. Two additional calls of duty in Pensacola brought McGhee in to play for the city's club. Bill was listed on Pensacola's roster at age forty-three in 1949 and once more for the Dons at age fifty-one in 1957.

Sandwiched in between his playing tours in Pensacola, McGhee carried two seasons with the Philadelphia Athletics under the direction of Connie Mack. During one of those seasons, in 1945, his connection to Pensacola was renewed playing alongside pitcher Charlie Gassaway. Bill McGhee played a total of twenty-one seasons in the Minor Leagues, managing in eight of those years. At age thirty-nine, Bill McGhee became the oldest player to hit a home run, a record that stayed intact for fifty-nine years until broken by Randy Johnson in 2003. McGhee would ultimately make his home in Pensacola, selling sporting goods after he retired from baseball.

McGhee's teammate Frank Joseph "Lefty" Hoerst started out his athletic journey as a star basketball player for LaSalle University. He signed with the Phillies organization in 1939, playing for the Class-D Mayodan Millers. Hoerst went to Philadelphia at the beginning of the 1940 season, making six relief appearances and earning one win. The Major League club sent him to Pensacola for the remainder of the year, and Lefty kept his ERA to 2.56 in twenty-three games.

Returning to Philadelphia in 1941, Hoerst's career with the Phillies continued through 1947 with a three-year stint in the U.S Navy wedged in between. After Lefty Hoerst retired from professional baseball in 1948, he became the head baseball coach at his alma mater, LaSalle University, and later refereed basketball games in the NBA.

The Fliers' season, even with the 1940 personnel changes, started out with on-field festivities that were now commonplace at Legion Field. The "Clown

Prince of Baseball," Al Schacht, visited the Fliers' fans on May 8, as if to further validate Pensacola's standing as an accepted baseball town. Dashiell himself stated that although his on-field staff had a new face, he "would not stand for a losing club." If successful during the season, manager/ owner Dashiell would capture the seventh championship flag of his career. Pensacola's versatile sportswriter Frank Pericola echoed the sentiment, but the young 1940 Fliers team came up short by just one game at the end of the season, finishing in second place.

Kinner Graf pitched for Pensacola from 1937 until 1941. With thirteen seasons under his belt, Graf took over the position of skipper while still throwing in thirty-eight games in 1941. Pensacola lost their Major League affiliation but continued to forge forward in the Southeastern League. The '41 Pensacola roster, as always, listed a few players on their way to the big leagues with a nice stopover on the white sands of Florida's Western Gate.

In Vic Frazier's professional career, Pensacola was the last stop after thirteen years on the mound. The pitcher from Ruston, Louisiana, hung up his spikes after 1941. Vic Frasier spent six seasons in the majors with the White Sox, Tigers and Boston Bees. Vic was a member of Detroit's bullpen when they won the American League Championship in 1934.

Just a few miles away from Pensacola's Legion Field, Gus Bebas was finishing up his flight training at Pensacola's Naval Air Station in 1941. Bebas, a Minor Leaguer from Chicago, pitched for the NAS ball team. Gus had most recently pitched for the Hickory Rebels of the Tar Heel League and later participated in the Battle of Midway as a pilot aboard the USS *Hornet*. A few days after the horror of Midway, Ensign Bebas was killed in a dive-bombing accident. The USS *Bebas* was named in honor of the NAS pitcher.

CHAPTER 4
THE INTEGRATION ERA: 1942–1960

PENSACOLA'S NEGRO LEAGUE

Through the course of the United States' involvement in World War II, more than 4,500 Major and Minor Leaguers placed their baseball careers on the back shelf while they defended their nation against the aggression of Axis powers. As a result, Pensacola was directly affected by the absence of the stars of the diamond entering service as navy and marine aviators. Names normally read about in national sports pages now became hometown news. Ted Williams, Bobby Kennedy and Nick Tremark, among others, trained for service at the auxiliary facilities attached to Pensacola's Naval Air Station.

With the advent of the war, baseball entered into a new age. Because so many of the men normally in baseball uniform were now putting on the colors of the armed forces, the level of play on the fields of Major League Baseball was notably diluted. Measures taken by club ownerships to keep gate receipts at a normal level ranged from circus-style antics to the return of retired veteran ballplayers. Other venues, to pull in fans, included the all-female rosters of the All-American Girls Softball League (later All-American Girls Professional Baseball League). A few league owners even began to muse about what was to some the unthinkable: enlisting blacks into the all-white leagues.

Although murmurings of employing players from the Negro Leagues had begun much earlier, baseball did not completely enter into its Integration

While baseball on a national level was viewed through black-and-white lenses prior to 1947, Pensacola's approach to segregated participation was much more moderate. Due to societal limitations, the color line was certainly in effect for the athletes on the Gulf Coast, but the fans of Pensacola placed no such restrictions on themselves. The all-black teams of Pensacola, such as the Seagulls, drew large numbers of white spectators to their high-level competitions. African Americans also filled seats at Legion Field, where they followed their favorite Fliers players with exuberant and dedicated passion. *Courtesy of Pensacola Historical Society.*

Era until baseball pioneer Branch Rickey signed former Negro Leaguer Jackie Robinson to a Major League contract with the Brooklyn Dodgers on October 23, 1945. Pensacola, being a southern city, was not any quicker to combine blacks and whites on common teams than any other town south of the Mason-Dixon Line. However, the relationship between the races in the context of baseball in Pensacola became a central point of unity much earlier than it did in neighboring municipalities.

The Negro League teams in Pensacola, Florida, garnered as much of a following for their high level of skill and athleticism as did any of the City League teams or the Southeastern League Pensacola Fliers. Negro League fields were located throughout the community, but the shared venues between blacks and whites at Legion Field and later, Admiral Mason Park, was a common element in the Snapper Capital. The two races shared field space, and both blacks and whites turned out in notable numbers for color-specific games. Baseball for Pensacola became the color barrier eraser.

A game between the Negro League Brown Bombers from Montgomery, Alabama, and the Pepsi-Cola Stars of Pensacola took place at Legion Field on Sunday, August 9, 1942. General admission was thirty-five cents, and men in uniform paid a discounted twenty-five cents—all welcome, all admitted, all sitting together enjoying the game. Around town, Terry Wayne

East Park, Kiwanis Park, Granada Park, Lions Park, Pete Caldwell's Field and many other locations now lost to obscurity served as shining diamonds in the Negro League of Pensacola.

AVIATORS PLAY BALL

By 1942, Pensacola Naval Air Station and its surrounding auxiliary fields boasted flight training in both land-based and seagoing planes. Aquatic PBY aircraft and other "floatplanes" complemented the machinery of the ever-growing flight school. Nearing the end of World War II, over 2,800 naval aviators were designated by Pensacola NAS and the surrounding airfields. Pensacola aviation instructors were called upon for many specialized

Louis Armstrong's love for baseball drew him to Pensacola's Naval Air Station in the summer of 1942. Armstrong was an avid supporter of the game in his hometown of New Orleans and frequently sought out local matchups along his entertainment tour routes. The war-era military baseball squads representing Pensacola's main and auxiliary air bases were peppered with men who had known both the Minor and Major League diamonds. As a spectator, Satchmo was treated to a professional-level game miles away from any big-league stadium. *Courtesy of Gulf Islands National Seashore Archives.*

operations, including training the Doolittle Raiders in carrier take off maneuvers in B-25 Mitchell Bombers.

With so many men stationed at Pensacola NAS, off-duty activities increased in diversity, as did the need for entertainment and morale-lifting recreation. Baseball, as it had since the early 1900s, played a pivotal role in the physical welfare of the men stationed in Pensacola. However, the teams of Pensacola's military posts were now drawing a higher caliber of player and an increasing fan base. Pensacola's military ball teams attracted more than just the casual observer.

As America fully entered World War II, professional entertainers joined the ranks of other Americans to do their part in boosting the morale of service personnel "for the war effort." Louis "Satchmo" Armstrong interrupted his 1942 USO routine to take in a game between two of the Fort Barrancas squads. While in town, Armstrong performed at Abe's 506 Club and the Savoy Gardens in the Belmont-DeVillers neighborhood of Pensacola. Both the 506 and the Savoy attracted top-notch African American entertainers to perform for the segregated black servicemen. Louis Armstrong had a keen, personal interest in baseball and sponsored a baseball team in his beloved New Orleans called "Armstrong's Secret Nine."

PENSACOLA'S WARTIME BASEBALL

Pensacola Naval Air Station boasted a base team in 1942 that was heavily peppered with men with professional baseball experience. The 1942 NAS team consisted of players such as Lefty Stevens from the Southern League, Pete McGarry from the Three I League and Tommy Woodruff, who played with the Corpus Christi Spudders and Springfield (IL) Browns. George Earnshaw, who had pitched for the Philadelphia and Chicago American League franchises and Brooklyn and St. Louis of the National League, made a noteworthy appearance on the mound for Pensacola's navy squad. Earnshaw was decorated for "exceptional ability and judgment" by Admiral Nimitz in 1944 and later became a scout for the Philadelphia Phillies. Disgusted with the work habits of young pitchers during their days off, Earnshaw instituted the now common practice of having the starting pitcher of the next game chart pitches for the man on the mound.

Pensacola's navy club was not short on professionally experienced coaches either. Lieutenant Forrest Twogood had pitched for the Toledo Mud Hens of the American Association. Twogood, or "Twogie," as he was known on the

Pensacola's Naval Air Station (NAS) sits upon historical foundations. The calm waters surrounding the air station once offered a winter home for visiting Native Americans, a landing point for Spanish explorers and a fortified defense for both Union and Confederate soldiers. As an army installation, the area surrounding Fort Barrancas continued to be occupied by troops even through World War II. The soldiers offered their own baseball teams to the already grand mix of navy and marine personnel, making NAS a hotbed for off-duty club rivalries. *Courtesy of Gulf Islands National Seashore Archives.*

field, shaped a rather successful career out of guiding young athletes to their highest potential. Twogie, after fortifying Pensacola's navy team, became the head coach at the University of Idaho and later at the University of Southern California.

Catching for Pensacola's enlisted in 1942 was Herman Franks. Franks had begun his professional career with the Hollywood Stars of the Pacific Coast League in 1932. Moving up through the ranks of the Minor League system, he broke into the majors in 1939 with the St. Louis Cardinals. Franks caught for the Cardinals, Dodgers, Philadelphia Athletics and New York Giants during his career. Mentored by Twogood while in Pensacola, Franks pursued a lifelong mission of enhancing players' skills, beginning with Leo Durocher's 1949 San Francisco Giants.

Along with competing against regionally and nationally ranked organizations, Pensacola's Naval Air Station club took on a steady spring diet of collegiate-level adversaries. Pensacola's 1942 scheduled opponents included Illinois Wesleyan, Georgia Tech University, Jacksonville NAS, the Atlanta Crackers of the Southern Association and others. The Crackers came to Pensacola to open the navy's new baseball field on March 20, 1942, only to be defeated by the sailors 3–2 in ten innings. Pensacola's record at the end of the 1942 season stood at twenty-six wins and thirteen losses.

The 1942 Pensacola Fliers split their season's managerial duties between Charles "Buster" Chatham and Jake Baker. Entering the year unaffiliated, the Pensacola Fliers, still locally dubbed "Pilots" by the fans and newspapers, finished fifth place in the Southeastern League. With a dismal 59–84 record, neither player/manager Chatham nor Baker could pull Pensacola into a league championship position. The fact that both managers failed to lead Pensacola to a winning percentage could not be attributed to a lack of baseball experience.

Baker had spent nine seasons in Minor League play prior to coming to Pensacola, with two of those seasons spent with Double-A Minneapolis of the Red Sox organization. Chatham, a true veteran of the diamond, began his career in 1922, playing for seventeen teams and eleven leagues before arriving on the Gulf Coast. Buster Chatham played third base and shortstop for the Brooklyn Nationals in 1931 and 1932. He later worked as a scout for the Pittsburgh Pirates, San Francisco Giants, Detroit Tigers and Texas Rangers.

Bill McGhee was on hand in 1942 for one of several seasons he played for Pensacola. Lefty West, who would pitch for the St. Louis Browns two years later, won four games for Pensacola, earning a miniscule 1.95 ERA in eight appearances during the season.

Due to losing so many players to service in the war, the Southeastern League closed up shop after the 1942 season. This brought the end of organized play in most cities fielding a Southeastern League club, but not Pensacola. While the league would begin anew in 1946, during the war Pensacola had more than its share of top-ranked players and exhibitions even without Minor League representation in the city. The war itself ensured that baseball fans in Pensacola would see the best of the best challenge each other at the local naval air station and its auxiliary airfields.

Just nine days after the December 7, 1941 attack on Pearl Harbor, Pensacola's Naval Air Station responded with an adjusted training program to accommodate a 300 percent increase in flight student instruction. Midway through 1943, the increase in training produced almost twenty thousand pilots from Pensacola, many of whom were responsible for heroic efforts during the war.

NAS Mainside could in no way accommodate all of the personnel and equipment requirements to train the number of men coming through the flight program. To meet an increased demand for housing and specialized flight training, several local auxiliary fields were called upon. Among them was Naval Auxiliary Air Station Saufley Field, positioned on Perdido Bay just moments from the main base by air. Corry Field, originally designated in the early 1920s as an advanced fighter plane training complex, was re-designated in 1943 as an aviator school. Whiting Field, in Milton, Florida, was commissioned in July 1943, and Barin Field, twenty-three miles west of Pensacola in Foley, Alabama, focused on the fighter pilot program.

The U.S. Navy bought farmland north of Pensacola with the intent of building a supporting airfield for NAS. The newly constructed Ellyson Field was completed in 1940 and designated as an auxiliary training facility in January 1943. Ellyson's use as a training venue for pilots would be short-lived. However, during the course of the next few years, the Brooklyn Dodgers would use the field to train hundreds of emerging young players. Bronson Field, located on Pensacola's Perdido Bay, boasted land- and water-capable training aircraft. As one of only two auxiliary fields in Florida to have land- and water-accessible runways, Bronson Field was key in training marine and navy airmen.

With the influx of students to Pensacola Naval Air Station and its outlying training fields, the challenge of filling off-duty hours with engaging recreation was daunting. The City of Pensacola offered its military personnel any number of recreational activities from water sports to cultural and social entertainment. The navy also instituted leisure sports along with its physical conditioning regiment.

Each base fielded at least one ball team to compete among the other airfields. The Pensacola NAS baseball team had already proven to be a worthy competitor within military and civilian circuits. Not to be outdone by the navy, the army encampment at Fort Barrancas outfitted a club of ball-playing soldiers. However, during 1944 and 1945, none of the local bases or teams could boast the caliber of professional players as could Bronson Field. The Bronson Bombers baseball team roster read like a Major League All-Star lineup, and the fans in Pensacola rallied around it as such.

BRONSON'S ELITE TEAM

Bronson Field came into existence in 1939 when the navy purchased 640 acres for an outlying airfield to complement Corry Field's primary trainers. A larger runway was constructed in 1940, and by 1942, another 263 acres were acquired for a seaplane facility on Perdido Bay. With the VSB scouting and bombing training aircraft in place, the navy brought in the first forty water-capable PBY Catalinas, nicknamed "Flying Boats," on January 2, 1943. Each flight student arriving at Bronson had already logged a minimum of 160 hours in the air and would train for at least another 75 to 100 more, in addition to specialized flight training depending on the aircraft. While training hours took up a large portion of each student's day, time was always allotted for recreation.

Bronson Field offered an above-average recreational facility with an Olympic-size pool, indoor basketball court, weight and fitness rooms, steam bath and a well-groomed baseball field complete with bleacher seating. The ball field was part of a network of fields positioned on each air base to facilitate the navy's aviation league. The Pensacola Naval Air Training Center League consisted of six teams made up of airmen and flight crewmen from among the navy and marine students. While Mainside, Saufley, Whiting, Ellyson, Barin and Bronson all submitted worthy teams, Bronson Field was somewhat top-heavy in its talent, with no less than six men in its 1944 lineup who had already played professionally.

Second baseman for the Bronson Bombers was John Hutchinson, who had played for the Class-B Yakima Pippins of the Western International League. Third base was covered by Willard Sellergren, who had most recently come from the Americus Pioneers of the Georgia-Florida League.

Philadelphia Phillies right fielder Ray Stoviak covered familiar ground for the Bronson squad. Ray Stoviak was an outfielder with the Double-A Baltimore Orioles of the International League who had made his Major League debut with the Philadelphia Phillies on June 5, 1938. He stayed with the Phillies as a right fielder until August. While Stoviak's experience on the Major League diamond was brief, his service with the navy gave him the opportunity to play alongside Major Leaguers on Pensacola's Emerald Shore. As one of the Bronson Bombers outfielders, Ray Stoviak became an equal instead of a rookie.

Bombers player/manager and former Brooklyn Dodger Nick Tremark took position in the outfield. Nicholas Tremark developed his fielding ability while playing outfield for Yonkers High School in New York. His five-foot-

Bronson Field stood as one of the crowning jewels among the naval aviation auxiliary training facilities initialized during World War II. The training base also topped the list with a contending baseball team, fielding four veteran Major Leaguers and several Minor League players. Filling roster positions for the Bronson Bombers were Brooklyn Dodgers outfielder Nick Tremark (bottom row, fourth from the right), Chicago White Sox third baseman Bobby Kennedy (top row, third from the left), Philadelphia Phillies outfielder Ray Stoviak (top row, fourth from the right) and Boston Red Sox outfielder Ted Williams (top row, fifth from the right). *Courtesy Pensacola Naval Air Station MWR.*

five stature did not hinder him from leading his American Legion team to the New York State Championship, played at Yankee Stadium. During his first year in college, he played with both the freshman and varsity baseball team at Manhattan College, serving as captain during his senior year. Immediately after graduation, Tremark signed with the Brooklyn Dodgers, playing under manager Casey Stengel.

Nick Tremark made his Major League debut in August 1934, quickly gaining the attention of manager Stengel, who adopted Tremark as "his boy." At the time, Tremark held the distinction of being the shortest player in Major League history. Casey Stengel used him mainly as a pinch hitter, and in 1934, Nick delivered seven hits in twenty-eight at-bats for a .250 average. Backing up teammates Al Lopez, Hack Wilson and Dazzy Vance, Nick belted hits off of Dizzy Dean, Paul Derringer and others, compiling a .247 lifetime average with Brooklyn.

In 1943, Tremark joined the U.S. Navy and was given the select wartime rating of chief athletic specialist. In 1944, he was assigned to Bronson Field. After his service to his country, Nick Tremark played and managed with several semiprofessional ball clubs in the New York City metropolitan area.

Bob Kennedy joined the marines right in the middle of his successful career with the Chicago White Sox. Kennedy's quick infielder reflexes served him well in the cockpit but were also helpful for the Bombers. Bobby Kennedy was born on Chicago's South Side during the Capone era, and as a street-tough Irish kid, he grew up a White Sox fan. As soon as he was old enough to hold a job, he took a position as a vendor at Comiskey Park. The White Sox management took notice of their sixteen-year-old vendor's enthusiasm for the diamond, as he sometimes worked out with the team.

In 1937, the Sox were just beginning to build a structured farm system to sustain the future development of their franchise. Because of his noted abilities, Kennedy was signed to a Minor League contract to play for Vicksburg, Mississippi, of the Cotton States League. After spending a short two and a half seasons in the minors, Bobby Kennedy, less than one month after his nineteenth birthday, was sent to debut with the Chicago White Sox.

Kennedy spent a total of sixteen seasons in the Major Leagues with the White Sox, Indians, Orioles, Tigers and Brooklyn Dodgers. In 1948, Chicago traded Bobby to Cleveland during an era when the Indians were owned by legendary baseball promoter Bill Veeck. Along with teammates Satchel Paige, Bob Lemon, Bob Feller and Larry Doby, Kennedy contributed to a Cleveland World Series victory over the Boston Braves.

Boston Red Sox favorite Ted Williams completed the outfield on Bronson's roster. Only three Major League players have entered service in both World War II and the Korean War. Ted Williams, Jerry Colman and Bobby Kennedy all flew as fighter pilots, with Williams and Kennedy taking their early technical training in Pensacola. Bobby joined Ted Williams as a member of the Pensacola Naval Air Station's All-Star team, playing against NAS Corpus Christi, a team that featured Boston Braves pitcher Johnny Sain. Sain's Boston teammate Buddy Gremp was stationed at Whiting Field in 1944 and Saufley Field in 1945. The two Braves opposed each other in navy play as Gremp covered first base for Pensacola.

Well-known sports columnist Furman Bisher visited Bronson Field to interview Williams and Kennedy in 1944 and took a number of photographs of the Pensacola-stationed Major Leaguers standing by their planes and engaging in daily base activity. While it was a novelty for the American public to see images of Ray Stoviak and other baseball heroes preparing for the defense of the nation, the power of the Bronson team was no novelty. The Bronson Bombers won the league championship in 1944. Several members of the team were also selected for the Navy Air Training Base All-Star Championship Series.

AIR BASE ALL-STARS

During the middle of September 1944, the Pensacola and Corpus Christi Naval Air Stations each assembled an all-star baseball team from among their auxiliary base squads. Either lineup card would have made any Major League manager's mouth water with the taste of a pennant. Four games were played from September 16 to 24, with two contests at each city's main air base. Although the games were more for exhibition than anything else, the morale boost for the military personnel and local fans went without measure.

The starting lineup for Corpus Christi under manager Boyd SoRelle from the Toledo Mud Hens listed Dan Menendez from the Opelousas Indians at second base; John Phipps of the Montreal Royals in left field; Bob Bergstrom of the Portland Beavers at third base; Philadelphia Athletics veteran Sam Chapman in centerfield; Charley Sylvester from the Hollywood Stars at first base; Dick Kalal of the Louisville Colonels at shortstop; R.L. Vaughn, most recently from the University of Southern California, in right field; and Milan Kapusta with the Batavia Clippers behind the plate.

Corpus Christi's starting pitching rotation consisted of Ezra "Pat" McGlothin from the Elizabethtown Betsy Red Sox, Philadelphia Athletics hurler Joe Colman, R.D. Holland of the Jonesboro White Sox and Johnny Sain, just beginning what would become an all-star career with the Boston Braves and New York Yankees.

Pensacola's all-stars were no less loaded with professionals. Under the direction of NAS physical education instructor and team manager Herman Franks, the Pensacola squad was a stacked deck of talent. Franks had caught for the Brooklyn Dodgers and was a veteran of many Minor League seasons. He would later manage seven seasons in the National League, along with coaching, scouting and accepting a brief stint as the general manager for the 1981 Chicago Cubs.

Taking the field for Pensacola was second baseman Ted Ratenski of the Charlotte Hornets, first baseman Buddy Gremp from the Boston Braves, shortstop Bobby Kennedy of the Chicago White Sox, Boston Red Sox favorite Ted Williams covering center field, left fielder Bob Cowsar from the Lamesa Lobos, right fielder Tommy Neill of the Hartford Bees and third baseman Frank "Buck" Weaver of the Burlington Bees and, later, the Pensacola Fliers. Catcher Mendel Ramsey played with the Jacksonville Tars and reserve infielder Johnny Hutchinson for the Yakima Pippins. Pensacola's pitchers included the Southeastern League's Paul Petrich and Jim Ruark of the Sanford Spinners and Leonard Heinz, most recently from the Waterloo Hawks.

On paper, the teams seemed very evenly matched—this would prove to be true on the field as well. The first two out of four games were played in Pensacola at the Navy Yard, with Pensacola winning the first game on Saturday, September 16, by a score of 1–0. Johnny Sain was the losing pitcher, and Frank Weaver, who was also the athletic director at Whiting Field, hit the game-winning home run. During the second game on Sunday, September 17, Corpus Christi made a valiant attempt to beat the Florida boys on their home turf, but Pensacola responded in a 5–4 win.

Because duty called and the nation's defense training was primary, the All-Star series took place only on the weekends. The Pensacola team traveled to Texas the following Saturday and Sunday. On Saturday, September 23, Corpus Christi got even by overcoming Pensacola 2–1. However, the hottest contest of the four-game series came on September 24 when Pat McGlothin went the distance for Corpus Christi in a nineteen-inning brawl.

Pensacola scored one in the second inning, and Corpus Christi answered back with two. Texas scored again in the fourth, and Florida put up a run in both the sixth and the ninth to tie it up. Neither team would bring in a run again until both put one on the board in the seventeenth inning. The score was four runs apiece through the middle of the ninetieth until McGlothin, helping out his cause, drove in the winning run to defeat Pensacola 5–4.

Although the exhibition series was split at two games apiece, the atmosphere could not have been better. Servicemen and civilians alike were treated to a thrill of a lifetime, watching the very best ballplayers the naval air training bases had to offer. Consequently, many were the very best the Major Leagues had to offer as well, proving once again that baseball is America's game in wartime and in peace.

"TEDDY BALLGAME"

Boston slugger Ted Williams enlisted with the United States Marine Corps at the Department of the Navy's recruiting office in May 1942. Due to his extraordinary 20/10 vision, he was quickly assigned to naval aviation. Williams reported for ground school in Amherst, Massachusetts, in November 1942. The navy had waited until Major League Baseball completed its season before requiring Ted to report for preflight training. After several months of qualifying instruction, Ted was sent to Pensacola for specialized training, and on December 7, 1943, Ted Williams was assigned to Bronson Field.

Bronson Field was outfitted with excellent athletic facilities and accommodations for its students and instructors. The officers' club, with its sweeping veranda overlooking the bay, offered breathtaking views of sunsets and rollicking porpoises. The basketball court and workout area sat adjacent to the swimming pool. However, it was the baseball field with its wooden bleachers that played host to enthusiastic townspeople and sailors desiring to catch a glimpse of the pride of the Red Sox and other professional players.

Later in life, recalling his time on the diamond while training in Pensacola, Ted said, "I didn't have my heart in it at all and I played lousy." The fact was that he really did play well while in Pensacola, ripping big-league line drives and home runs. If Williams did have his heart elsewhere, it was not hard to understand why. "Teddy Ballgame" took his aviation defense career seriously, setting records in aerial gunnery. On May 2, 1944, Williams accepted appointment as second lieutenant and received his wings aboard Pensacola NAS. He was then assigned as a staff instructor for the naval air training bases, a post he held until June 1945. Just after his commission, Ted Williams married Doris Soule. Regardless of how Ted felt personally about his playing quality in Pensacola, he did help the Bronson Bombers to win the 1944 Training Command Championship.

It was apparent to those who served with Williams in Pensacola that he had become fond of the region. It seems that his time along the Gulf Coast was the beginning of Ted's love affair with Florida. Just months before Ted's death in 2002, Jack Reed, the operations officer for morale, welfare and recreation for Pensacola NAS, came across a photograph of Williams in his Bronson Bombers uniform. Reed played in the Red Sox organization himself and was an avid follower of Ted's career. Not knowing the deteriorating physical condition Ted was under, Reed made a phone call to Ted's home in Homosassa, Florida. Reed's thought was to speak to the veteran ballplayer and ask if he might like to have the photograph.

Ted's daughter Claudia, who was also his caregiver, answered the phone. Jack Reed explained the reason for his call and from where he was calling. Claudia quickly apologized to Jack. Her father was too ill to speak on the phone, but she asked if Jack would wait on the line for a few moments. After a short time, Claudia came back to inform Reed that she had told her father someone from Pensacola at the navy base was on the telephone. Claudia relayed to Reed that when her dad heard someone was calling him from Pensacola about the Bronson Bombers, tears came down his cheeks and a smile across his face. Claudia said, "Mr. Reed, I have not seen my dad smile like that in a very long time. Thank you for that memory."

THE FIRST "DODGERTOWN"

By 1945, the navy began to streamline its training operations at Ellyson Field. As the de-escalation of the war decreased the need for aviators and support staff, Pensacola's auxiliary fields reduced the number of instructors and ground school facilities. In response, Ellyson's basic and primary training operations were relocated to Corpus Christi, Texas. The navy eventually deactivated the airfield in 1947 but not before catching the attention of Brooklyn Dodgers president and general manager Branch Rickey.

Branch Rickey was a baseball innovator in the truest sense of the term. He had played in the majors for four seasons, managed the St. Louis Browns and the St. Louis Cardinals and held the office of general manager for the Browns, Cardinals and, now, the Brooklyn Dodgers. With four World Series titles under his belt, Rickey had introduced and implemented batting cages, pitching machines, batting helmets and the first full-time spring training facility and streamlined the farm system to ensure the health, productivity and preservation of the affiliate Major League club. It was with the idea of player development and procurement that Rickey looked to the Gulf Coast for room to grow.

Not satisfied with the Minor League system alone, Branch Rickey's organizational genius set into motion a project that would pull local talent from strategic locations across the country. However, the idea was not only gleaning the best prospects from amateur tryouts but also to mold player abilities to the "Dodger Way." Traveling in his private Beechcraft airplane, Rickey flew into Pensacola to survey the facilities at Ellyson Field and communicate his intentions.

Future Dodgers legends Walter Alston and Carl Erskine were among the many who participated in the very first "Dodgertown." Positioned north of town atop the bluffs of Pensacola Bay, the Ellyson Field flight-training facility was one of the first to be decommissioned after the conclusion of World War II. Brooklyn Dodgers general manager Branch Rickey saw an opportunity in the location and amenities of Ellyson for a player development camp. *Courtesy of the author.*

In Pensacola, the Dodgers' GM met with Fliers owner Wally Dashiell and Rear Admiral Frank Wagner. Ever the innovator and strategist, Branch Rickey soon recognized Pensacola's advantageous geographical location. Rickey and the Brooklyn front office would in short order breathe new life into Ellyson Field and bring future stars to the Port City in the form of Dodgers Minor

Leaguers. Ellyson provided adequate facilities for the Dodgers' amateur training camp, but the success of the location would prompt Brooklyn to add the venue to their Minor League spring training program. The Triple-A affiliate Montreal Royals trained in Havana, Cuba, with the main club, but more than ten clubs from the remainder of the Dodgers' farm system were sent to Pensacola for preseason exercises.

The Double-A Fort Worth Cats were sent to work out at Pensacola's Legion Field, taking in scrimmages against the Fliers. The rest of the Dodgers' farm clubs were stationed at Ellyson to train against each other. The training began on March 1, with no less than 125 men in exercise. Teams from Ashville, North Carolina; Danville, Illinois; Nashua, New Hampshire; and Cambridge, Massachusetts, were among those Brooklyn sent for spring training on the Gulf Coast.

Many future Major League stars ran the base paths at the Dodgers' Pensacola facility. Toby Atwell, Danny Ozark, Ed Chandler, Carl Erskine, Pat McGlothin and Herman Franks were featured among the Dodgers' junior circuit personnel. Future actor Chuck Connors, playing for the Dodgers' Mobile, Alabama affiliate, spent the spring soaking in instruction from the Ellyson Field coaching staff, which included Walter Alston, George Sisler and Pepper Martin. A young former Negro League pitcher from the Nashua Dodgers by the name of Don Newcombe was just starting his victorious climb up the Major League ladder. During his time in Pensacola, Newcombe began to show the prominent talent that would win games and the hearts of fans while he built relationships that would serve him in years to come.

In addition to the spring venue, the *Sporting News* reported that Branch Rickey was stocking the Brooklyn farm clubs from specialized training camps in Thomasville, North Carolina; San Bernardino, California; and Ellyson Field in Pensacola, Florida, all emphasizing "quality out of quantity." Each camp, including Pensacola, held open trials for local players and then selected a large number of them to form scrimmage teams. After the teams were formed, the Dodgers went to work on selecting and instructing the best of the amateurs, fully intent on growing the next generation of Brooklyn's finest. Rickey's framework for a Dodgers camp in Pensacola was described by the *Sporting News*:

> *At Pensacola, the players were divided into nine teams. Each team had a manager who was responsible for familiarizing himself with the players' capabilities and personalities. Scouts watched every workout and game, and*

then gathered with Dodgers' staff at the end of each day to analyze the talent well into the night. At the beginning of the Minor League season, more than a thousand men had been evaluated.

Branch Rickey's influence in Pensacola persisted from the late 1940s well through the early 1950s. However, one Brooklyn farmhand's early experience with Pensacola had a negative outcome. Newly signed second baseman Jackie Robinson's Minor League assignment was with the Montreal Royals. As the Royals were a farm club of the parent Brooklyn franchise, Rickey broke through a sixty-five-year "gentlemen's agreement" among Major League club owners to bar blacks from playing for any of their teams. While Robinson's signing was the beginning of desegregation within the ranks of the majors, Branch Rickey's bold move, along with Jackie's presence, was met with much opposition.

Bound for the Royals' spring training grounds in Daytona Beach, Florida, Robinson and his new wife, Rachel, boarded an airplane in Los Angeles, California, on March 1, 1946. From the outset, the Robinsons' trek was fret with difficulty. The plane flew from California to New Orleans, landing for what was to be a brief stop. According to Jackie Robinson's autobiography, he and his wife were asked to leave the plane and take their belongings with them into the terminal. Robinson felt the "bumped" flight was racially motivated, although reasons contrary to his thoughts were given. The Robinsons were denied the right to eat in the airport coffee shop, and twelve hours later, Jackie and Rachel were once again in the air after their "brief" layover.

The next stop was for refueling in Pensacola. Again the Robinsons were delayed. Their seats were twice given to white passengers, and it quickly became evident they would have to stay the night in town. This fact brought with it its own level of challenges, as there were no nearby accommodations for black guests. An airport porter called for a car, and the driver took them to a local hotel in hopes that he might find a bed for the couple. When none was available, the hotel doorman suggested an inquiry for an overnight stay with a black family he knew downtown.

Jackie Robinson later retold the story, stating that the Pensacola family extended grand hospitality and offered them a place to sleep. Jackie said that although the family was "warmhearted and willing to share what little they had," the family was quite large and the home was quite small. The Robinsons thanked the family for their kindness but opted to catch the next bus to Jacksonville and then on to Daytona Beach.

THE LEGACY OF LEGION FIELD

Adding to the chronological list of Major and Minor League teams that have enjoyed the inviting climate and latitude of Pensacola, the 1946 Boston Braves and the World Champion Detroit Tigers made the city a spring training exhibition location. On April 2, 1946, Tigers pitcher Frank "Stubby" Overmire bested the Braves in a 9–6 victory at Legion Field. The win in Pensacola marked the third straight for the Tigers over the Braves in 1946 preseason play, with Hank Greenburg and Pinky Higgins belting home runs for Detroit.

Pensacola fans were treated to championship-level competition featuring Greenburg, Birdie Tebbetts and George Kell for the Tigers and Tommy Holmes, Tommy Neill and Citronell, Alabama-born Bama Rowell for the Braves. The April 2 event brought Tommy Neill and Jonny Sain back to a Pensacola, Florida diamond for a second time after their wartime diamond appearances. Also in attendance in their respective bullpens for the Pensacola contest were future Hall of Fame inductees Warren Spahn and Hal Newhouser.

With the end of World War II and men returning from domestic and international duty, the Southeastern League, like many of its Minor League counterparts, resumed normal operations. Players who had just recently defended their country on the field of battle were now ready to defend their town ball teams on the field of play. Pensacola joined Anniston, Vicksburg, Montgomery, Jackson, Gadsden, Selma and Meridian to form the reorganized Southeastern League.

The Pensacola Fliers returned to play under their familiar nickname, along with the American League Washington Senators signing Pensacola as their Class-B affiliate for the 1946 season. In having a Major League benefactor, Pensacola fared somewhat better in support than did many of the other teams attempting to regain momentum after the war. Pensacola's 1946 team featured men who were returning from service in the military and those who would serve the squads of Major League teams. After a preseason workout for the Fliers in Winter Garden, Florida, the player combination was a winning hand, and Pensacola secured its fourth pennant since 1937.

Veteran Bill McGhee, born in Shawmut, Alabama, had become an institution in Pensacola. McGhee returned to the City of Five Flags to manage and play first base in 1946. Working alongside McGhee was Saul Rogovin, who later pitched for the Tigers, White Sox and Phillies and threw twenty-two games for Pensacola. Also joining McGhee's '46 Pensacola staff were Tigers and Browns pitcher George Gill and Cuban-born Freddy Rodriguez, who would later play for the 1958 Chicago Cubs and 1959 Philadelphia Phillies.

Included on Pensacola's reorganized team were catcher and former army corporal Jim Vance and third baseman and navy recreational director Frank "Buck" Weaver. Vance had played for the Eighth Air Force All-Stars in the 1943 European Theater. Buck Weaver coached the Whiting Field baseball team and also oversaw the welfare and morale of navy airmen through athletic activity. During Weaver's brief career in professional baseball, he also played for the St. Louis Cardinals and Cleveland Indians organizations.

Buck Weaver dedicated his life to the physical and mental well-being of student aviators. The longtime Milton, Florida resident spent thirty years in navy recreation and worked for Pensacola-based Biggs & Kupfrian

Located at the corner of Gregory and G Streets in downtown Pensacola, Legion Field was the home grounds for the Fliers and the Seagulls, as well as a spring training venue for multiple professional franchises. The formerly named Maxent Park was originally built on community interest and later expanded with citywide backing. The wooden stands at Legion Field afforded a ringside view of the world of baseball and, at times, future Hall of Famers such as Babe Ruth, Max Carey, Dazzy Vance and Mel Ott. *Courtesy of Pensacola Historical Society.*

Sporting Goods. Weaver passed at the age of ninety-six with interment at the Barrancas National Cemetery at Pensacola's Naval Air Station. The combination of veteran players and determined rookies in 1946 not only won a championship for Pensacola but also drew a record 126,000 fans during the season.

Legion Field pulled fans, both black and white, to root for the Fliers. Left fielder Neb Wilson was a particular favorite among those in the segregated bleachers along the left field line. As Wilson would come up to bat, a particular cadence and rally stomp would arise from the left-side onlookers. Pensacola resident Bobby Martin recalls, "A home run from Wilson would result in almost hysteria." Fliers' owner Wally Dashiell sought ways to bring the black and white communities together under the banner of baseball, but it would be another three seasons before he would accomplish that.

Pensacola was without a Major League affiliate in 1947. While the year began with promise for the Fliers working out the preseason with Brooklyn's students from the Ellyson Field camp, their own season in the Southeastern League was less than stellar. Pensacola finished in the middle of the league devoid of a title. However, not having a national-level affiliation did not prohibit the Fliers from building a quality team. American League veteran Carl Fisher, Pensacola favorite Neb Wilson and Bronze Star recipient Minor Scott performed for the fans, leaving none disappointed.

In 1948, Branch Rickey's instructional school continued at Ellyson Field. *Baseball Digest* described the operation as "huge" but also stated the school was an "entirely separate enterprise" than that of Rickey's twenty-five Minor League training operations. Brooklyn had become a part of the Pensacola community by the spring of 1948, and young men from across the Gulf Coast were honing their skills and living out their dreams at the Dodgers' baseball school. The spring training experiment of "one big camp" was paying off for Branch Rickey and changing the mindset of preseason conditioning. While the school and the spring encampment were completely different operations, combining it all at one facility set an example for other franchises.

During the years in which the Dodgers utilized Pensacola for their Minor League spring training grounds, local baseball fans unknowingly watched the burgeoning careers of some of the game's greatest legends. Walter "Smokey" Alston managed the St. Paul Saints club for six seasons. Alston had himself played in the Major Leagues for the Cardinals but became known for his achievements as a manager within the Dodgers' system. Alston managed several Brooklyn farm system teams while training in Pensacola. When

Walter Alston got the call to become the Brooklyn Dodgers field manager in 1954, his position in St. Paul was filled by Pensacola native Max Macon.

Dodgers pitching legend Carl Erskine spent several spring exercises in Pensacola. Erskine knew Walter Alston from their time together on the Emerald Shore. The men furthered their relationship in 1950 as members of the Montreal club, and later, Erskine played six years under Manager Alston with the Dodgers Major League franchise. Carl Erskine reported to *Baseball Digest* that after a good spring training in Pensacola he was prepared for a successful season. Erskine went 19–9 pitching against regular season opponents in 1948.

The city of Pensacola was buzzing with baseball activity even before the Fliers' 1948 season began. The Dodgers were en masse north of town, and Legion Field was the gathering place for much excitement as well. The Nashville Volunteers of the Southern Association opted to make Pensacola their 1948 spring training destination. The Vols were managed by former Boston Braves outfielder Larry Gilbert, and the team featured Gilbert's own son, Charlie, along with future Major League All-Star Smoky Burgess. The Nashville club provided quality opposition for the Pensacola Fliers preseason training.

The Fliers had spent a couple of seasons rebuilding a contending team. Neb Wilson, future Major Leaguers Bob Thorpe and Davey Williams and veteran Bill Burgo were part of the foundational infrastructure initiated by Pensacola's front office. As much an oddity as it was indicative of Pensacola's intention to construct a winning combination, the club changed managers three times during the 1948 season. The year began under the managerial direction of seasoned baseball veteran Otto Denning, changing to adopted Pensacola son and team owner Wally Dashiell and finishing under Minor League journeyman Clyde "Rabbit" McDowell. Each had an impact, but none could deliver a pennant.

Sportswriter Wesley Chalk praised McDowell in his *Chalk Lines* editorial for Rabbit's ability to get Pensacola's pitchers back in shape and smooth the ruffled feathers of teammates not speaking to each other. But regardless how much of a peacemaker McDowell turned out to be, another would fill his shoes the following season in hopes of a winning combination on the field and on the bench.

TRIUMPH OF 1949

The Fliers drew more than just the attention of the Pensacola faithful by the beginning of 1949. Although the club had not captured a title for the past two seasons, the Fliers were still known for competitive play. The Southern Association's Atlanta-based club followed in Nashville's footsteps the previous year by choosing Pensacola for its spring workout headquarters. Jack Taylor and Davey Williams, who were now with the Atlanta Crackers, had played for Pensacola the previous season.

Pensacola's 1949 team was basically a collection of no-names with no Major League affiliation, requiring a relatively small payroll. Most of the men who played for the Fliers in 1949 would never reach the Major Leagues. However, the results of the season would later prove that it did not take a big-league benefactor to build a team that would become one of the greatest clubs in Southeastern League history.

Bill Herring, a thirty-nine-year-old Minor League veteran, signed on as the Fliers' manager in '49, sharing some of the pitching duties as well. Pitcher Bert Heffernan posted a 2.56 ERA in thirty-five games and threw a perfect game against Montgomery. Now at age forty-three, Minor League legend Bill McGhee batted .287 for Pensacola alongside friend and teammate Neb Wilson, who slugged sixteen home runs and a .324 batting average.

Pensacola boasted a pair of twenty-plus-game-winning pitchers in 1949. Alvin Henencheck went 22–6 and Ken Deal threw 21–5. Left-hander Joe Kirkland won an ERA crown, with six shutouts in eighteen starts. Kirkland's ERA was a minuscule 1.62. Jack Hollis and Joe Kirkland were named to the Southeastern League's All-Star first squad, while Neb Wilson, Minor Scott, Bob Thorpe and Alvin Henencheck were named to the second squad.

The 1949 Pensacola Fliers finished the season with the highest mark in the history of the league, sixteen games ahead of the second-place team. Their .700 winning percentage is testimony to the determination of what some would call an underdog team. This club was not only well balanced—it functioned with single-minded purpose, proving that excellence can grow from meager resources.

The Fliers swept Jackson in four straight games in the playoffs and delivered a pennant-winning blow to Vicksburg in a four-games-to-one championship tournament. A short time later, the Class-B teams of the southeast held an invitational matchup called the Little Dixie Series. During the series, the Fliers defeated the Tampa club of the Florida Internationals, taking four out of six.

During the eighteen-year Minor League career of hard-slugging Neb "Hack" Wilson, six seasons were spent as a member of Pensacola's home teams. Neb predominantly covered the outfield for Pensacola, becoming a fan favorite, especially with the African American community sitting in the left field bleachers. Each time Neb came up to bat, a chant arose from his left-corner cheering section, accompanied by a stomping cadence that was said to sound like rolling thunder. Whether wearing a Fliers uniform or that of the Dons, Wilson was a Pensacola mainstay. Neb's .324 batting average in 1949 helped the Fliers to a league championship. *Courtesy of Diane Crona.*

Not to be outdone by the adults, the 1949 Pensacola Little League All-Stars traveled to Williamsport, Pennsylvania, to participate in the August national classic. Pensacola was defeated by Hammonton, New Jersey, and settled for second place in the third annual Little League World Series. However, a precedent had now been set, and Pensacola was also becoming a hard-playing youth baseball town.

SEAGULLS, PEPSI-COLA STARS AND ARTHUR GIANTS

Tucked away in a grove at the corner of Fairfield Drive and Market Street, just north of Pensacola Catholic High School, sits the remnants of Pete Caldwell's Field. Caldwell's Field held the distinction of being the home field for the Pensacola Arthur Giants. The Giants were one of the city's most illustrious Negro League teams during the mid-half of the twentieth century. The Arthur Giants organization had weathered the rigors of a color-restrictive baseball culture and survived the demise of many elite all-black teams following the game's desegregation. The Giants were such a part of Pensacola's black community that the team's fans and followers would not allow them to slip away into obscurity.

Pensacola physician and Giants owner Dr. E.S. Cobb had developed the team into a highly respected squad throughout the 1930s, offering competitive baseball that attracted the roving eyes of national-level Negro League scouts. In the 1940s, controlling interest of the Giants was transferred to Arthur Lee Weathers, who took the team to new heights in family entertainment and fostered a sense of community ownership. Longtime Pensacola resident Gloria Coleman recalls the excitement of seeing games at Caldwell's Field: "It was something like a county fair every weekend, with all of your friends and family around you at every turn. We called Mr. Weathers 'Daddy Bob' and we called his wife 'Ma Bella.' They were just like a second set of parents to all of us kids."

Cars lined up along Market Street waiting for the park gates to open before games. Vendors selling hotdogs, popcorn and other ballpark fare offered families a festive atmosphere and a getaway from everyday life. Gloria says that one of the popular fixtures in the stands was a peanut barker with a withered arm. "He would yell 'Hot Peanuts,' and if you held up your hand he would throw you a sack with his good arm," Gloria recalls. "And he was spot on target every time." Daddy Bob and the Arthur Giants players were

Traveling in a streamline air-cooled bus, the Seagulls were not limited to local or even regional competition. Barnstorming road trips carried the Gulls as far as San Francisco to match up against nationally ranked Negro League teams. As one of Pensacola's premier all-black clubs, the Seagulls played a level of baseball that easily kept up with Buck O'Neil's Kansas City Monarchs and Walter Gibbon's Indianapolis Clowns. *Courtesy of Pensacola Historical Society.*

role models for the young people, as they interacted with the children before and after games, giving life instruction and athletic tips.

The Giants, Seagulls, Pepsi-Cola Stars and other Emerald Coast Negro League clubs played well past the era when most southern black teams ceased existence. However, in Pensacola, it was not due to continued segregation that the organizations stayed intact but because of the incredible patronage and support by both black and white fans.

The Seagulls were a feeder affiliate for the Negro Southern League and remained a functioning organization after the parent league folded. Indianapolis Clowns pitcher Walter "Dirk" Gibbons remembers playing in Pensacola as a visiting opponent and not seeing much more than the ball field in "The Bottoms" area north of the Brownsville neighborhood. "I didn't even know you had a downtown until I came back to Pensacola years later. We weren't allowed to roam down that way," recalls Gibbons. However, "roaming" became a regular occurrence with the Seagulls, as the team traveled across the country barnstorming their way as far as San Francisco, where they once again faced the Clowns.

The families of Pensacola Negro League players David Colman, William Bell and Charles Marvray recall fondly the experiences and memories surrounding the teams before and after baseball's desegregation. While the personal stories and exploits of many Negro Leaguers have been lost to obscurity, Pensacola's legacy has been kept alive through the passing of oral history from one generation to the next.

David Colman played second base for the Seagulls during the era when the Clowns came to play in Pensacola. Colman was a respected member of the Pensacola Naval Air Station civilian workforce, a Pensacola church leader, youth baseball coach and a loving father and husband. But beyond those attributes, David Colman was a part of the city's baseball heritage. Prior to Colman's service to his country as a soldier between 1950 and 1953, David played for the Pensacola Seagulls club.

David Colman's son Ed returned to Pensacola for his father's funeral in 2011. When asked how he thought his father would like to be remembered, Ed answered straight away: "Dad would want people to know that he loved his family, loved his country, loved his Lord in heaven, loved to sing…and most certainly that he was a home run king."

Seagulls catcher William "Pit" Bell played alongside David Colman and later kept up with many of the relationships he made during his playing days. A thirty-six-year veteran of Armstrong World Industries, Bell continued his passion for the game, attending local competitions and reminiscing about the Seagulls' coast-to-coast exploits. Just before his death in 2006, Hall of Fame member Buck O'Neil visited the Port City to take part in a Negro League memorial celebration hosted by the Pensacola Pelicans. O'Neil and Bell quickly found each other to rekindle memories of the time the Seagulls faced O'Neil's Kansas City Monarchs.

Pit Bell's widow recalls with fondness the way the ladies and gentlemen would dress in grand attire to come watch the Seagulls play at Legion Field. "It was such a lovely time with all the folks. You just felt like you were a part of something very big and proud to be a part. It didn't hurt that I was one of the team wives and got special attention, including riding the bus," Mrs. Bell chuckles.

Booker T. Washington High School graduate Charles Jefferson "Hawk" Marvray began his baseball career several seasons prior to his senior year. Graduating in 1946, Marvray played football for his school but took up baseball under the coaching direction of Vernon McDaniel and Emory Williams with the Pensacola Giants. Garfield Pugh, partial owner of the Pepsi-Cola Stars, wooed Marvray to become a member of the elite team for the 1945 and 1946 seasons.

Charles earned the nickname "Hawk" for his keen attention to the game and defensive maneuvers on the field. Hawk also held firm ownership of the plate each time he stepped up to bat. Marvray had made a name for himself in his hometown and among the teams who played the Stars. Upon graduation from high school, an opposing team once again contracted Hawk. This time it was the Panama City Blue Sox. The Blue Sox, like Marvray's Pensacola clubs, competed against nationally ranked Negro League organizations. Hawk spent three seasons in Panama City, where he was scouted by the Cleveland Buckeyes and signed his first professional contract in 1949.

Following Branch Rickey's pioneering act of signing Jackie Robinson, other National and American League clubs began to make their own scouting expeditions into the fertile Negro League circuits. Charles Marvray's .315 batting average in 1950 caused the Chicago White Sox and St. Louis Cardinals to feature his exploits in their field reports. However, the scouts were a little late in enlisting the Pensacola-born athlete because Hawk was drafted into army service in 1951. The U.S. Army appreciated Marvray's playing skills and allowed him to continue his passion as a member of the Special Services Baseball Team.

Upon returning to Pensacola after his service to his country, Hawk joined the Pensacola Seagulls and was reunited with several old teammates. He also began coaching Little League Baseball and took a position with the N. Goldring Corporation. Two years after Charles Marvray's death in 1998, over three hundred people gathered at the former site of Legion Field to honor the memory of Hawk as a monument was set in place just a few yards from where he once drove home runs over the back fence.

George Agee, Charles Thompson, Johnny Dixon, Charles Mobley and Purvis Lewis are among the names of Pensacola Negro League players who will never grace the halls of Cooperstown. But each made a mark in the game just the same. Agee pitched for the Giants under Daddy Bob Weathers. Weathers, who played third base for the Pepsi-Cola Stars, remembered the Kansas City Monarchs on a spring tour through Pensacola: "We played against Jackie Robinson's Monarchs, which came down here. We played them right out there at Legion Field. Those games drew big crowds too."

While Wally Dashiell was managing the Fliers, he saw Charles Mobley playing shortstop for the Stars one afternoon. As the Fliers and the Stars shared the field, Dashiell approached Mobley about coming out to play a few innings with the Fliers to show appreciation for the black community and their support of Pensacola baseball. When the city police chief got wind of Dashiell's idea, he advised both men that although there was an accepted arrangement to share the field, mixing the races on a single team may cause an uproar too strong for local law enforcement to put down. Dashiell was extremely disappointed, as Mobley's batting average was quite high at the time. Dashiell exclaimed, "If I could just paint you white, I would have you as our shortstop tonight." Charles Mobley says that Dashiell's statement, although not racially sensitive, made him feel good because he knew Wally genuinely wanted to have him in the game with the Fliers.

Undaunted by the color hurdle, team owner Dashiell formulated a new plan. An invitation was accepted to play the Wilkes-Barre Indians, an integrated team, in 1949. The Indians fielded several former Negro League talents such as Harry "Suitcase" Simpson and Al "Fuzzy" Smith. Mild public protest arose initially, but it was quickly silenced as Simpson hit for the cycle. Amidst the throngs of spectators, Wally Dashiell opened the grandstands up to all patrons, eliminating segregated seating.

LITTLE LEAGUE ALL-STARS

St. Petersburg hosted the 1950 Florida Little League State Championship, with the last game being played on August 16. The bid for the title came down to a final game between Fort Lauderdale and the Pensacola Tangerine Stars. Pensacola manager Jack Peerson led his boys to a 4–2 victory, securing a spot for the second year in the Little League World Series. Although Pensacola lost to Kankakee, Illinois, in the quarterfinals of the series, the Tangerine Stars returned home to a hero's welcome.

Building on their past success, the Pensacola Little League All-Stars advanced to the World Series for a third consecutive year in 1951. Hall of Fame legend Cy Young threw out the first pitch to open the tournament. Pensacola was defeated in the quarterfinals by Fairmont, West Virginia, in a heated 5–4 battle, but the city of Pensacola could not have been more proud of their boys if they had brought home the pennant. A special parade awaited the boys upon their return home.

Throughout the history of the game in Pensacola, the city has produced an above-average number of professional ballplayers for a town of its size. Quality youth league experiences, along with caring and attentive coaches, have resulted in a foundation for multiple Major League contracts being signed by Pensacola athletes. Greg Litton, Kevin Saucier and Don Sutton are among the multitude that began their early advances into the game with Pensacola's Little League, Dixie Youth, Babe Ruth League and Bill Bond Baseball programs. *Courtesy of Pensacola Historical Society*.

THE FLIERS SAY GOODBYE

The Fliers' 1950 season opened with lingering momentum from their 1949 championship. Now managed by twenty-eight-year-old catcher George Dozier, Pensacola stormed ahead toward another victorious year. Along with Charles Weathers, Neb Wilson returned to his position in Pensacola's outfield brigade. Pensacola's dangerous slugging outfielder duo was joined by up-and-coming Minor League star Jim Rivera. Born in Puerto Rico, "Jungle Jim" spent a total of ten seasons in the majors beginning in 1952. Predominantly playing for the Chicago White Sox during his big-league career, the quick and aggressive Rivera is regarded as one of the most popular players in White Sox history.

On July 3, 1950, the All-Stars of the Southeastern League were pitted in a mid-season exhibition against the reigning champion Fliers. Jungle Jim drew first blood with a first inning home run. Pensacola tacked on another in the third, and in the fifth inning, they scored four more runs. The All-Stars scored in the second, third and sixth innings, but it was not enough, as they succumbed to the Fliers 6–3. During the contest, Pensacola out-hit their competition twelve to seven. At the plate, Pensacola's Bobby Lyons, Ray Williams and Charley Weathers each collected a single, while Neb Wilson collected a double.

The Fliers secured the league's championship pennant once again in 1950, winning eighty-two games with a .612 winning percentage. Anniston, Alabama, pulled their team out of the league before the end of the season, and the remaining seven teams of the Southeastern League faced the possibility of being without a circuit to play in for 1951. For the third time in forty years the Southeastern League talked of closing its doors and ceasing operations. However, Pensacolans were not going out without a fight to keep their team securely in place.

Dodger great Tommy Lasorda once stated, "Baseball is about the fans, for if it were not for the fans, there would be no reason to play."As a last-ditch effort to gain funding and attract spectators, team owner Wally Dashiell held a lottery for a 1950 Chevrolet convertible. For his efforts, Dashiell collected $2,100—and a fine for not having a license to hold a lottery. Wally's daughter Diane says that the city had mercy on her father and penalized him just $1.

With the looming demise of the Southeastern League circuit, the fans of Pensacola rallied around the last gleaming light of a dying fire. According to the Sunday November 26, 1950 edition of the *Palm Beach Post*, "Pensacola baseball fans scraped together $17,620 in pledges" to assure their team would play the following season. If the Southeastern League itself would have carried the same support as did its Pensacola franchise, the history of the league would be significantly different.

The Fliers' 1951 season opened on a shaky foundation. In late April, future Pensacola franchise owner Joe Panaccione umpired one of the Fliers' last games. Shortly thereafter, the league halted operations. As the Fliers had most recently become a feeder team for the Double-A Atlanta Crackers of the Southern Association, they were under the general direction of the Georgia club. The Crackers, who were affiliated with the Boston Braves, incorporated the Fliers with their Class-B Miami Beach Flamingos, and in doing so transferred several players to Miami. Pensacola manager George Dozier was set in as the new Flamingos skipper for the remainder of 1951. Fliers Forrest Kennedy, Charles Ehlman, Morton Smith, Robert Lyons and Richard McMillin donned Flamingos uniforms and played again under the command of Dozier.

THE WARD ACES AND THE ESCAMBIA COUNTY LEAGUE

The grand experiment of the Dodgers having the lion's share of Brooklyn's farm system in one place for spring training worked so well that they took lessons learned on the Gulf Coast and transferred them to an even larger venue. Although Branch Rickey had been pushed out of his position by new Dodgers owner Walter O'Malley, the spring conditioning program that Rickey began in Pensacola was now in full swing but on a larger scale in Vero Beach, Florida. Dubbed "Dodgertown," the facility brought together Minor League farm teams, free agents, semi-seasoned players, Class-D clubs and the stars of the Brooklyn franchise under the banner of a single springtime facility. O'Malley saw the operation as "extravagant," but the value of the Dodger family gathering proved its worth time and time again, becoming a model for other clubs.

Even with the Dodgers vacating Ellyson Field and the Fliers winging south, every corner of the city of Pensacola expressed love for baseball during the

The Escambia County League offered men from Escambia and Santa Rosa Counties an opportunity to play hardball at an amateur yet highly competitive level. The competition was stout enough to give men like Francis Waters the ability to hone his craft toward his first Minor League contract. Waters and the Ward Aces won the 1951 ECL Championship. *Front row, left to right*: Willford Polley, Robert Watson, Clint Cravey, Noble Boyette, Jack Fell, Ken Boykin and Jimmy Booker. *Back row, left to right*: Dub Reagan, Melvin Pittman, Francis Waters, Chick Backus, Hoyt Heathington, Gayle Boykin and Budda Fillingim. *Courtesy of the Waters family.*

early 1950s. The Seagulls saw no decrease in fan support and continued to pull in nationally ranked opponents. And Pensacola's new semipro Escambia County League teams had no concerns about being transferred, only of winning a pennant.

The Escambia County League was represented by teams such as the Brent Boosters and Ward Aces. Clubs from Pleasant Grove, Ensley and Ferry Pass entered the fray to test their abilities against other Pensacola hopefuls. The Escambia County League became a backdrop for a few players to further their careers in baseball. Aces hurler Francis Waters accumulated a large enough reputation as a strikeout master to garner a Minor League contract with the Monroe Sports of the Cotton States League. The Ward Aces stormed their 1951 competition and took home bragging rights in the league's championship.

Beginning in 1951, Pensacola Junior College offered fans yet another opportunity to support local baseball. PJC opened its doors in 1948 with an enrollment of 128 students. Shortly thereafter, a quickly increasing student body placed a demand on the college for interactive extracurricular activities. Rising to the occasion, social science instructor Lou Ross began PJC's inaugural intercollegiate sports program. In 1951, Ross coached the college's first baseball team and served as the regional vice-president of the National Junior College Athletic Association.

BILL VEECK SURRENDERS TO THE NAVY

In an August 19, 1951 home double-header against the Detroit Tigers, St. Louis Browns owner Bill Veeck and manager Zack Taylor pulled one of the most memorable stunts in baseball history. During the second game, Veeck and Taylor substituted three-foot-seven Eddie Gaedel as a pinch hitter for their slightly injured outfielder, Frank Saucier. Eddie, of course, drew a walk, as the pitcher found it hard to locate Gaedel's meager strike zone. The legally contracted Gaedel was substituted for a pinch runner while the crowd and Frank Saucier roared with delight watching Bill Veeck's perfectly executed gag.

Bill Veeck later admitted that he always felt guilty about taking Saucier out of the game because Frank played very little during that year—his only one in the Major Leagues. Veeck's guilt may have prompted his 1952 visit to Pensacola's Naval Air Station. Saucier had served as a navy deck lieutenant in World War II and was recalled for two years active duty in January 1952 in response to the Korean Conflict. He was sent to Pensacola to begin his tour of duty. Bill Veeck still had Saucier under contract in St. Louis and thought he might secure Saucier's release from the navy by pulling a few strings he had in Washington. After going through two admirals and his contacts in D.C., Veeck was unable to get Frank's release. Although Frank Saucier never played the game professionally again, he served his country with pride at the air station.

During the season Saucier was at Pensacola, the base hosted the Atlanta Crackers of the Southern Association for the 1952 spring training camp. Under the managerial direction of Dixie Walker, the Crackers sparred with the navy club, working on fundamentals and shaking off winter pounds. Pensacola's air station persisted in putting together competitive teams to challenge regional Minor League franchises and college squads.

The following year, the NAS and Saufley Field teams trained with the Northwestern University Wildcats in March 1953. The Saufley Field Seminoles bested Wheaton College in a double-header in April. By August, the base teams were involved in the Eastern Division Navy Baseball Tournament. Pensacola conquered the base club from Quonset Point, Rhode Island, 4–2 and then rolled over Great Lakes in a 3–2 eleven-inning contest. In a championship closer to home, the 1953 Tate High School baseball team secured the runner-up position in the state high school series.

BILL McGHEE PLANS FOR A NEW BALLPARK

According to the January 13, 1954 edition of the *Daytona Beach Morning Journal*, the city council and supporting citizens of Pensacola were in discussion about the possibility of building a new baseball park and inviting professional team representation back to Pensacola. Pensacola sports editor Barney Waters wrote in his column that former Fliers manager Bill McGhee would present a proposal to the city council for a waterfront stadium and entry into the Class-D Alabama-Florida League, should the park become a reality. The idea was for a seven-acre waterfront lease in the Hawkshaw neighborhood on Pensacola's bay front.

On January 19, McGhee and over one hundred Pensacola representatives turned out during a city council meeting in support of the new ballpark proposal. The current team lineup for the Alabama-Florida League included

Panama City, Marianna, Graceville, Fort Walton and Dothan. Pensacola and Crestview put forth interest in joining the league, should they be able to secure proper playing facilities.

The league itself was ailing, and disbanding the organization had been discussed prior to Pensacola's interest. The Alabama-Florida League began in 1936 as a Class-D circuit with intermittent success. The proposal of a Pensacola team joining the league brought new hope for prosperity of the Alabama-Florida League. Pensacola was not only looking to add a team to the league but also to add innovation. McGhee's proposed Pensacola ballpark would include lights for night games, which was an attraction that would bring more fans and new revenue.

IT WAS IMPORTANT THAT THEY PLAYED

Like numerous communities across America, Pensacola has been blessed by unsung heroes in the form of coaches and sponsors of youth sports. Many of these men and women have influenced Pensacola athletes to reach their highest potential and have guided players toward professional careers. Some have even taken a stand for their teams in social and controversial issues.

By August 1955, Pensacola NAS employee Fred Hicks had managed his African American Little League team to a championship position in the Florida Panhandle. Bringing his team to the regional tournament in Northwest Florida, Hicks found that the other eleven teams refused to play his all-black team. The refusal of all eleven opponents to play a legitimately qualified contender also meant the forfeit and disqualification of any team who refused to compete. The result of the forfeits was that Hick's team became the Northwest Florida champions and thus advanced to the state finals in defense of their title. The Pensacola Little League team arrived in Orlando ready to play only to face the same prejudice they had received at home.

After much deliberation by Orlando city councilmen, just prudence prevailed. The council stepped aside after Orlando city attorney Donald Sentersitt declared there was neither state law nor city ordinance that would prevent a black team from meeting a white team on the field of play. This ruling allowed Little League officials to make the judgment call on behalf of the tournament.

The question of allowing Pensacola to play in the state tournament was put to a vote—a vote that included every boy concerned in the tournament and their managers. The teams all voted that Pensacola should remain in the tournament and play for the championship. All of the boys participating in the tournament voted together to welcome Fred Hick's team, although one of the managers resigned afterward. Pensacola was eventually eliminated fairly during the tournament, but according to *Afro-American Newspaper* columnist Sam Lacy, "It was important that they played."

ADMIRAL MASON PARK

During the month of August 1956, young men from Pensacola took part in a varied array of baseball competition throughout the United States. Rising as the cream of the crop from summer youth programs, Pensacola all-stars took on state and national opponents to prove their skills. The Pensacola/Cantonment Junior American Legion team played in the Florida American Legion Finals in St. Petersburg, facing opposition from Clearwater, Gainesville and West Palm Beach. In Conway, South Carolina, the Pensacola Babe Ruth championship team competed against South Carolina's best for the southeastern title. Alexandria, Louisiana, hosted the Dixie Boys series, with West Pensacola in the lineup. On August 4, 1956, Pensacola returned the hospitality by opening its fields to the Florida Little League Junior and Boys Major League Program tournament. In the second year of operation, the Florida Little Major League youth baseball organization elected Pensacola's Jimmy Hitzman as league president.

As the local youth leagues stayed active, plans continued to bring Minor League baseball back to Pensacola. Fans desired it, Pensacola's geographic location welcomed it and the need for downtown economic redevelopment demanded it. Although the city's predominant arena of commerce centered on or near the downtown area, by 1956, an ever-widening influence of shopping and business venues spread out away from the shoreline of the bay.

A major entertainment attraction infused with Pensacola's historic downtown charm was just the prescription for commercial resurgence and citizen participation. Local businessman Fred Davis, building on Bill McGhee's proposal and envisioning what downtown Pensacola could be once again, purchased a club within the Class-D Alabama-Florida League. If the league agreed to the finalization of the purchase, baseball would be

Pensacola's rebirth as a Minor League town in 1957 came with a new team, a new league and a new ballpark. The concrete-and-steel structure of Admiral Mason Park gave fans a view of their bay while they watched the Pensacola Dons of the Alabama-Florida League take on all comers. Another new addition, absent at Legion Field, was lights for night games. No longer were contests restricted to daytime events, allowing for a growing number of spectators to join in the action. The outfield fence sat close enough to the shoreline that a well-hit ball at high tide would get dropped in the drink. *Courtesy of Pensacola Historical Society.*

a renewed reality for the City of Five Flags. The people of Pensacola had spoken resoundingly over time; baseball was their entertainment of choice.

Years later, Buck Showalter stated, "There has always been a constant in Escambia County and the Pensacola area, and that is baseball. There has been a flux of football back and forth, basketball back and forth, but baseball has been a constant here. It has always been a thing that you put up on a pedestal to try to be good at." Although Buck's words came over fifty years after McGhee and Davis sought inclusion in the Alabama-Florida League, the statement is true concerning the love affair between Pensacolans and their game.

Since the close of the Southeastern League, former Fliers outfielder Neb Wilson continued playing throughout various circuits across the country. In

1956, at age thirty-three, he let it be known that he would like to try his hand at managing. The New York Yankees Class-D affiliate St. Petersburg Saints began looking for a replacement manager after their 1956 season ended. Club president Herb Smith felt that he had the position that would be perfect for Neb Wilson. The Saints were more than willing to assist in Neb's aspiration because a home run slugger such as Wilson could have a positive influence on young Yankee players. There was one hitch, and that was Mrs. Lillian Wilson.

Neb's wife, "Lil," loved Pensacola, and while a tentative position elsewhere was agreeable to her, a long-term contract that would move the Wilson family away from the area was not. President Smith negotiated at length with Neb over the phone, only to realize that the devoted husband would leave the final decision up to his wife. Not desiring the Yankees to cause a marriage break-up, Smith spoke with Mrs. Wilson directly. The end result was no long-term contract for Neb Wilson and the Yankees franchise. Neb Wilson managed the Saints for one season in 1957 and returned to Northwest Florida in 1958 to participate in the Alabama-Florida League. Saints president Herb Smith was quoted as saying, "Well this proves one woman is stronger than the entire New York Yankees organization."

The January 11, 1957 edition of the *Sarasota Journal* reported that after the Dothan, Alabama; Donaldson, Georgia; and Crestview, Florida clubs dropped their teams from the Alabama-Florida League, only four franchises remained. Montgomery and Selma, Alabama, had both shown interest in joining the league, however neither had committed two weeks prior to the January 27 deadline. Pensacola had been officially accepted as a member of the circuit during the November 1956 league meetings.

Since the beginning of the Alabama-Florida League in 1936, the organization traveled a bumpy road of existence. There were seasons that the league did not have enough support to field any teams. However, by Opening Day in April 1957, the league boasted a 120-game season, guaranteeing fans 60 home games. The 1957 Alabama-Florida League was composed of the Fort Walton Beach Jets, Graceville Oilers, Montgomery Rebels, Panama City Fliers, Selma Cloverleafs and Pensacola Dons.

Fred Davis's new team was commissioned as the Dons in honor of the Spanish conquistadors who had made their mark in Pensacola during exploration and settlement. Dons Tristan de Luna y Arellano, Panfilo de Narvaez and Hernando de Soto each set foot on the shore of Pensacola Bay, a location that now boasted a brand-new ballpark and a fresh group of Dons wielding bats (rather than swords) and conquering flags. *Pensacola News*

Journal sports editor Earle Bowden had a direct hand in naming the team, as the moniker fit structurally into the daily news type.

To complement the incoming team, Bill McGhee and other Pensacola investors partnered with the city to construct a new stadium on the shoreline. The completed project was named for then Pensacola mayor, Vice Admiral Charles Mason. Admiral Mason Ballpark featured a concrete-and-steel framework, lights for night games and, eventually, two thousand seats to accommodate spectators. The park sat at the southernmost point of Ninth Avenue on current Bayfront Parkway. Situated on five and a half acres, Admiral Mason Ballpark opened to a view of Pensacola Bay over the outfield fence. Joe Panaccione, who would later own the Pensacola Senators, said that home run balls would sometimes land in the lapping water of the bay when the tide was up.

In years to come, Admiral Mason Ballpark offered opportunities for youth leagues to utilize the facilities in tournament play. Buck Showalter said that playing at Admiral Mason as a teenager was a great experience. "I loved hearing my metal spikes clack on the concrete of that old park. For me it was like being at Yankee Stadium," Showalter recalls. Despite the ever-present summer humidity, throngs of mosquitoes from the nearby marsh and the pungent aroma of the sewage treatment plant across the street, Admiral Mason became a starting point for multitudes of big-league hopefuls.

THE DONS ESTABLISH A BEACHHEAD

With a new ballpark, new team, new league and newly energized fans, Pensacola entered a fresh era of baseball. The atmosphere in the city was thick with anticipation over the Pensacola Dons. And even though the Alabama-Florida League was a Class-D endeavor, for Pensacola it was as if a Major League club had just been dropped onto its shore. There were in 1957, as there always are, skeptics who pondered the staying power of this new experiment. But for most it was like the return of a long-lost friend.

Dons ownership sent in Donald "Rex" Ford as player/manager in 1957. With no formal Major League affiliation, playing against four affiliated teams in the six-team circuit, Pensacola built its team from mostly "local" money for the first season. This did not stop the roster from including a nice string of athletes for Pensacola's first leap back into organized ball since 1950. New manager Rex Ford had rattled around the St. Louis farm system for five seasons prior to coming on with Pensacola. Although Rex was a novice at managing, Fred Davis thought he saw enough moxie in Ford to give him a turn at the freshly cut reigns of the Dons. Ford did not measure up to what ownership expected and was replaced with Lou Fitzgerald a short time into the 1957 season. Davis did not have far to go to find Fitzgerald, as Lou was Fred's brother-in-law.

Lou Fitzgerald was the exact opposite of Ford in regards to experience, with a total of twelve years in the minors. Lou was "all baseball," and this was not his first experience as a player/manager. Nor was it his first experience in Pensacola. Lou Fitzgerald played outfield for the Pensacola Fliers in 1946 and 1947, and managing in Pensacola was a building block for both the Dons and Fitzgerald. Lou Fitzgerald brought a wealth of knowledge to the budding team, and in return the Dons would shape skills in Fitzgerald that he would later use to help the careers of future Major Leaguers. During many of the coming seasons, Lou coached and managed players such as Johnny Bench, Rusty Staub, Joe Morgan, Bernie Carbo and Dusty Baker. Before completely retiring from baseball in 1993, Lou Fitzgerald was a scout for the Atlanta Braves and the Florida Marlins.

Under manager Lou Fitzgerald, the 1957 Dons pitching squad combined for a 4.33 ERA. The bullpen featured Minor League veteran Marshall Renfroe, who brought steadiness to the younger members, and up-and-coming Bo Belinsky, whose off-the-field actions were unpredictable at best. Dons pitchers left nothing to the imagination of opposing batters—they were all business. *Courtesy of Frank Hardy.*

Although most of the 1957 Dons' players were raw talent, Lou Fitzgerald oversaw an exceptional group of men. This team included a few with Major League ties, both past and future. Bo Belinsky, Pensacola regular Bill McGhee and Marshall Renfroe represented the elite brotherhood of the 1957 Dons who touched the green diamond of the Major Leagues.

Robert "Bo" Belinsky grew up in Trenton, New Jersey, where he was known as a "street rat" and a pool hustler. Belinsky was a charismatic standout in the Trenton street scene, which carried over into his fledgling baseball career. Bo began his climb through the minors in 1956 with the

Brunswick Pirates, the Class-D Pittsburgh affiliate of the Georgia-Florida League. After pitching in eleven games for the Pirates, Pensacola picked up Belinsky for the next season. Bo became an immediate favorite among the Pensacola fan base with his dominance on the mound and personal charisma; it was like drawing moths to a flame.

Joe Panaccione remembered Belinsky as having a good arm and enjoying the attention it brought him. "He was a high-profile kid who loved the limelight," Panaccione states. Bo Belinsky captured a 13–6 record for Pensacola in 1957 with 202 strikeouts and a 3.00 ERA. Bo certainly was not destined to stay in the lower leagues and was purchased by the Orioles franchise in 1958. However, it only took him one season to work into the hearts of Pensacola's baseball culture. And fortunately for them, the Orioles' farm system would bring him around again in 1959.

Working his way up through Baltimore's Minor League system, Bo continued to create many fans, as well as his share of enemies. His overconfident ego caused him to be a holdout during contract negotiations. The Los Angeles Angels purchased Belinsky for the 1962 season, during which he won ten games with a 3.56 ERA for his first season in the majors. The Angels were only in their second year as a Major League club and played their home games at Dodger Stadium. On May 5, 1962, Bo Belinsky pitched a 2–0 no-hitter against the Baltimore Orioles. Bo's no-hitter was the first one in Angels' history and the first one in Dodger Stadium.

Belinsky's fame skyrocketed, ensuring overnight celebrity status in Southern California and making him a sought-after companion in the L.A. nightlife scene. Bo began to date well-known starlets prior to marrying *Playboy* Playmate Jo Collins. Belinsky moved over to the National League in 1965 with the Phillies, joined the Astros in 1967 and the Pirates in 1969 and finished his career with the Reds in 1970.

During his pro playing days, Bo was known for his flippant attitude toward the press and sometimes the fans as well. But second-generation Pensacola photographer Frank Hardy Jr. remembers his own locally famous dad sitting in the outfield stands at Dodger Stadium and calling out to Belinsky in the bullpen. "Bo, it's Frank Hardy from Pensacola," he yelled while holding up a photo of Bo clad in a Dons uniform. Bo not only acknowledged his acquaintance from Pensacola but also signed autographs and regaled fans with memories of the Florida Panhandle.

Also pitching for the Dons was Marshall Daniel Renfroe, born in Century, Florida, on May 25, 1936. He began his professional career in 1954 with the Phillies organization. The left-handed pitcher bounced from

Philadelphia's Appalachian League affiliate to their Crestview, Florida team in the Alabama-Florida League. After being purchased by the New York Giants, Marshall honed his skills on the mound with four different teams in as many leagues between 1955 and 1956. New York sent Renfroe to Class-D Greenville, Texas, of the Sooner State League for the first portion of the 1957 season. Then, in what was a homecoming for the fans of Escambia County, Florida, Marshall Renfroe was assigned to the Pensacola Dons' bullpen for the remainder of year.

Marshall's pitching record with Pensacola was four wins and six losses with a 3.21 ERA. But twelve games on his home turf helped bolster the loyalty of the populace in a renewed position in the baseball world. Renfroe would spend another full season in the minors before getting his taste of the majors. Marshall's debut for the recently relocated Giants came on September 27, 1959, against the St. Louis Cardinals. Renfroe returned to the minors in 1960, spending three more seasons in various farm systems, including those of San Francisco, Baltimore, Minnesota, Washington and the New York Mets.

Renfroe finished his nine-season career with a 3.99 ERA after pitching 1,131 innings. Returning to the Pensacola area, Marshall became a welder for the Westinghouse Corporation, located just minutes from the old Dodgers' training camp. Driving home from work on December 10, 1970, Marshall stopped on a bridge to help a stalled and stranded motorist. While attending to the vehicle's needs, he was struck by an oncoming gas truck and died from his injuries. Marshall Renfroe was interred at Pensacola's Bayview Memorial Park. Marshall's younger brother Dalton played professionally as well, predominantly as a catcher for the Washington Senators and Cleveland Indians farm systems. Dalton caught for the Pensacola Senators in 1962.

EARLE BOWDEN AND DON GRIFFITH PROMOTE PENSACOLA BASEBALL

Two prominent Pensacola residents became as responsible for the popularity of the Dons as the new ballpark and player personalities. James Earle Bowden and Don Griffith each in their own way helped to weave the character and charm of Pensacola baseball into the hearts of the people. Don Griffith became known as the voice of Pensacola's teams throughout the city's Alabama-Florida League years. Griffith was a broadcaster for WCOA, located in the *Pensacola News Journal's* downtown offices. Over the course of fifty years, Don Griffith announced games for Pensacola's Minor League teams, local high school football games and the Pensacola Naval Air Station's Goshawk football team, a team once served by future Football Hall of Fame quarterback Roger Staubach.

Don Griffith announced all home and away games for the Pensacola Dons, Angels and Senators. Home games were broadcast from Admiral Mason Park, while away games were a bit of a smoke-and-mirror affair. Stationed in front of a microphone at the WCOA studio, Griffith would receive play-by-play Teletype messages from someone sitting in the press box of the Dons' road opponent. With every Teletype communication received, Don would recreate each play over the Pensacola airwaves, adding sound effects of a bat hitting a ball or a pitch landing in the catcher's mitt. He even produced crowd noises, turning them up for big plays and home runs. It has been reported that due to Griffith's ability to capture the passion and fervor of the live event, most listeners were not aware that he wasn't even at the game.

Earle Bowden captivated Pensacola audiences through the power of the pen. Bowden joined the *Pensacola News Journal* team in 1953. Initially working as a sportswriter for the paper, Earle covered the Dons and other local athletics, bringing to Pensacola a unique form of journalism through his distinctive political cartoons. However, Bowden did not limit his drawings to a single subject—he also caricatured countless Pensacola citizens and familiar themes.

Bowden's hedcut cartooning style brought a feeling of inclusion and insightfulness for his readers. Along with his interpretation of Dons' players and coaching staff came a picture into the life around the green diamond, which was foreign to many *News Journal* subscribers. Earle Bowden's influence on the Gulf Coast has reached far beyond the written, or in his case, drawn page. Bowden was a spearhead in the campaign to establish the Gulf Islands National Seashore, which was signed into law by President Nixon in 1971.

Mrs. Babe Ruth

The July 26, 1957 installment of the *Sarasota Journal* reported on the opening game of the Babe Ruth League State Championship, with Pensacola facing Sarasota County in the first-round bracket. The Pensacola team, composed of thirteen-, fourteen- and fifteen-year-old boys, overcame Sarasota and each Florida opponent thereafter.

Pensacola's Babe Ruth League state pennant sent them to the league's World Series competition held in Ann Arbor, Michigan. The event began in late August and featured a three-round venue for the title. Pensacola, while fielding a competent team, was limited to a two-man pitching staff of Lou Vickery and Don Griffey, who pitched their way through three opponents to capture the crown.

The Pensacola Babe Ruth team had arrived in Ann Arbor with lively bats as well, finishing off their last adversary, Stanford, Connecticut, in a 9–0 trouncing. Pensacola brought home the Babe Ruth World Champion title to a very proud community crowd, proving 1957 to be a fine year for baseball in the Port City.

Pensacola's championship team was managed by former Twilight Leaguer and Chicago Cubs farmhand Gilbert "Lefty" Lybrand. Lefty, who was a switch foreman for the Frisco Line Railway, dedicated his entire life to the development of players and the perpetuation of the game. Lybrand's Pensacola PONY League rosters were often dotted with names that would later be listed on professional contracts. Dabo Renfroe, Lou Vickery, P.J. Smith, Dave Partrick, Bill Vickery, Otto Knowles, Johnny Lewis and Don Sutton each performed under the watchful direction of Lefty Lybrand. Lefty's expertise in player evaluation was later enlisted by the Washington Senators and the Major League Scouting Bureau as Lybrand scouted Alabama and the Florida Panhandle.

The Kansas City Athletics secured spring training accommodations in Pensacola in 1958 for several of their Minor League clubs. Athletics' farm director Hank Teters brought his players to Pensacola in March but was not alone in utilizing Pensacola as a preseason stop. The St. Louis Cardinals and the Chicago White Sox made Pensacola one of their exhibition game destinations, just after breaking spring camp. The practice game on April 3 once again brought big-name players to Pensacola. The Cardinals and White Sox arrived by rail, ready to face off in the confines of Admiral Mason Park. The special spring training event drew over seven thousand fans to the downtown ballpark. A section of right field had to be roped off to accommodate additional seating. Fans were poked into every available corner of the park, all in high hopes of catching a glimpse of their favorite players.

White Sox manager Al Lopez sent Early Wynn to the mound for Chicago. The Associated Press, in an interview with Lopez, reported that Wynn would be allowed to pitch as far into the game as he could. Among the teammates backing up Wynn were Ray Boone, Nellie Fox, Luis Aparicio and, returning to Pensacola from his days as a Flier, Jim Rivera.

St. Louis skipper Fred Hutchinson fielded Don Blasingame, Curt Flood, Ken Boyer, Eddie Kasko and the beloved Stan Musial. Although in May 1958 Stan became the eighth player in Major League history to reach three thousand hits, he was only able to achieve one during his game in Pensacola. Musial's hit was a normally executed single that was ruled a ground rule double as it rolled into the cordoned-off area in right field.

The White Sox beat the Cardinals 4–3, but the Pensacola fans were the true winners in the historic hosting of two great teams. It has been rumored that the Chicago White Sox front office attempted to wrangle Don Griffith away from his small Gulf Coast broadcasting market into a radio contract for the Sox. As the story goes, Griffith turned them down flat, not wanting to leave the town and the team he loved.

The Alabama-Florida League added two teams in 1958. The Dothan Cardinals returned to the lineup, while the Dodgers new Columbus, Georgia affiliate also joined the ranks of the league. Pensacola secured a player development agreement with the Baltimore Orioles and retained Lou Fitzgerald as their manager. In the Orioles, the Dons gained a partner for strengthening a contending team. New faces along with a familiar friend took the field in front of Pensacola's hopeful fans as Neb Wilson rejoined the ranks of Pensacola players. Neb's return to a Pensacola team delighted the community and Wilson's wife.

In addition to his popularity on the diamond, Neb Wilson brought his mighty bat. The once formidable Pensacola hitter lost no time in slugging his way into the rafters of the Alabama-Florida League. Now thirty-five, "Hack" Wilson punched twenty-four home runs, hit for an average of .396 and attained a slugging percentage of .680 in 1958. Wilson was two years older than his manager and five years older than the next-oldest teammate, but the veteran Minor Leaguer held his own in support of the Dons.

The Dons carried on their pitching roster a twenty-year-old right-hander by the name of Jim Lehew. The Orioles had placed a fair amount of stock in Lehew as an up-and-coming arm that would deliver his share of winning games for the franchise. During his development in Pensacola, Lehew did not disappoint. In his first season of professional baseball, Jim Lehew won twenty games and lost only nine, culminating in a 3.11 ERA.

Jim Lehew had signed as an amateur free agent pitcher with Baltimore just before the 1958 regular season. The St. Louis Browns moved east in 1954 to become the Baltimore Orioles, and club president Clarence Miles wanted to operate as a new expansion team rather than a relocated one. Scouts near and far searched for young talent and definitive trades in order to clear out old St. Louis Browns roster names. In locating Jim Lehew, Baltimore scouts found a unique prospect. Jim had an unorthodox submarine pitching delivery that baffled batters. Jim worked just three seasons in the minors before being called up to the parent club for a look. He spent two of those seasons with Pensacola, where he received good developmental training from Fitzgerald and great support from the fans.

Pensacola's backbone in 1958 may have been Wilson at the plate and Lehew on the mound, but the rest of the Orioles' farm club brought their best to the diamond as well. The Dons were in the hunt for the pennant all season, standing as hardy opponents for all who faced them. Pensacola fought right down to the wire to grasp the title, but it was the Selma Cloverleafs who finally overcame the Dons in the playoffs. In a startling season-ending upset, fourth-place Dothan won the championship.

The Pensacola Dons finished their season with a 67-55 record, and although the league pennant was not flying over Admiral Mason, the City of Five Flags flew a banner of victory, as baseball had returned in earnest. In

In town to commemorate the Babe Ruth League World Championship title secured by Pensacola's stalwart team, Mrs. Babe Ruth functioned as ambassador for the organization named for her deceased husband. The Babe himself had posed for pictures with the Fliers thirty years earlier. Now standing in for the Sultan of Swat, Mrs. Ruth joined the 1958 Dons for a few photographs. *Courtesy of Frank Hardy.*

yet another homecoming of a different nature, Mrs. Babe Ruth visited with the Dons during their regular season on a goodwill tour. Claire Merritt Ruth was the Babe's second wife, marrying him in 1929. Babe Ruth had passed away in 1948, leaving Claire his estate and winter home in Florida. Claire Ruth had four years earlier authorized the use of her late husband's name for the Babe Ruth League youth baseball program. Pensacola's own Babe Ruth League players had once again shown themselves worthy opponents during the 1958 championship competition, and Claire Ruth honored the team in proxy for the Bambino. The Dons paid homage to the Yankees' legendary slugger by hosting Mrs. Ruth for a day at the ballpark and remembering the Babe's visits to Pensacola in the 1920s.

Remembering former stars of the diamond continued with a special "Oldtimers' Game" held on August 13 at Admiral Mason Park. Announcing the all-star line-up for the bout, the *Pensacola Journal* exclaimed, "Parade from the past. Old Pros, ex-Fliers battle in 'liniment' clash Thursday." The Fliers' roster included Red Barnhart, Joe Szuch, Babe Hosler, Garrett McBryde, Bill McGhee, Wally Dashiell, Buck Weaver, Trader Horne, Ralph Hendricks, Mallory Tennant and Joe Panaccione. The Old Pros were no less stacked off their bench with Lefty Lybrand, Bill Ellis, Jelly Jones, Dude McCrory, Jim Soward, Russ Scarritt, Monte Barrow, Donnie Tidwell, Ralph Chaudron, Bob Duncan and Fred Harrell. The field was filled with a grand example of Pensacola's contribution to the world of baseball, and the stands were filled with fans bursting with nostalgia and pride.

BUCK, BO AND "WHITE LIGHTNING"

Former Negro League All-Star John "Buck" O'Neil began scouting for the Chicago Cubs in 1955. Buck O'Neil had a gift for reading young talent and signed many players like Lou Brock and Billy Williams to professional contracts. Florida-born O'Neil was at ease in working his way across the southern States and the Gulf Coast, as he was used to the high humidity and relentless heat from his days in the celery fields of Carabelle, Florida. Buck's scouting travels frequently brought him to the Emerald Coast and inevitably to look in on amateur Pensacola players.

Robert Davidson had been a standout senior at Pensacola's Washington High School in 1955 before going on to play for Southern University in Baton Rouge, Louisiana. While at Southern University, Davidson achieved a .420 batting average in 1957. Before leaving for school in Louisiana, Robert spent four seasons with the Pensacola Seagulls and was employed by the Spearman Brewing Company. On May 22, 1958, Buck O'Neil, seeing potential in the Seagulls' hard-hitting infielder, signed Davidson to a contract with the Cubs that included a $10,000 bonus.

"I have always wanted to play professional baseball and I only hope I have good luck," Davidson told reporters in a June 6, 1958 interview. When asked if he thought he would eventually take over Ernie Banks's position as the Cubs' shortstop, Robert laughed and replied, "Well that may be asking a little too much, but with the right breaks I hope to break in somewhere." Davidson reported to the Class-D Paris Lakers farm club the following spring.

A letter from the Topps Chewing Gum Company dated April 30, 1959, arrived at the home of the Davidsons prior to Robert's twenty-first birthday. The letter was addressed to Mr. Daniel Davidson, Robert's father, due to the fact that Robert was considered a minor in the context of signing a legal contract. The letter stated that the intent of the Topps Company was to include Robert in a forthcoming card collection upon his arrival to the Major Leagues. Robert's dream of playing professionally had arrived, and the very company that had produced cards featuring his heroes of the past was now asking him for an agreement—just like other Major Leaguers.

Just months before Buck O'Neil's death in October 2006, he visited Pensacola one more time. On this occasion, however, his trip was as a goodwill ambassador for the Negro League Museum in Kansas City, Missouri. While in Pensacola, Buck visited with local youth leagues, made an appearance at Jim Spooner Field and gave one of his last interviews to Sandra Averhart of WUWF radio. Sitting in the studio on the campus of the University of West Florida, O'Neil reminisced about his playing days with the Kansas City Monarchs, becoming the first African American coach in the Major Leagues and his scouting experiences with the Chicago Cubs. Buck recalled that he could always count on finding good talent when he came to the Florida Gulf Coast.

The Alabama-Florida League dropped back to six teams in 1959. Pensacola retained affiliation with the Orioles, but by the end of the season, owner Fred Davis determined that he had gone as far as he could financially with the Dons and sold the team. The Dons were purchased by local tavern owner and former Minor League outfielder Joe Panaccione. The 1959 Dons were stocked with what could be considered their best potential pennant-winning team to date. The Orioles had several good scouts in their arsenal searching out and signing great talent. One Orioles scout was former big-league hurler Hal Newhouser. Newhouser not only scouted his perspective players with a discerning eye but also helped in their personal development during the off-season and spring training.

Two of the players on the Dons' roster Newhouser took special interest in were Bo Belinsky and Steve Barber. Barber, along with several other Dons, also credited manager Lou Fitzgerald with helping them make monumental strides on the field. Notable standouts for the 1958 Dons included Cal Ripken Sr., George Stepanovich, Steve Dalkowski and George Werley. To the delight of Pensacola fans, Jim Lehew and Neb Wilson were once again suited in Dons uniforms.

Bo Belinsky came back to Pensacola for a second tour, but this time his off-the-field antics had become well known. Belinsky's street-savvy ways had begun to catch up with him as pool halls, rowdy bars and loose women filled his off hours. The pitcher often took up with prostitutes and participated in less-than-virtuous business dealings. During the early portion of the 1959 season, Belinsky's frequent companion was a young woman who claimed to be eighteen years of age. Bo, not interested in having her prove her age, paid for the oversight shortly after the affair ended. The girl, who was in actuality only sixteen, threatened to claim statutory rape unless Belinsky married her.

Belinsky later recalled that he quickly went into hiding and called Fred Davis. Davis told Bo that he could not have made a more grave error, as the girl's mother was a school crossing guard in Pensacola and the mother's boyfriend was Pensacola's chief of detectives. A week later, Fred Davis, in what was a huge favor to Belinsky, intervened to sell his contract to Aberdeen, South Dakota, under manager Earl Weaver. Bo later said, "I bet he [Weaver] had no idea how he suddenly came up with a new left-hander that late in the season." Belinsky pitched nine games for the Dons in 1959, compiling an ERA of 3.00 before he was ushered away in scandal.

Steve Barber, on the other hand, was cantankerous with coaches and hard on himself. He often threw tantrums on the mound and sailed wild pitches past his catchers. After the Orioles broke their Minor League spring training camp in 1959, a frustrated Barber went AWOL, heading back to his home in Maryland. He cited that his reason for leaving was that Baltimore had invested too little time and money into his career. After further consideration, Barber decided that he desired to play baseball more than anything else. He called Orioles' farm director Harry Dalton to let him know that he wanted to come back. Steve Barber reported to Pensacola's skipper Lou Fitzgerald.

Hal Newhouser helped Barber by getting him involved directly with Fitzgerald, as Fitzgerald knew how to handle players. "Fitz really got me squared away," recalled Barber. "I respected the man, and I knew that the things he was doing for me were in my best interests. I felt that in Fitz I had not only a manager but a friend I could rely on."

In an interview before his death, Steve Barber told a story about how Lou Fitzgerald got through to him and around his hotheaded antics. Fitz was tough but caring in his methods. During a particular match, Barber was having trouble focusing on the mound. Fitzgerald told him that he was going to keep him in the game for all nine innings, even if he walked 500 batters. "In the third inning, I walked the bases loaded and Fitz came out to the mound. He said, 'Okay Steve, you got 499 to go. I settled down and started throwing strikes. I believe we won the game two to one in ten innings," Steve stated.

Under Fitzgerald, Steve Barber participated in two no-hitters and four two-hit games. Lou made all the difference in Barber's career, and after Pensacola, Barber went on to play fifteen seasons in the majors. His fastball was said to exceed ninety-five miles per hour, and he was the first twenty-game winner in modern Baltimore Orioles history.

Cal Ripken Sr. caught sixty-one games for Pensacola in 1959, carrying a batting average of .292 along with two home runs. Catching for the Dons during the last season of the 1950s was a challenge for the twenty-three-year-old. From Belinsky and Barber to Lehew and Dalkowski, the bullpen contained a myriad of styles for Ripken to learn. Catching Dalkowski alone was like taking on a small swiveling cannon.

Steve Dalkowski pitched just seven games in Pensacola but made a mark on the team during his brief stay. Dalkowski, nicknamed "White Lightning," has been hailed as possibly one of the fastest pitchers in baseball history. Although his pitch speed was tested at the Aberdeen Proving Grounds military installation, no official result was recorded due to prior fatigue in Steve's arm. However, some experts, along with Cal Sr., have speculated that his pitches attained speeds of 105 miles per hour. While the pitch velocity was an estimate, Steve's unpredictable violent behavior and hard drinking habits made his pitching control equally speculative. Screenwriter Ron Shelton loosely based the character Nuke LaRoosh on Dalkowski in his 1988 film *Bull Durham*. Steve's speed and wildness frightened even the bravest batters. Ted Williams once matched up against Dalkowski in a spring training game. Williams said that Dalkowski was the fastest he ever faced and never wanted to see him again.

Ripken was always ready take on a challenge and accepted Pensacola pitchers in stride. Cal Sr.'s own coaching and managerial career began in 1961, spilling over into four decades. Reflecting the lessons learned in Pensacola under Fitzgerald, Ripken was famous for bringing young recruits through a discipleship referred to as the "Oriole Way." The process emphasized hard work, professionalism and a strong understanding of baseball fundamentals. He frequently summed up the Oriole Way by stating, "Practice doesn't make perfect. Perfect practice makes perfect." Cal Ripken Sr. to date stands as one of the most influential instructors of the game, with countless players owing their careers to his tutelage.

Despite the notable talent on the 1959 Pensacola Dons ballclub, they were hastily eliminated during the playoffs and finished their season with a 59–66 record. Across town, the Pensacola Colt team of the YMCA's PONY League had put together a champion fifteen-/sixteen-year-old club. Qualifying for the third annual PONY League World Series held that year in Ontario, California, Pensacola went on to defeat La Mesa and win the title. Locally, Major League Baseball scouts roamed the stands as Tate High School senior Otto Knowles signed a professional contract with the St. Louis Cardinals. Knowles reported to the Cardinals' Florida State League affiliate in Daytona Beach the following spring.

THE WATERS WAY

The Chicago White Sox picked up Pensacola as a Class-D affiliate in 1960. With the Major League organizational change from Baltimore to Chicago, the Pensacola club also changed its team name. The Pensacola Angels took the field under not only a new name and a new parent club but also with completely new ownership. Pensacola businessmen Joe Panaccione and Bennie Barberi acquired the Snapper Capital franchise and retained Doc McCormick as the general manager.

Joe Panaccione had been an outfielder with the 1941 Cambridge Canners and the 1942 Johnson City Cardinals within the St. Louis farm system. Joe then became an umpire for the Southeastern League, giving him the opportunity to become fully acquainted with the town and citizens of Pensacola. The City of Five Flags beckoned to Joe, and thus he made his home there in 1950, adopting the people and community as his own. Panaccione opened an Italian pizzeria and sandwich shop that quickly became the social spot for a unique mixture of locals, theater performers, jazz musicians and ballplayers.

If Panaccione's old baseball acquaintances were anywhere near the area, a stop at the pizzeria and pub was a must. Former players like all-star Andy Seminick and legendary pitcher Johnny Vander Meer knew where they could find Panaccione for a chat about games of the past and current prospects. In the early 1960s, Vander Meer worked as a goodwill ambassador for the Schlitz Brewing Company and was managing the Reds' Tampa Class-D affiliate. On one of many occasions while visiting with Panaccione, Vander Meer told Joe that they had this brash street kid from Cincinnati playing infield for the Tampa Tarpons. "If we can get the 'street' out of him, he's going to make one hell of a ballplayer. You ought to keep your eye out for him," said Vander Meer. "His name is Pete Rose."

As a former outfielder, Joe Panaccione had a unique perspective on player development. One of the immediate implementations was to ramp up the involvement of quality instructors. This implementation included high school baseball coach and professional player Fred Waters. Waters took the same care with the Angels' pitchers as he did with his own boys in Pensacola's school system. His coaching job for Pensacola's Alabama-Florida League franchise was complemented with a legitimate position in their bullpen as well.

The league still featured six teams in 1960, with every team in the circuit boasting a Major League association. Beyond Fred Waters lending his experience, Panaccione set J.C. Dunn as the Angels' skipper. Dunn was also a product of the Cardinals' farm system, having his first professional season in 1949. Dunn's contract with Pensacola was as a player/manager, sharing first base with Bob Vostry. Dunn tutored the Angels in the finer art of hitting, ending his own 1960 season with a .301 batting average.

Pensacola's 1959 and 1960 seasons suffered in attendance and gate receipts, although quality athletes filled the roster, such as Ney "Speedy" Gonzalez and Jim Schuda. The fans who did attend games clamored for a pennant, and the Angels seemed initially to be a disappointment to the faithful of Admiral Mason. The Angels completed their year fourteen and a half games behind first-place Panama City. However, the Angels qualified for post-season play and entered into the finals. In what would be an unlikely turn of events, Pensacola upset Panama City three games to two and then went on to defeat Selma three games to one. The Angels won the championship while breathing new life into their fans and grabbing the attention of the Washington Senators front office.

The venerable Fred Waters became one of the most recognized names in the Pensacola baseball community. Fred's die-hard commitment to the success and development of players set the high-water mark for all coaches that came after him. Waters pitched and coached for Pensacola's Minor League teams of the 1960s, all the while coaching and mentoring area high school players. Numerous Pensacola athletes owe their existence in the professionals to the direction and assistance of Coach Fred Waters. *Courtesy of Pensacola Historical Society.*

There are few names in the annals of Pensacola's baseball history that are remembered with as much affection and admiration among the players than that of Fred Waters. Waters, accepted by many as the face of baseball in Pensacola, set the precedent for individual skill training on the Gulf Coast. Over the course of Waters's coaching career, many of the most notable players emerging from the Pensacola region were in some manner positively affected by his personal guidance. Fred Waters's early experiences with the Dodgers organization and later Pittsburgh prepared him to undertake his life's call.

Waters was born in Benton, Mississippi, and attended the University of Southern Mississippi, splitting his attention between football and baseball. After being drafted by the Dodgers as an amateur free agent, he reported to Brooklyn's spring camp in 1949. The young pitcher was immediately impressed by the attention the Brooklyn coaches gave their prospects, and it was during this initial experience into the world of professional baseball that Fred Waters knew his future calling. Waters worked his way up through the Dodgers and Milwaukee farm systems before being traded to the Pirates in 1954. His Major League debut with Pittsburgh came on September 20, 1955, alongside fellow rookie Roberto Clemente.

Fred's Major League career lasted only up until 1956, after which he settled back into the minors for another five seasons. An injury during winter training in the Dominican Republic ended an otherwise promising rise to stardom. What would have meant certain disillusionment to others spurred Waters forward to his calling.

Fred Waters played and coached with the 1960 Pensacola Angels, compiling a 2.55 ERA, all the while overseeing the instructional obligations as a local high school baseball coach. Waters continued his juggling act of athletic duties well into the late 1980s, adding even more opportunities for involvement into the lives of those just beginning their careers. In 1964, Waters accepted the position as the Minnesota Twins Rookie League manager in Elizabethton, Tennessee. He also continued to coach high school baseball. For twenty-two years, Fred Waters stood as one of the first instructors most players experienced in the Twins organization. Many players like Hall of Fame members Rod Carew, Kirby Puckett and Bert Blyleven owe their early training in part to Waters.

The Twins desired to involve Waters deeper into their organization, knowing that Fred's insight brought a level of player development understanding that surpassed most. As a prime example, Hall of Fame pitcher Bert Blyleven said that Fred Waters taught him more about pitching than anyone else he had ever encountered. Fred turned down a front office job with the Twins because it would take him away from coaching high school ball in Pensacola and his job as skipper in Elizabethton.

It was during his role as a high school coach in Pensacola that Fred Waters shared his knowledge and love for the game with rising Emerald Coast stars. Prior to their professional occupation, Dennis Lewallyn, Preston Hanna, Jimmy Hutto and Kevin Saucier gained direction under the watchful eye of Coach Waters. After Fred Waters's death in 1989, his legacy continued through the Fred Waters Baseball Clinics. Professional scout Squeaky Parker took up the charge to continue the excellence begun by Waters for baseball development in Pensacola through the annual Fred Waters Clinics. Former Catholic High School and San Francisco Giants pitcher Billy Sadler continues the legacy of Fred Waters as he conducts frequent clinics patterned after the ones he experienced through the inspiration of Parker and Coach Waters.

CHAPTER 5
THE EXPANSION ERA: 1961–1976

TED WILLIAMS RETURNS TO PENSACOLA

After 1961, Major League Baseball made changes to how the nine innings of a regulation game were played out. With intentionality to speed up the game and ensure spectator excitement, several innovations, such as the widening of the strike zone, were enlisted. During the Expansion Era, new cities entering into the Major League Baseball market caused the National and American Leagues to split into two divisions and employ an end-of-season league championship before the World Series.

As a response to a heightened dominance of the pitcher over the batter, mounds were lowered and the American League employed a designated hitter in place of the pitcher's spot in the lineup. New player selections were gained through the use of a mid-year amateur draft, and scouting reports became available through Major League Baseball's centralized agency. It was during this era of baseball's regeneration that Pensacola became a player export machine, as many of the young men developed under Fred Waters and other area coaches grew into professional maturity. The Cradle of Naval Aviation now had athletic representation in a multitude of baseball's franchises.

During this era, player endorsements in the media reached a new height. Riding on America's love of its baseball heroes, the Sears and Roebuck Company enlisted Ted Williams to promote a line of sporting goods carrying his name. "Teddy Ballgame" traveled across the country as his own

It has been said that Ted Williams's love of Florida began while he was stationed at Bronson Field as a flight instructor. Ted's passion for game fishing and outdoor sports paralleled that of his devotion to baseball. Ted returned to Pensacola after his retirement from the Boston Red Sox to endorse and demonstrate the Sears and Roebuck sporting goods line that carried his name. *Courtesy of Pensacola Historical Society.*

product line ambassador, giving tips on equipment use and greeting fans. Sears included Pensacola on one such tour, bringing Williams back home again, so to speak. Now making Florida his full-time residence, Ted Williams returned to Pensacola sharing stories of the Bronson Field Bombers and the pilots who trained at the air station.

THE SENATORS TAKE OFFICE

The December 7, 1960 early edition of the *Daytona Beach Morning Journal* ran a short article stating that the Chicago White Sox had opted to release Pensacola as their Class-D Florida affiliate for the coming season. This decision by Chicago's team executives was part of the overall plan to get the White Sox embedded deeper into the Florida baseball landscape. Following the success that teams like the Dodgers and Orioles had with permanent camps in the Sunshine State, the White Sox moved their endeavors a little more south by taking over the Daytona Beach club formally associated with the Cardinals.

It was uncertain during January 1961 as to whether or not Pensacola would sign an agreement with a new Major League parent club. However, Bill Moore, the president of the Alabama-Florida League, was not at all concerned. While the rest of the teams in the league had either retained their previous season affiliation or acquired new ones, an independent Pensacola would still play in the 120-game season. Concern may not have been on President Moore's mind, but club expenses and the possible lack of scouts and players offered by a parent organization were in the thoughts of Pensacola's owner, Joe Panaccione.

The sparks from the 1960 championship were certain to kick up the coming season's attendance as owners Panaccione and Barberi began negotiations with the Baltimore Orioles and Washington Senators as possible affiliates. The '61 Senators club, located in Washington D.C., was considered an expansion franchise in the American League. The original Senators club had relocated to Minnesota to become the Twins. On February 10, the new Washington team secured its first link in a needed farm system by completing negotiations with Pensacola's ownership. In the signing of a contract with Washington, the Pensacola Senators were born.

Pensacola adopted the name of its parent club, adding the benefit of utilizing uniforms sent from Washington's equipment manager. The uniform care packages from D.C. immediately cut down on expenses for season startup costs. Another addition implemented by the Washington Senators into their Pensacola farm team was skipper Archie Wilson. Wilson had spent fourteen seasons playing professionally before coming to Pensacola. Washington front office executives felt that Wilson would become one of their main organizational managers, and Pensacola would be a perfect place for him to cut his teeth. Archie Wilson and Fred Waters oversaw a team of young hopefuls, including four players placed directly by Washington for quick conditioning. Two of those four would see almost immediate placement on the Major League roster.

Relief pitcher Don Loun threw in twenty-two games for Pensacola in 1961 and twenty-three in 1962. The Senators signed Don Loun as an amateur free agent out of Frederick, Maryland. Loun excelled under the guidance of Fred Waters for two seasons before advancing to Class-A Hampton, Virginia, in 1963 and then on to Double-A and Triple-A for the first half of 1964. Loun's Major League debut on the mound for Washington came

Beginning with the 1961 season, under new owner Joe Panaccione, Pensacola gained a Major League benefactor in the form of the reestablished Washington Senators. The Washington club backed their Pensacola Class-D franchise with as much support as possible. Pensacola fans backed their Senators with unbridled exuberance. *Courtesy of Frank Hardy.*

on September 23, 1964. Loun posted a relief record of 5–3 in 1961 and an 11–9 record as a starter in 1962 for Pensacola.

Shortstop John Kennedy played 115 games for Pensacola and fielded for Washington, D.C. the very next season. Kennedy's first professional at-bat came as a member of the Pensacola Senators, and during that season he hit .254 and collected 171 putouts. Kennedy started with Raleigh in 1962 in the Carolina League and stayed on for a good portion of the season, but by September, he had arrived to join his former Pensacola teammates in Washington. John fielded second base and shortstop for twelve years in the majors with teams including the Senators, Dodgers, Yankees, Pilots and Red Sox. Kennedy and former Pensacola pitcher Steve Barber were among the roster of players for the short-lived single season of the 1969 Seattle Pilots.

Pitcher Carl Bouldin took the mound in only three games for Pensacola, and third baseman Ed Brinkman took part in but twenty-eight before being called up to Washington. Both men started out together with the Middlesboro Senators before moving to Pensacola. Bouldin's stay on the Gulf Coast was much shorter than Brinkman's, with Carl Bouldin winning all three games in which he pitched.

Ed Brinkman stood out as one of Washington's top prospects in respect to growing their new expansion franchise. Ed became noticed as slick infielder who could cover more than his share of the diamond. Pensacola was a great proving ground for Brinkman, and by the end of the 1961 season he was in Washington at just nineteen years of age. The quick roster changes for Manager Wilson, in regard to players being sent up the line, must have made the Class-D club seem more like a Triple-A franchise. Pensacola finished second in the league behind Selma, posting a 70–47 record.

YOUTH LEAGUE SUCCESS

Professional baseball scouts make their living by knowing where to find raw talent. Some of that knowledge comes from hours of observation, but even more of it comes from the inner gift of pure instinct. However, when there is a ripe field bursting with fruit, even the greenest of baseball men know where to pick up prospects.

For several decades, Pensacola has been one of those ripe fields—and not just for baseball players. The region has produced such notable athletes as professional boxer Roy Jones Jr., NFL running back Emmitt Smith, WNBA center Michelle Snow, softball phenom Charity Butler, former South Carolina State kicker Blake Erickson and hundreds more. The above-average-level sportsmen and sportswomen signing professional contracts have kept the City of Five Flags as a circled point on the maps of many professional athletic scouts.

In 1954, Charles Winston Dungan signed a Minor League contract with the Cleveland Indians, and Arthur Roberts signed with the Orioles; both players graduated from Tate High School. Additionally, White Sox scouts watching Tate High School teams picked up senior Stover McIlwain in 1956. Calvin Otto Knowles signed with the Cardinals' Gulf Coast scout in 1959, and David Lloyd Partrick was selected by Washington scouts stationed in Pensacola for the 1961 season.

As a recipient of the high-level training offered by Pensacola's numerous high school baseball programs, Stover "Smokey" McIlwain became a forerunner for players turning skills learned on area diamonds into professional careers. McIlwain saw his first game in a big-league uniform just three days after his eighteenth birthday. While Smokey's Major League career consisted of just two games from 1957 to 1958, his occupation with the Chicago White Sox organization lasted through 1963. Stover McIlwain's baseball profession and life were cut short, as

Representing the best that Pensacola's Babe Ruth League had to offer during the summer of 1960, a formidable all-star squad was sent to compete against their peers at the friendly confines of Admiral Mason Park. Among the players on game day was a young pitcher who would one day grace the halls of Cooperstown. *From left to right*: Gary Goodwin, David Ivey, Jerry Lambert, Stan Wolf (kneeling), Joey Miller, Don Sutton and Dabo Renfroe. *Courtesy of David Ivey.*

he died of cancer at age twenty-six. McIlwain was interred at Spruell Memorial Cemetery in Cantonment, Florida.

One of the reasons attributed to the large number of professional baseball players arising from the Pensacola Bay area is that of an abundance of coaches taking a personal interest in the future of their young people. From college to high school to community leagues and personal instruction, Pensacola coaches have made a difference in the development of countless athletes since the earliest city sandlots. Many names that have been printed on Little League, Babe Ruth League and other Pensacola youth organization uniforms have gone on to grace the backs of Major League jerseys. During the summer of 1960, sixteen-year-old Don Sutton pitched his way onto the Pensacola Babe Ruth All-Stars. The scouts were watching.

TWIG AND THE 1962 SENATORS

The Alabama-Florida League made a small change to its 1962 team lineup. The Dodger-affiliated Panama City Fliers moved to Andalusia, Alabama, to become the Andalusia/Ozark Dodgers. This left only Pensacola and Fort Walton Beach as Florida representatives in the league. Pensacola made a slight shift for the new season as well. The Senators replaced manager Archie Wilson with baseball legend Wayne Terwilliger. "Twig" had played for the old Washington club in 1953 and 1954, and with over thirteen years of professional baseball experience, he went straight to work with Pensacola's boys as soon as he hit town.

The *Pensacola News Journal* reported on May 11, 1962, "Terwilliger's got a good bit of everything—good pitching, good hitting, and a lot more of that blazing speed." Hal Keller, Washington's farm director, set Terwilliger in at Pensacola with the assurance that he had given Wayne a team that could win. Twig had managed Keller's nephew Don during the previous season with the Greensboro Yankees. Hal's brother was former Yankee slugger Charlie "King Kong" Keller. All three Kellers agreed that Terwilliger had what it took to bring Pensacola a pennant.

In what would become Pensacola's last professionally affiliated franchise season until 2012, the 1962 Senators delivered a victorious season. Wayne Terwilliger, set in as manager by the Washington farm director, brought a wealth of experience and determination. Although Pensacola's 79–38 record carried them into championship play for 1962, the folding of the Alabama-Florida League caused Admiral Mason Park to fall silent of Senators the very next year. *Courtesy of Pensacola Historical Society.*

Twig broke into the majors with the Chicago Cubs in 1949, while playing later for the Brooklyn Dodgers, Washington Senators, New York Giants and Kansas City Athletics. As the new manager for the 1962 Pensacola team, Terwilliger brought a wealth of experience to the already strong club. Had the Alabama-Florida League continued beyond the 1962 season, it is anybody's guess as to what Pensacola could have achieved. However, with Panaccione, Terwilliger, Waters, general manager Howard Schulman and the high caliber of players assured by Washington, Pensacola had the opportunity to become a Minor League empire town.

Wayne Terwilliger's lifelong occupation in baseball eventually spanned nearly seventy seasons, with fifty years as a manager or coach in sixteen franchises. Terwilliger has been listed on the coaching staff for the Washington Senators, Texas Rangers, Minnesota Twins, St. Paul Saints and Fort Worth Cats. He has worked alongside such greats as Ted Williams, Don Zimmer and Bobby Valentine. At age eighty, Twig held the distinction of being the oldest active manager in baseball and became the only man besides Connie Mack to manage past eighty years of age.

Pensacola fielded several players in 1962 that eventually saw time in the majors: Bob Baird was promoted to D.C. by September, and Berry Moore would reach Washington's bench in 1965 along with the returning Don Loun and Roy Heiser, who had already pitched a few games for the big-league Senators in 1961. Fred Waters remained on retainer as Pensacola's pitching instructor, but his time on the mound in 1962 would bring back memories of his prime. Pensacola was stocked with a few other weapons in its arsenal that were direct complements of the Washington farm director.

According to Twig's autobiography, *Terwilliger Bunts One*, he had a core of ten returning players from the 1961 season, six of whom were pitchers, including the previous season's ace, Fred Waters. Wayne characterized Waters as "a lefty who still knew how to get 'em out with a little of this and a little of that, he went 11–2 for us." Carlos Mendoza was a right-handed slider-throwing reliever. Mendoza's "little" slider was a huge advantage in Class-D baseball because many of the players at that level had never seen a slider let alone knew how to hit one.

Catching for Twig was Dalton "Dabo" Renfroe, brother of former Pensacola Dons and Pittsburgh Pirates pitcher Marshall Renfroe. Dalton's son Randy would later play in the California Angel's organization. Dabo proved to be a good battery mate for Pensacola's bullpen and a decent hitter at the plate. One of the now common and everyday practices that Terwilliger implemented with Pensacola's pitchers was a chart showing every throw a pitcher tossed, even the warm up pitches before and during the game. The strategic effort was to keep from burning out Pensacola's hurlers.

The team structure implemented by Joe Panaccione, Wayne Terwilliger and Fred Waters, along with the Washington Senators farm director, paid off in spades for Pensacola. From the beginning of the 1962 season, regional newspapers ran large stories about the possibilities for Pensacola to win the championship. Local businesses were supportive of the team, and advertising around Admiral Mason proved it. A parade through the city streets on opening day with convertible automobiles carried Senators players, staff and executives amid the cheers and enthusiasm of Pensacola baseball fans. On opening night, Pensacola mayor Charles Overman Jr. threw out the first ball, and the city of Pensacola sensed victory from the season's first singing of the national anthem.

Pensacola won its initial game of the season 9–2 behind Waters's pitching. Good hitting, three stolen bases and a team unified secured the victory. Just one week into the Alabama-Florida League season, Pensacola took a firm hold of first place. It was a position that the Senators would keep for the remainder of the year. Pensacola kept its momentum through the determination of the staff and players and an energetic fan base that believed in the team itself. Sports blogger Todd Kaufmann once wrote, "Fans are what makes the game great. The fans are what make the players try harder, and they're the reason that the ninth inning is the most exciting inning in baseball." The fans of Pensacola's 1962 Senators were alive with every ninth inning.

As the finals approached, Pensacola was well on top of the league with a 79–38 record and was twenty-two games ahead of second-place Fort Walton Beach. The Senators also led the league in attendance and quite possibly fan exuberance, although there is no way to gauge such a fact. Nevertheless, it was the Pensacola fans that generated the energy to infuse the excitement demonstrated by Twig's Senators. The Pensacola Senators easily carried home the Alabama-Florida League's 1962 pennant, defeating Selma 3–1.

Terwilliger said that he built the 1962 team around speed, as they did not have the greatest power at the plate. "I taught my players everything I knew about base running and we poured it on all year," he later remembered. Twig recalled the base-running efforts of the Pensacola Senators in his autobiography:

We ran in close games and it helped many times. We ran when we were behind and we ran when we were ahead. If it was early in the game, we ran. When we were ten runs ahead, we ran. It drove the opposing managers crazy. When the Ft. Walton Beach manager got on me one day, I just said, "You manage your way and I'll manage mine," and he shut up.

Wayne Terwilliger structured Pensacola on quickness and agility, the same way a power-hitting team focuses on big bats at the plate.

Although Pensacola had been given a gift from its parent club in the form of Terwilliger and a great core of players, the actual organizational budget did not allow for luxury perks. The players and coaching staff traveled in a broken-down school bus, painted in a dull black overcoat to hide the rust. There were holes in the floor that had to be stuffed with newspaper when it rained to keep the players from getting wet. The windshield wipers had to be moved by hand by none other than the skipper himself, and team trainer Paul Raibon doubled as the Senators' bus driver.

There were absolutely no expendable funds for anything such as fireworks at the end of a victorious game. So as the final win of the championship rolled around, Terwilliger did the next best thing. He had worn an old pair of huge polka-dot boxer shorts that the players had teased him about all season long. In response to their triumphant year, Twig ran the shorts up the flag pole to celebrate their position as champions. Twig said that when he came back into Pensacola many years later in 2004 with his Fort Worth Cats playing the Pelicans, he could still see those polka-dot shorts flying in the breeze.

Pensacola was riding what has been considered by some as the best season in all of Pensacola's baseball history. But the Alabama-Florida League was approaching its demise. On November 29, 1962, league president William Moore was quoted in the *Tuscaloosa News* as saying, "We are out. We cannot get working agreements because we do not play Negroes in our league." As a product of the Old South, the Alabama-Florida League would not roster any player of African American descent. Although Major League Baseball had made its transition toward amending its segregated ways, there still existed into the early 1960s pockets of color-restricted athletic competition.

The oldest Class-D circuit in existence was facing extinction due to the restrictive nature of its original bylaws. This, along with professional baseball's re-alignment toward a new tiered classification for the Minor League system, meant inevitable reevaluation for teams such as Class-D Pensacola. Three of the existing Alabama-Florida League teams actually did have working agreements in place for the 1963 season: Fort Walton Beach (Minnesota Twins), Selma (Cleveland Indians) and Pensacola (Washington

Senators) were settled with their parent clubs to continue with the current agreement. However, insomuch as the remainder of the teams could not establish proper fulfillment of contract, the league could not continue.

Pensacola had become a dominant force in a fading league. "I asked for more time to work out the problem, but it was fruitless," lamented Moore. "I hope we can come back in 1964. We are going to try," he stated with a wavering hope. The Alabama-Florida League was no more after the 1962 season. With the intention to exclude black players, its existence had no place in the new era of desegregated and inclusive baseball. Although Panaccione himself desired and voted to enlist African American players, Pensacola became a peripheral casualty with the folding of the league.

The Washington Senators, not willing to cut their ties on the Gulf Coast just yet, returned with three of their Minor League clubs for spring training in 1963. "Baseball has always been such a natural fit for Pensacola," said Joe Panaccione. As Washington's Minor Leaguers were due to roll into town, Joe sat in the dugout of an empty Admiral Mason Park for an interview with Pensacola sportswriter Gene Pullen. Gazing out toward the right field fence, Panaccione unknowingly prophesied over the City of Five Flags. "It's a shame this park will not be used the way it should be this year. What Pensacola needs is not Class-D baseball; this city needs a Double-A ball club. One it can be proud of and one worthy of support," Joe projected. In reference to the spring exercises that would be held by Washington that year, he continued by saying, " Maybe when people see these Major League level teams training here this spring, they will realize what they're missing and get the ball rolling for baseball's return to Pensacola. Let's hope so anyway."

Unfortunately, Pensacola would not be represented by a professional baseball team for another forty years, and the city would not host an affiliated club until 2012. However, it would not hold back the bountiful harvest of diamond-worthy talent still bursting from the Port City. The Seagulls continued utilizing Admiral Mason until the park's condition demanded otherwise. Pensacola Junior College and local company leagues drew enough spectators to raise a following. Youth leagues and high school teams grew in popularity. On the north side of town, Don Sutton's J.M. Tate High School won its state championship. And thus on a smaller scale, baseball harbored a healthy continuance in Pensacola, as the city unknowingly awaited fulfillment of Panaccione's prophesy.

JOHNNY JOE LEWIS

After the disbanding of the Alabama-Florida League, Fred Waters settled back into his role as the baseball coach for Pensacola High School in 1963—not that his focus had been taken away from his high school boys while he executed his duties on the mound for the Senators. As the Senators chased the Alabama-Florida League pennant during the 1961 and 1962 seasons, Waters managed the Pensacola High Tigers in back-to-back Big Five AA Conference baseball championships. In 1963, the Tigers carried a 22–2 record, taking them to Sarasota for another crack at the title. Although Pensacola took the second-place spot in 1963, Waters and his Tigers had become statewide celebrities from the Panhandle to the Keys.

Pensacola's Booker T. Washington High School, founded in 1916, was an all-African American school until its desegregation in 1970. Washington High Wildcat alumni, such as Florida State Supreme Court Judge Kenneth Bell, NFL linebacker Derrick Brooks and decorated Air Force pilot General Daniel "Chappie" James are but a few who have risen to great achievement after graduating from Booker T. Washington. The Wildcats' Johnny Joe Lewis had begun to make his mark as an impressive outfielder in the late 1950s. Lewis played outfield for the Pensacola Seagulls during his high school years, and while he was fielding for the Gulls, onlookers easily noted that Johnny Lewis was on the rise to his own achievements on the diamond.

The year that Johnny finished his studies at Washington High, the Detroit Tigers held a tryout camp in nearby Atmore, Alabama. Lewis traveled to Atmore to participate and try his hand at catching the eye of professional scouts. After Johnny Lewis performed the prescribed drills instituted by the Tigers, their field scout lost no time in approaching the Pensacola player. Lewis was offered an almost immediate contract with the Detroit organization. Just after signing the contract, Johnny was traded to the Cardinals and was sent to Class-D Wytheville, Virginia, in 1959.

Johnny Joe Lewis worked his way quickly through the minors, achieving a slugging percentage over .500 in four different seasons. He arrived in St. Louis for his Major League debut on April 14, 1964. That year, he hit .234 in forty games, helping the Cardinals to a National League championship. Although Johnny did not take the field during the 1964 World Series, his Cardinals gained the title four games to three over the New York Yankees.

Lewis was traded to the New York Mets for the 1965 season, where he stayed until his last Major League game in 1967. After the following season

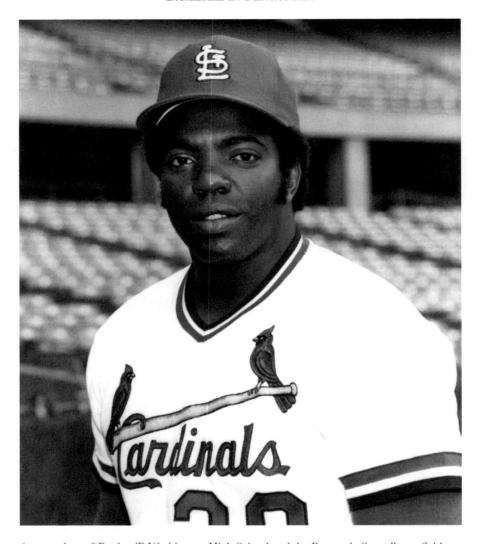

As a product of Booker T. Washington High School and the Pensacola Seagulls, outfielder Johnny Joe Lewis gained the attention of Major League scouts. First signing with the Detroit Tigers, Johnny was traded to the St. Louis Cardinals in a 1959 transaction. Upon his big-league debut in 1964, he entered the Cardinals' clubhouse with eyes fixed on a championship. Lewis's initial experience in the majors was one filled with a World Series trophy. *Courtesy of the author.*

in the minors, Johnny Lewis retired from playing professionally, although his days in baseball were far from over. At various levels and at a number of strategic positions, Lewis was employed by the Cardinals from 1970 to 1998. He scouted during the early 1970s and coached and managed several

Minor League affiliates. From 1973 to 1976, he coached for St. Louis, and then again from 1985 to 1989. In 1999, Johnny Lewis became the Minor League hitting coordinator for the Houston Astros and was named their roving hitting instructor after the 2001 season.

This City Needs a Double-A Ball Club

As Johnny Lewis was making his debut with the Cardinals, Tate High School graduate Don Sutton was just stepping into his career, signing with the Los Angeles Dodgers as a free agent in 1964. Even with Pensacola celebrating local players in the ranks of professional baseball, there was more stirring in the game closer to home. The Associated Press released a report that the Double-A Knoxville Smokies of the Southern League were strongly considering pulling out of Tennessee. The reason cited for the Smokies possible withdrawal was a lack of gate receipts. Knoxville had attracted only a little over twelve thousand patrons in the first twenty-three games of the year. The report was not just about a notion by ownership wishing to relieve themselves of operational challenges. The process of relocating the team was already in the hands of league president Sam C. Smith, who was helping to guide offers from qualified cities. Pensacola officials echoed Panaccione's sentiment and made it known that the town would like to host a Double-A club.

Smith had been instrumental in forming the Southern League, which had been remodeled from the remnants of the old South Atlantic League and the defunct Southern Association. His goal was to see the new league flourish. Cities that were in the running to receive Knoxville's franchise were Memphis, Tennessee; Montgomery and Mobile, Alabama; and Pensacola, Florida. Pensacola was seemingly ready to refurbish Admiral Mason Ballpark to accommodate the Double-A team. The opportunity did not materialize for Pensacola, as Knoxville changed affiliates from the Detroit Tigers to the Cincinnati Reds, breathing new life into its Tennessee host. But there were those in Pensacola who subscribed to the vision spoken by Joe Panaccione, and they would continue to hold on to the hope of professional baseball returning to their town.

JACKIE MOORE COACHES CHAMPIONS

Jay, Florida, located north of Pensacola, is a small 233-household community and, as athletes go, has produced its share of quality high school players. But in 1957, Jay, Florida–born Jackie Moore took a step toward reaching the aspiration of many small-town boys in signing a professional baseball contract. After contracting with the Tigers, Jackie worked predominantly as a catcher. Making his way through the farm system, he arrived in Detroit during the 1965 season.

Jackie Moore's skills developed on the Gulf Coast landed him behind the plate in Michigan. It was not long before the life Jackie may have imagined in the majors took a turn into a whole new field. Moore played in only twenty-one games for Detroit in 1964 with fifty-three at-bats, achieving a meager .094 average before being sent back to Triple-A.

Shortly after retiring as an active player, Jackie Moore found his true specialty in baseball. Moore's ability to bring out productivity in others ushered him into coaching and managing. His first managerial duties began with Boston's New York–Penn League affiliate in 1968. Jackie stayed with Boston for another year and then signed on as a coach for the Milwaukee Brewers in 1970. Moore's big-league career covered player developmental positions in the Rangers, Blue Jays, Expos, Reds, Rockies and Astros organizations.

Among the long list of achievements that mark Moore's career are managing the Oakland Athletics, coaching for the 1990 World Champion Cincinnati Reds and managing the Round Rock Express owned by Nolan Ryan during their inaugural season in 2000. Reunited with Ryan in 2008, Moore was named bench coach for the Texas Rangers, a position that would allow both men to see their team win the 2010 and 2011 American League championships.

COOPERSTOWN BOUND

Legendary pitcher and baseball broadcaster Dizzy Dean visited Pensacola during the first week of March 1966 as a participant in the pro-amateur prelude to the Pensacola Open PGA tournament. The Hall of Fame hurler held a press conference after arriving, talking about his personal feelings on the current deterioration of the game. His specific topic of discussion

Tate High School's baseball program has turned out numerous Major League-quality players, but none more illustrious than pitcher Don Sutton. The rural, hardworking upbringing that Don experienced north of Pensacola served him well on the mound with good work ethic and determined grit. Sutton's accomplishments during twenty-three years on the Major League diamond landed him a place in the Hall of Fame. But it was the way "Black & Decker" carried himself among teammates, opposing players and fans that landed him in the hearts of thousands. *Courtesy of the author.*

was about modern baseball and those Dean phrased as the "greedy people running it." Dizzy Dean's opinion may have been the slightest bit tainted, as he was recently released from his broadcasting position under less than agreeable conditions.

On the top of Dizzy's list of gripes was the excessive amount of time, effort and people it was taking to decide whether the Braves would continue in Milwaukee or be allowed to move to Atlanta. "Seventeen judges and fifty lawyers haggling over where the Braves ought to play—in Milwaukee or Atlanta," Dean said with a little exaggeration. He offered his opinion that the team should take up residence and play in Seguin, Texas. Seguin was where Dizzy had broken into baseball some forty years earlier. Just a bit over a month after Dean's Pensacola press conference, another future Hall of Fame pitcher was emerging into the Major Leagues. Don Sutton made his debut with the Los Angeles Dodgers on April 14, 1966.

Sutton, born in Clio, Alabama, moved with his family to the rural community of Molino just a few miles north of city center Pensacola. Sutton's father, Howard, instilled a strong work ethic in his son, which became apparent even in Don's early years of youth baseball. Also apparent in the young righty's ability with a baseball was the personal instruction given to Don by his sixth grade teacher Henry Roper. Roper had once pitched for a Class-D club associated with the New York Giants. But that might as well have been a Major League club in Sutton's mind, and he asked Roper to teach him the finer points of pitching. "Everything I know about the game I learned originally from Henry Roper," contends Sutton.

Many of the local tournaments that Don participated in were held at Admiral Mason Ballpark. Names such as Jim Whittington, now a key figure in Pensacola real estate; Sacred Heart Hospital employee and Blue Wahoos staffer David Ivy; and future NFL quarterback Kenny Stabler were listed on the rosters of challenging teams playing alongside Sutton at Admiral Mason.

Retired professional scout George Zuraw marks Don Sutton as one that got away from him, claiming that he initially spotted Sutton at Tate while he was canvassing the southeast for the Pirates. During Don's senior year, Zuraw approach the emerging right-hander with a contract and a signing bonus of a few thousand dollars. Don was looking for a higher offer in order to cover college tuition. The Pirates offer fell short, and Don went on to Gulf Coast Junior College in Panama City, Florida. After signing with the Dodgers, Don's first assignment was with Class-A Santa Barbara, were he posted an 8–1 record in ten games. Moving quickly to Double-A the same season, Sutton went 15–6 in twenty-one games for Albuquerque. That would be it for his initial acclimation into the pros. Don Sutton saw his first Major League batter just twelve days after his twenty-first birthday.

Sutton joined a Dodgers team already stacked with talent. Under manager Walter Alston, pitchers Sandy Koufax and Don Drysdale welcomed Don to the staff. Infielders Jim Lefebvre, Wes Parker, Maury Wills and former Pensacola Senator John Kennedy backed up the young pitcher to help him achieve his rookie season ERA of 2.99, with twelve wins and twelve losses. Kennedy and Sutton shared their Pensacola connection, while Drysdale taught Sutton the most, according to Don. With his rookie year behind him, Don Sutton never looked back. He stayed with the Dodgers for fifteen years and four National League titles before being traded to Houston in 1981.

Don's career took him from the Dodgers to the Astros and then to the American League with the Brewers, Athletics and Angels, ending up back with the Dodgers in 1982. While Sutton was with the Brewers in 1988, Milwaukee won the American League pennant, but it was not until playing in his sixth World Series experience that he took home a ring. The 1988 Dodgers beat the Yankees in a four-games-to-three contest, ending Don's playing career on the highest note. During Sutton's twenty-three years of Major League service, "Black & Decker" was a four-time National League All-Star, 1977 All-Star Game MVP, National League ERA leader in 1980 and shutout leader in 1970. In twenty seasons, he pitched two hundred or more innings, and in five seasons, he threw two hundred or more strikeouts. Don finished his career on the mound with 324 wins.

The full list of Don Sutton's achievements is extensive and worthy of his election into the National Baseball Hall of Fame Class of 1998. Immediately after retiring from playing, Sutton became a baseball announcer for both radio and television. Don had some experience in this field, working as a radio personality in Pensacola prior to his life as a professional pitcher. Sutton is most remembered for his broadcasting years with the Atlanta Braves, but he also took the booth for the Washington Nationals in 2007 and 2008. Today, Don Sutton Park in Molino encompasses five baseball and softball fields, servicing the youth leagues close to Don's childhood home in the northern Pensacola area.

BILL BOND ALL-STARS

The Bill Bond Youth Baseball League evolved into more than just a Pensacola institution, as it transitioned from earlier years as a Florida Little Majors franchise. Founded in 1969 by Mr. Bill Bond and a number of Pensacola businessmen and community leaders, Bill Bond Baseball set a standard in high quality and competitive play for the participants, parents

For decades, Pensacola boys have had an advocate for their development in becoming successful young men—that advocate has been Bill Bond. The one-time director of navy civilian human resources at Pensacola's Naval Air Station launched Boy Scout troops and baseball leagues in order to give area boys a place to excel and achieve personal success. Bond's 1960 all-stars were a shining example of how seeded inspiration could turn into achievement. *Bottom row, left to right*: Chuck Scruggs, Howard Roberts, Roddy Morris, Jim Hall and Bill Bond. *Middle row, left to right*: Bobby Sheets, Ronnie Overstreet, Robert Ashler, Sandy Sansing, Fred Yilling, Gordon McCraw and Reily Roberts. *Back row, left to right*: Andy Gordon, Mike Leatherwood, Eddie Bates, Ernie Martin, Bill Barrow and George Poulos. *Courtesy of Bill Bond.*

and league officials. The league was formed from the remnants of previous baseball programs that did not meet the requirements demanded by the caliber of youth players produced in the Pensacola community. The new league was also formed in response to the disallowance of minority players by other youth organizations. Bill Bond instantly produced a surpassing level of competition, helping to develop skills and fundamentals for all races of young people.

Bill Bond Baseball is associated with United States Specialty Sports Association and Dizzy Dean Baseball, although the league plays postseason all-stars with Dizzy Dean. Bill Bond offers coach pitch for six- to eight-year-olds, minor and major leagues for nine- to twelve-year-olds and a juniors league for thirteen- to fourteen-year-olds acquired from the North Pensacola Optimist Club in 2008. From its earliest inception, Bill Bond Youth Baseball League has developed the training needed for those who desire to reach their fullest potential. Many Pensacola boys who would later go on to lace up Major League spikes gained their earliest knowledge of the game on the fields of Bill Bond.

The league was named for seventh-generation Pensacolan and director of navy civilian human resources William "Bill" Bond. The new organization honored the legacy of one who had given his life to the excellence of Pensacola's youth and many years to building opportunities for the boys living throughout his beloved city. Youth sports and Boy Scouts topped Bill's list of outreach endeavors, but it was baseball that held his heart. Major Leaguers Billy Sadler, Travis Fryman, Jay Bell, Phil Hiatt and Talmadge Nunnari each spent precious seasons in the Bill Bond League honing their future trade.

After playing in the majors, Talmadge "T" Nunnari returned home to ultimately take a pivotal role with the independent Pensacola Pelicans. On the occasion of an invitational day clinic sponsored by the Pelicans, T stood before a group of children and parents and recalled his early baseball experiences in Pensacola. In each hand, T held up a jersey. In one hand was his jersey from the Montreal Expos, and in the other was his Bill Bond uniform.

As he spoke to the young people who had come to work out with the Pelicans' players and coaches, T talked about the importance of learning good habits early and following instructions from parents, teachers and coaches while enjoying the days as just being a kid. He said that both uniforms he held before them brought memories of accomplishment and teamwork, but of the two, his jersey worn while playing for the Bill Bond League brought him the highest sense of pride.

During the formulating era of Bill Bond Baseball, Escambia High School won the AA Division State Baseball Championship for the second year in a row in 1966, and Tate High took the A-Class pennant in 1968. Through the fundamental instruction garnered from organizations like Bill Bond and personal training from local coaches and high school programs, Pensacola had become something of a baseball player factory.

Ken Wright and Jim Hutto

LaDon Boyd signed with the Kansas City Athletics organization in 1967 after his senior year at Escambia High. Charles Sutton of Tate was drafted by the Dodgers in 1966. Skippy Gibson was selected by the Cleveland Indians in the 1968 Amateur Draft along with fellow Tate graduate Dennis Franklin, who was picked up by the Pirates. The Indians also chose Escambia High's James Hobgood in 1968. In 1969, the Padres selected Donald Keenan from Pensacola High and Aubrey Anderson from Escambia High.

Kenneth Warren Wright, born September 4, 1946, grew up in the Warrington community just across Bayou Grande from Pensacola Naval Air Station. Ken Wright developed his ball-playing skills on the local sandlots while the navy's elite Blue Angels exhibition flight team practiced their aeronautics overhead. Ken attended Escambia High School and became a threat to be reckoned with on the mound against rival schools. Escambia teammate John Hinkley says that Ken was the hardest-throwing pitcher anyone had ever seen. "I ought to know. I had to catch him," says Hinkley. The same observation about Wright's iron arm is echoed by Ken's underclassmen and fellow Major Leaguers Dennis Lewallyn and Kevin Saucier.

Ken signed with the Boston Red Sox as an amateur free agent in 1964, staying with Boston's Minor League system through 1969. On December 1, 1969, Wright was drafted by the Kansas City Royals in the Rule 5 Draft. At age twenty-three, the right-hander from Pensacola made his first Major League appearance on the mound for the Royals on April 10, 1970. Ken's starting salary as a member of the Kansas City bullpen brushed just over the $7,000 mark; however, Ken had reached his goal of throwing in the big leagues.

Among Ken Wright's teammates during his years with the Royals were Cookie Rojas, Buck Martinez, Dick Drago, Hal McRae and George Brett. Ken had the opportunity to work under the managing styles of both Bob Lemon and Jack McKeon. According to Wright, one of the highlights of being on the Royals was rooming with fellow Floridian Lou Piniella. Road trips with Ken and "Sweet Lou" became quite interesting, as Wright recalled: "As a pitcher, I was always ready to settle in for the evening and get a good rest before the next day's work. Lou would often be keyed up and have trouble falling asleep. I would generally drift off first, only to wake up with a jolt to a loud crash and Lou standing across the room with a bat in his hand." Ken explains his story by saying that:

When Piniella was not satisfied with his performance at the plate, he would stand for long lengths in front of a mirror, looking at his stance and critiquing his own swing. On more than one occasion, Lou would get up in the middle of the night to experiment with new hitting techniques

he had just envisioned. Taking swings inside our hotel room in the small
hours of the night, a lamp or vase sometimes became an accidental victim
of Piniella's desire for perfection. Of course, the crash brought me out of a
dead sleep, only to see my old pal in a way too familiar picture.

Wright and Piniella were traded to the New York Yankees on December 7, 1973, for veteran pitcher Lindy McDaniel. The trade was the beginning of a long and wonderful relationship for Sweet Lou and the New York Americans. For Ken, it meant just five innings of pitching with the Yankees and a trade to the Phillies the next season. Wright spent the remainder of 1974 back in the minors and subsequently retired at the end of the season. After Ken's return to Pensacola, he became the director of Warrington Emergency Aid Center, a community assistance organization founded by his mother.

Pensacola High School's baseball program held its head high with a sense of pride and accomplishment in 1970. Pitcher Terry Bowman, just months after his senior commencement ceremony, walked onto the field in Bradenton, Florida, as a member of the Pittsburg Pirates Gulf Coast League affiliate. Bowman was traded to the Twins in 1971 and was sent to Minnesota's Gulf Coast League club under Manager Fred Waters. Also during 1970 season, the East Brent Dixie Youth majors become their league's World Series champions, and Pensacola High graduate Jim Hutto made his Major League debut.

Hutto was signed by the Boston Red Sox as a seventh-round pick during the 1965 Amateur Draft. Jim's first assignment was in Waterloo, Iowa, of the Midwest League for 1965 and 1966. After being sent to Winston-Salem of the Carolina League in 1967, Hutto made a trek west to the Pacific Coast League (PCL) Tulsa Oilers in a 1968 trade to St. Louis. That year, Jim and his Oiler teammates under manager Warren Spahn played into a 95–53 season record. The Cardinals held onto Jim for just a single season before dealing him to Philadelphia for Bill White. The Phillies saw potential and extreme versatility in Hutto but determined that Jim needed just a bit more refining. He stayed in the PCL for one more year, proving his worth as a valuable utility man. During Hutto's four seasons in the Minor Leagues, he covered the outfield and all three bases and caught a number of games.

Beyond his diverse fielding skills, Jim posted a .256 batting average in 1968 and a .306 average in 1969. The Phillies hastily called up Hutto to the parent club for the 1970 season as a needed pinch hitter and catcher. Jim had been considered by some as still a bit raw for the big leagues, but manager Frank Lucchesi was in a bad way with the loss of both of his catchers. During an early-season game against the Giants, starting catcher Tim McCarver broke his hand while hitting a foul ball in the top of the sixth inning. In the bottom of the sixth, backup catcher Mike Ryan's hand was broken under the spikes of Willie McCovey in tag-out at the plate. Jim platooned the position behind the plate with several others, participating in fifty-seven games. On May 26, 1970, Hutto made a rookie mistake by committing a base-running error—Official Major League Baseball Rule 7.08(h), better known as passing a runner.

Playing against Montreal, the Phillies had two on with no outs in the ninth inning. Terry Harmon stood at third for Philadelphia, and Jim Hutto was the runner on first. At the plate, Byron Browne hit a fly ball into short right field, where it was trapped by Rusty Staub. Leading off at first and not paying close enough attention to either the play or the first base coach, Hutto thought the ball had been caught for an out. Jim returned to first just as Browne was rounding the bag, resulting in a called out. The Phillies won the game, but for Jim, the sting of the mistake would be turned into the benefit of others in the years to come.

Jim Hutto made restitution for his base-running blunder on July 19 when he slugged a pinch-hit grand slam against the Dodgers. McCarver and Ryan came back in early September, and the Phillies found themselves with a wealth of catchers. Jim Hutto, the rookie utility player, now became valuable as a tradable commodity. On December 16, 1970, the Phillies exchanged Hutto, Grant Jackson and Sam Parrilla with Baltimore for utility man Roger Freed. The Angels selected Hutto in the 1971 Rule 5 Draft, only to trade him back to the Orioles in June 1973. Jim bounced around the Orioles' farm system for a couple of seasons before seeing Major League play again in 1975.

After retirement in 1976, Jim Hutto put his experiences on the diamond to work developing the careers of other players as a Minor League manager. Jim entered the game as a professional at the age of seventeen, knowing well the stress and toils of one so young entering a man's world. Even lessons learned from the mistakes that he made, like the one in 1970 against Montreal, were used to guide his boys toward perfecting their skills and disciplines. In 1985, Hutto was part of a unique arrangement in the Florida State League. The Houston Astros relinquished their affiliation with the Daytona Beach club to become a co-op for the Orioles and Rangers. The newly christened Class-A Islanders fielded such players as Billy Ripken and Kenny Rogers under Hutto's management.

As a player, Hutto understood the reality of the hazards surrounding baseball. During the year he was attached to the Angels, that truth materialized back home in Pensacola in 1971. Although the game of baseball is not often thought of as a dangerous sport by the casual observer, the physical risk and the uncertainty of injury are quite real. On March 20, 1971, during a game between Woodham and Washington High Schools, seventeen-year-old senior William Bogan stepped to the plate in the fourth inning for Woodham. Bogan, the team's shortstop, wheeled himself around and squared for a bunt. A fastball cleared contact with Bogan's bat and hit him firmly in the chest. William Bogan died from the injury of the impact eight days later.

Later during the summer of 1971, Pensacola's Babe Ruth All-Stars brought home the state championship, defeating West Palm Beach 9–0 in the finals. Also, Fred Waters began coaching the Escambia High School baseball squad, bringing with him his already proven training methods. The Escambia club responded by delivering Coach Waters a Florida 4A Championship in 1972. Future Major League pitcher Preston Hanna commanded the mound for Escambia in their grasp of the 1972 title.

SCOUTING PENSACOLA'S ALL-STARS

Mirroring Escambia High from the previous season, Pensacola High School won the 1973 4A cup while Pensacola Christian High brought home a state 1A pennant. Over the years, Pensacola became home to more than just championship trophies, as the city won the hearts of ballplayers who played through on tour. Several were so taken by the southern hospitality that they eventually made Pensacola their residence. Former St. Louis Browns relief pitcher Ernie Manning was one such player. Ernie had first experienced Pensacola during his Southern Association days with the Montgomery Rebels. After living many years in his adopted town, Manning passed away in Pensacola on April 28, 1973.

By the 1974 season, Coach Fred Waters had seriously ramped up Escambia High's baseball program. Pulling triple duty as high school baseball coach, junior varsity football coach and guidance counselor, Waters directed his boys toward personal and athletic achievement. Fred Waters and company claimed another 4A victory in 1974. Fred's '74 championship team was stacked with talent, including catcher Pete Perkins, who batted .275 for the season, just behind leftfielder Charles Sapp's .290 average. First baseman Tim Wadsworth and shortstop Steve McGowan both slugged their average to just under .330 during the year. Waters's starting pitcher for the May state championship had also been the ace of Escambia's bullpen. Future Major Leaguer Kevin Saucier listed an 11–2 season during 1974, culminating in Saucier signing a Minor League contract with the Philadelphia Phillies one month after graduation.

Knowing that player development among Pensacola's high schools was an above-the-mien endeavor, representatives from many Major League organizations trolled the fields of Northwest Florida hoping to land a big catch. Just as Branch Rickey did many years prior, professional scouts used Pensacola as a staging ground to view regionally grown prospects. Cincinnati Reds scout Larry Doughty held a try-out camp in Pensacola during the summer of 1974. The camp attracted players from west of Mobile, Alabama, and those from eastern towns down the Florida coast, all looking for a shot at a professional contract. Doughty's future career in baseball spanned several clubs as a scout, farm director, vice-president of player personnel and general manager. As general manager of the Pittsburgh Pirates, Larry oversaw the team to two division titles in 1990 and 1991. Playing shortstop for the Pirates during Doughty's years with Pittsburgh was Tate High School's Jay Bell.

As the autumn of 1974 was approaching, the Pensacola-area Dixie Youth elite team was on the road once more defending its title. The Dixie Youth World Series held their finals in Decatur, Alabama, where Pensacola squared off against Columbia, South Carolina, for the pennant. During the final game, Pensacola was down by a run in the ninth inning. Coming from behind, Pensacola brought two across the plate to record a 3–2 win and bring home the series trophy. Pensacola's Tony Kinley took the series batting title with a .625 average.

PRESTON HANNA SIGNS WITH THE BRAVES

The summer of 1975 was filled with youth baseball leagues and company team softball competition throughout Pensacola. Without a professionally affiliated team in town since 1962, local fan following was reserved to an almost neighborhood scale. While high school and college bleachers were filled with parents and alumni, for a short time through the mid-1970s, an adult hardball league attempted to grab a hold of Pensacola's eye.

A semiprofessional league, consisting of seven local teams with players' ages as diverse as their level of experience, made a run at bringing upper-level baseball back to Pensacola. Teams were composed of men too old to be active professionally and younger fellows desiring a taste of hard-hitting competition. Steve Williams, playing out of Milton, Florida, had once been selected by the Houston Astros in an amateur draft, while player/manager Lewis Parker played in Pensacola's Negro League. Former Pensacola Seagulls owner Purvis "Pearl" Lewis came out of semi-retirement to coach in the league and hoped the venue would catch on with fans. However, with a lack of sponsorship and weekend-only games, financial and fan support was too small for a legitimate run at success.

Although the semipro league did not succeed in its long-term aspirations, Escambia High School's Preston Hanna did see the fruition of his hard work. Hanna came up under the tutelage of Coach Fred Waters. As with many area players, Waters had given Hanna not only a "leg up" to attaining a professional baseball career but also a unique perspective on the game. In the June 1972 Amateur Draft, the Atlanta Braves selected Hanna as their eleventh pick in the first round of the draft. Preston was assigned to Wytheville, Virginia, Atlanta's rookie-level franchise, where he struggled some to find his consistency. The Minor League players were different than what he had experienced in Pensacola. Not only were there hitters who could overcome his pitching, but now there was no familiar home crowd to cheer him forward.

During his last year at Escambia, Preston went 13–0 with a 0.31 ERA. He was voted all-state in baseball and Outstanding Athlete of the Year in his own hometown, none of which mattered to the teams he was assigned to now. All of Preston's high school achievements were yesterday's news, and he would have to live up to being the bright prospect that Atlanta had invested in. With his ERA hovering around 3.50 during 1973 and 1974, Hanna won eleven games in Double-A Savannah. After twenty-six games and 10 more wins the next season for Triple-A Richmond, the Braves brought Preston to Atlanta for a look at the big leagues late in 1975.

Over the next two years, Preston's pitching time was divided between Atlanta and Richmond, plus Savannah for seven games in 1977. But by spring training of 1978, Pensacola's Preston Hanna found his way onto Atlanta's bullpen roster as a regular. Hanna was still working out "a bad case of the butterflies," as he put it, prior to taking the mound against the Giants on April 26, 1978. He had beaten San Francisco on their home turf during the week prior, holding them to a one-hit shutout in seven innings. That was just not enough to curb his nerves twenty-four hours before pitching them again.

Preston Hanna, #49, discusses strategy with Braves infielder Larvell Blanks during the Braves 1980 spring training exercises in Orlando, Florida. Yet another protégé of Fred Waters, Preston Hanna made his mark on the mound at Escambia High School. The Atlanta Braves signed Hanna in the first round of the 1972 Amateur Draft. Preston's time under Escambia's coach was reflected once again after retirement, as Hanna mirrored his old mentor in working in player development. *Courtesy of Pensacola Historical Society.*

Preston's wife was the one who really brought him the peace to go forward. "She said that I would be fine once I reached the mound, and she was right," said Hanna. Preston held the Giants to three hits and no runs through five innings, allowing Atlanta to win their fourth game in their first five meetings with San Francisco. Former Major League pitcher and fellow Escambia High teammate Dennis Lewallyn says that no one knows just how much a baseball wife can affect a player positively or negatively.

Mrs. Hanna in no way could affect the events that would come Preston's way during the next few years.

By the end of the 1970s, Preston's pitching arm began to give him trouble with soreness and flexibility. It was during this time he later reported that his club began pressuring him about taking medication to relieve the pain and tension. The mounting pressure to perform, coupled with the physical challenges of his arm, changed Preston's game. By 1980, he was seeing only a few starts and pitched mainly in relief. After speaking his mind publicly about Atlanta's front office, Preston made a few enemies with the Braves' brass. Oddly enough, Hanna became a favorite of the Braves' enigmatic owner Ted Turner.

On June 12, 1981, Major League players stopped work in a strike that had been voted on unanimously by the Baseball Players Association. The work stoppage surrounded arguments over free agency and owner compensation. Out-of-work Preston Hanna began looking for opportunities to make ends meet, as the length of the strike was anticipated to extend throughout negotiations. In a quirky twist, Ted Turner offered Hanna a position at his Cable News Network as a sports production assistant. Although the job would have placed him working directly for the same owner he was striking against, there was no conflict with Major League Baseball, as the position was unrelated.

The media had a field day with the obscurity of the story. Turner favored Preston personally, but the bad publicity the job offer brought to Turner and CNN kept the position from ever materializing. Fortunately, the strike came to a close at the end of July, and Hanna, along with the rest of Major League Baseball, returned to work. Unfortunately, Preston had created an undercurrent with his front office leadership, and with Ted Turner out of the country during mid-season 1982, Preston was given his unconditional release. He played out the rest of the year with Oakland, which signed him as a free agent. After the 1983 season in the minors, Hanna retired from playing professionally, as his arm continued to give him discomfort. Preston Hanna's son Warren played for the Chicago Cubs organization in 2001 and 2002.

LEWALLYN'S DETERMINATION

Beyond Preston Hanna, Escambia High's baseball legacy continued as each player drafted represented his school, his town and the life lessons instilled by the coaching staff. Right-handed pitcher Dennis Lewallyn also credits Fred Waters with getting his career started. Lewallyn, whose father had played service ball during World War II, grew up playing Little League in the Warrington area of Pensacola. During those years of youth baseball, he played with and against Preston Hanna, Kevin Saucier, Joe Cannon and other Pensacola boys who would see professional competition.

"Even though I made All-Star teams in PONY League, I was never the best guy on the squad," recalls Lewallyn. He continues, "I was pretty skinny and did not start developing power until about my sophomore year at Escambia." Dennis was not an overpowering pitcher, and he was surrounded by a high school varsity team that continually produced winners and caught the eye of area scouts. During Lewallyn's freshman year, a coach suggested that Dennis might try football as a backup due to his good speed and six-foot-four stature. The coach sent Lewallyn to see Fred Waters about the possibility of playing on Escambia's football squad.

As an underclassman, Dennis did not yet have a relationship with the legendary varsity baseball instructor. "I did not even know that he knew who I was or that I played baseball," said Dennis. Not only did Coach Waters

Initially not seeing himself as an accomplished pitcher, Dennis Lewallyn considered going out for football at Escambia High School. But with a little encouragement from Coach Waters, Dennis applied himself to what would be his career craft. After throwing for the Dodgers, Indians and Rangers, Lewallyn has helped to shape the professions of young pitchers within several Major League franchises. As a natural mentor, Dennis Lewallyn has positively affected the lives of ballplayers in multiple countries, giving them over four decades of professional experience. *Courtesy of Dennis Lewallyn.*

know about Lewallyn, he advised him that if he played high school football all he would ever be was a high school football player. But if he would come out to play varsity baseball, he was certain that he would go on to achieve a Major League roster spot. Dennis says that he had always dreamed of playing Major League ball, but no one (including himself) had ever given him the notion of attaining that dream. Coach Fred Waters became the first to believe in him. Dennis married his high school sweetheart Kathryn, and together, with his selection by the Braves in the 1971 Amateur Draft, they began their life as a baseball family.

Lewallyn did not sign with Atlanta, deciding to first get in some college ball at Chipola Junior College in Marianna, Florida. He was picked up by the Dodgers in the first round of the 1972 Amateur Draft and posted an 11–6 season with Daytona Beach. Class-A Bakersfield in 1973 and Double-A Waterbury in 1974 proved a bit tougher for Dennis, but personal determination won out—something that does not always show up in a box score. Dennis and future Pensacola Blue Wahoos manager Jim Riggleman shared living space as Waterbury teammates.

Dennis now ponders if not being the best player on his early teams caused him to work all that much harder. "It may have actually been a blessing in disguise, as it pushed me to be better without the added pressure of undue expectations," says Dennis. In reality, he knew where he wanted to go and what it would take to get there.

Dennis began the 1975 season pitching for the Dodgers Triple-A affiliate in Albuquerque, New Mexico. As an Albuquerque Duke, Lewallyn posted a 3.90 ERA and tucked thirteen wins under his belt. Nearing the end of the season, Los Angeles wanted to see if Dennis could compete in Dodger Blue, and on September 21, 1975, in the Houston Astrodome, Dennis Lewallyn was brought in to throw in the bottom of the seventh inning. With two outs and the Dodgers behind 6–2, Dennis faced J.R. Richard, the Astros' starter. Richard took the first pitch for a four-hundred-foot foul, which narrowly missed adding to Houston's score. Gathering his nerve, Dennis pitched his way out of the inning and headed into the visitor's dugout.

On the Dodgers bench, pitching coach Red Adams worked a little angle to calm Dennis down. Adams asked, "You got another inning in you?" When Lewallyn replied that he did, Red asked what he felt was his best pitch. Dennis said, "Sinking fastball." Dennis later realized that Red's conversation with him was purposely spoken within earshot of catcher Steve Yeager. Adams then queried with a cocked eyebrow, "So why don't you throw it?" The rookie stated that Yeager kept asking him for different pitches, so he yielded to the starting catcher. Red boomed, "Aw, don't listen to him. He's just calling off that pitch 'cause he can't hit it himself." Yeager hit the roof; Lewallyn got a chuckle and settled into his work.

Dennis enjoyed five seasons with the Dodgers, although he spent a good portion of his time on the Minor League roster, being brought up for brief periods. In 1980, he was traded for cash to Texas, and then in 1981, Lewallyn became a middle reliever for Cleveland. Dennis reflects on his time in the majors and his Minor League experience as a great way of life. Skills picked up along the way from teammates, coaches and, most assuredly, Fred Waters helped shape the rest of his career in baseball. After retiring from active pitching at the end of 1982, Dennis became a pitching coordinator in the Dodgers organization, a position he held for twelve years.

In 1996, Lewallyn accepted the position as pitching coach for the Lethbridge Black Diamonds, an affiliate of the new expansion Arizona Diamondbacks. Lethbridge, Alberta, was a far cry from Pensacola, but the opportunity to help roll out a new club held a wealth of excitement. In Los Angeles, Dennis shared a common Northwest Florida upbringing with Don Sutton. In Arizona, the new organization would link Lewallyn to three other Escambia County boys in manager Buck Showalter, hitting instructor Jimmy Presley and shortstop Jay Bell. Dennis served as pitching coach for several Arizona affiliate teams and eventually took over as Minor League pitching coordinator through 2006. The Chicago Cubs Southern League club contracted Dennis in 2007 as its pitching coach. The Cubs enjoyed the veteran knowledge that Dennis brought to the organization and promoted him as their Minor League pitching coordinator in 2011.

TATE HIGH WINS AGAIN

During the 1976 4A Florida State High School Championship in Tampa, the Tate High baseball team secured another cup for their school's trophy case. Defeating South Dade in an 8–6 final game, Tate rallied behind their all-star pitcher Ronnie Stryker to win the title. During the tournament, a day after Stryker had pitched a complete game, he stood at the plate in the top of the sixth inning with his team down by one run. The bases were loaded with Tate Aggies with two outs on the board. The count on Stryker was one ball and two strikes. Digging in under pressure, Ronnie hit a rope double, scoring all three base runners. The score held at 8–6, and Stryker finished his second complete game in less than twenty-six hours.

Ronnie Stryker's regular-season record was 17–0, and upon returning home he was greeted with a hero's welcome and an offer from the World Champion Cincinnati Reds. Ronnie was not the only pick for the Reds out of J.M. Tate High in 1976; Scotti Madison was drafted by Cincinnati but did not sign. The Texas Rangers selected power-hitting catcher Alphonso Lewis from Pensacola High along with Escambia High left-handed pitcher Greg Eason in the June Amateur Draft.

On July 26, Babe Ruth League teams from all over the state of Florida gathered at Brent Ballpark for the 1976 Dixie Boys State Baseball Tournament. Brent hosted the tournament, while Gulf Breeze hosted the Babe Ruth World Series in August. Brent manager Joe Massingale and Coach Terry Madden guided their boys to another successful year in Pensacola, along with their team of all-stars, which included future Major Leaguer Jimmy Presley.

CHAPTER 6
THE FREE AGENCY ERA: 1977–1993

J.J. CANNON

Young men emulate their baseball heroes as they step up to the plate or take the field on diamonds across the country. Summer is filled with dreams of reaching the big leagues and fulfilling their hopes of donning the uniform of their favorite team. Statistically, few fully achieve that fleeting notion, but for those that do, the realization that baseball is a business is often an abrupt wakeup call upon arrival in the professional clubhouse.

Due to baseball's reserve clause, it was not until the waning years of the 1970s that Major League players acquired the contractual rights to bargain for release from their team. Players were bound to their signing team unless club ownership decided otherwise. In 1969, Cardinals outfielder Curt Flood determined to guide his own career course and refused to report to the Phillies after a trade by St. Louis. In the years to follow, and with representation from the players' union, more athletes challenged the old guard. In 1975, pitchers Andy Messersmith and Dave McNally played without a formal signed contract and later argued that their contract could not be renewed if it was never signed. An arbitrator agreed, and they were declared free agents. With the reserve clause changed, the players' union and the owners then agreed on the structure and rules that would now govern player free agency.

In Pensacola, front office politics was the farthest thing on the minds of those running the bases on Dixie Youth and Babe Ruth fields throughout town. The free agency era of Major League Baseball history is laced with artificial turf, media-fueled controversy and more and more fans viewing televised games with the advent of cable television. On the fertile diamonds of the Gulf Coast, baseball kept its firm popularity, as the Florida sunshine turned teenage boys into Major League All-Stars and time-honored citizens.

Although Pensacola boasts numerous professional athletes who attribute their success to their upbringing in the City of Five Flags, still other players have the town listed on their birth certificate. Pensacola-born Jim Morrison attended high school in Tampa prior to being drafted by the Phillies in 1974. Morrison played second base for Philadelphia beginning in 1977 and during the 1978 season, during which Jim and fellow Pensacolan Kevin Saucier both made the club roster. Jim Morrison's career in professional baseball has spanned thirty-seven years as a player, coach, instructor and manager.

Pensacola's Joseph Jerome "J.J." Cannon was born at Camp Lejeune, North Carolina, but moved to the Florida Gulf Coast during his tenth grade year. Cannon says that he began playing Little League baseball at the age of eight, with his dad teaching him everything he knew about the game. After high school, J.J. enrolled in Pensacola Junior College and was accepted to its baseball program. While at PJC, Cannon caught the eye of the Houston Astros, who selected J.J. as the sixteenth pick in the first round of the Winter Amateur Draft of 1974. Cannon has the distinction of being the first player in the history of Pensacola Junior College to be chosen in a Major League Amateur Draft.

After batting .300 in seventy-seven games during his Rookie League assignment, Cannon was sent to Cedar Rapids, Iowa. After just over three and a half seasons in Houston's farm system, at age twenty-three, Cannon took the outfield for the Astros on September 22, 1977. Cannon spent a large portion of the 1978 season with Triple-A Charleston before being traded to Toronto with two other players for catcher Alan Ashby.

Cannon found a true home with the Blue Jays organization, remaining with it for twenty years as a player, coach and manager. Upon arriving in Toronto, J.J. found a friendly face from his surrogate Gulf Coast home. Blue Jays announcer Tom Cheek had risen from humble beginnings in Pensacola to become a much-beloved voice in Canadian sports. Cannon's occupation as a Major League player ended on October 5, 1980, although that day became the first step toward an incredible career as an advocate in the advancement and development of baseball players for over two decades.

J.J.'s initial taste of coaching came with the 1983 Kinston Blue Jays as a player/coach. Cannon continued working throughout Toronto's affiliate clubs until 1991, when he became the skipper of the Medicine Hat Blue Jays. While later managing the St. Catherine Blue Jays to a 49–29 record and a spot in the 1993 playoffs, Cannon was named Manager of the Year for the New York–Penn League. In 1999, he moved to the Braves' farm system, taking their Appalachian League club to a second-place divisional finish, followed by an Eastern Division Championship the next year. With the beginning of the new century, J.J. found himself coming full circle and returning to the Houston Astros organization, which named Cannon as the manager of the Lexington Legends. In return, Cannon delivered a 92–48 record and a South Atlantic League title.

DO YOU KNOW FRED WATERS?

The Minnesota Twins picked Stan Cannon and the Seattle Mariners selected Jeff Cary out of Pensacola Junior College during the 1977 Amateur Draft. PJC had become a school worth scouting by the Major Leagues, and with Fred Waters offering his opinion on players that he watched on a regular basis, Pensacola continued to produce. Waters was considered by many as one of the "Grand Old Men" when it came to player evaluation.

Dennis Lewallyn said that when he reached Cleveland in 1981 and was getting to know now Hall of Fame pitcher Bert Blyleven, that he happened to mention that he was from Pensacola. Blyleven responded immediately with, "Pensacola! Do you know a guy named Fred Waters?" Lewallyn said that he did and relayed what his relationship was to him. In turn, Blyleven said that Fred had instructed him during Bert's early years with Minnesota. "He made all the difference in my pitching career," Blyleven told Dennis.

VOICE OF THE BLUE JAYS

Beyond producing players, coaches and managers, Pensacola also boasts being the home of one of Major League Baseball's most popular and revered announcers. Tom Cheek found a love for baseball at an early age, not unlike his neighborhood friends. But Cheek's participation in the sport went beyond playing pick-up games near his home on J Street. Tom's widow, Shirley, paints a picture from her husband's shared memories of early days in Pensacola. She said that Tom would often perch on the sidewalk curb and call the game as if he were in the press booth while the other boys played out their big-league fantasies during a stickball game. Tom was introduced to his first tape recorder when he was fourteen years old—he never looked back.

Cheek served his country in the United States Air Force, where he became acquainted with Yankees broadcaster Red Barber. With a newfound interest in sports broadcasting, Tom invested in himself by enrolling in the Cambridge School of Broadcasting in Boston. Beginning in 1962, Cheek found work as a disc jockey but quickly started cultivating his passion by calling on-air baseball, basketball, football and hockey games for the University of Vermont. The 1969 Montreal Expos expansion team was looking for a second announcer

Many children who play a friendly game of baseball with their friends in the schoolyard or neighborhood street often envision themselves becoming like one of their big-league heroes. Growing up in Pensacola, Tom Cheek was no different in his dreams to reach the professional diamond. However, Tom's vision was that of a seat in the broadcast booth. From calling mock games on J Street for his friends to becoming a legendary broadcaster for the Toronto Blue Jays, Tom Cheek prided himself in his Pensacola beginnings. Anyone who ever met Cheek in his official capacity was certain to hear about the whitest beaches in the world and the hospitable people of the Snapper Capital. *Courtesy of the Toronto Blue Jays.*

to complement Dave Van Horne, their primary play-by-play man. As his Burlington home was just over sixty miles from the new team, Tom tried out for the position. The Expos opted for a rotating guest announcer format, and Tom frequented the Montreal booth throughout the 1976 season.

Now accustomed to the demands of Major League Baseball broadcasting and gaining a growing listenership with Canadian baseball fans, Cheek was enlisted by another expansion team across the border. The Toronto Blue Jays hired Tom Cheek to call games full-time alongside pitching legend Early Wynn. This began Cheek's over-twenty-seven-year relationship with the Blue Jays and their loyal followers. Although Tom would change broadcast partners, the Toronto baseball faithful never changed their love for the "Voice of the Blue Jays."

While with the Jays, Cheek announced 4,306 consecutive games through his retirement in 2004, securing him a place of enshrinement in the Canadian Sports Hall of Fame. Tom Cheek was honored by being selected as an announcer for both the 1980 and 1984 Winter Olympics. But Cheek's most famous call came during Game 6 of the 1993 World Series, as Toronto gained its second crown in back-to-back series wins. As Joe Carter slugged a walk-off home run to defeat the Phillies 8–6, Tom Cheek exclaimed with unbridled enthusiasm, "Touch 'em all Joe! You'll never hit a bigger home run in your life!"

Tom Cheek died of brain cancer on October 9, 2005. The tumor had forced retirement far too early for the legendary voice. No matter where Tom Cheek had an audience, he was always willing to identify himself with Pensacola and brag about the world's most beautiful beaches. Tom authored *Road to Glory*, which chronicled his life as the Blue Jays announcer and continues to be an inspiration to those aspiring to sports broadcasting. Prior to his death, Tom used his strong voice as an advocate for the Cooperstown enshrinement of Don Sutton. Tom posthumously won the National Baseball Hall of Fame's Ford C. Frick broadcasting award in 2013.

THE VERSATILE BUCK SHOWALTER

William Nathanial "Buck" Showalter's memories of playing baseball in Escambia County are numerous. Buck recalls traveling from his home in Century to Pensacola in order to take part in tournaments at Admiral Mason Ballpark. Showalter would encounter players in Pensacola with whom he would later share the field during his professional career. Players like J.J. Cannon, Hosken Powell, Kevin Saucier and others would join in what Buck describes as a "special brotherhood" of those who hailed from Pensacola.

Buck's dad was the high school principal and an athletic coach for Century High. The Showalters were a family ingrained in sports, which was reflected in Buck as he played baseball, basketball and football. He contends

Buck Showalter lived in the north end of Escambia County, but baseball tournaments and all-star competitions frequently brought the Showalter family to Pensacola. The games placed him in direct contact with other boys from the Pensacola area who he would later know on the professional diamond. "Because we had that connection of playing together on the Gulf Coast, it was like being in a special brotherhood," contends Showalter. *Courtesy of the author*.

that the multi-sport lifestyle added greatly to his well-rounded ability as a baseball player and manager. "I was always outside," says Showalter. "We played outdoors from morning 'til night. And because we live in a climate that allows us to, it meant most months out of the year." Showalter states this as the reason that the Dominican Republic has so many top players coming from their country, as the children play outside and play multiple sports.

After competing against each other as kids in Pensacola, Hosken Powell and Buck Showalter roomed together during their playing days at Chipola Junior College. Powell contends that Showalter was a top-rung ballplayer and that everyone on the team knew Buck was poised for a management or front office job one day. "He was always in control and could get anyone to do anything he asked of them," recalls Hosken. Powell offers the following anecdote as proof:

> *Once, Buck got this crazy idea to cover his shoes with glow-in-the-dark paint so that he would stand out during night games. When he approached our manager about it, he told Buck that he could paint his shoes as long as everyone else on the team did likewise. I think our manager felt that was the end of the notion, as nobody would do it. All I can say is we all glowed in the dark that night. We knew he would make a great big league skipper.*

Buck added to his basic fundamental skills at Chipola and then Mississippi State College, after which Showalter signed his first professional contract with the Fort Lauderdale Yankees of the Florida State League in 1977. Buck's introduction into the Yankees farm system would take him on a lifelong journey of the diamond, giving him the ability to share his experience and knowledge with multitudes of players. The same season Showalter entered the world of Minor League Baseball, the Brent Dixie Boys All-Stars brought home their state pennant and the Myrtle Grove fifteen- to sixteen-year-old Dizzy Dean All-Stars won the Florida title.

Showalter's career as a Minor League player lasted for seven seasons, all attached to the Yankees' franchise. His best year at the plate was his first, posting a batting average of .362. His career average compiled at .294, and his fielding percentage in seven seasons ranked .947. During his Minor League years, Buck hit seventeen home runs and drove in 336 RBIs. Buck did not see Major League play due to the fact that he predominantly played first base—a position that Don Mattingly was covering for New York at that time.

Buck retired from play in 1983 and was hired by his old club to manage the Oneonta, New York affiliate in 1985 and 1986. There he won 114 games during the course of the two seasons. He managed his former club in Fort Lauderdale the next year, leading the league with 85 wins. Moving to Albany, New York, of the Eastern League in 1989, Showalter was named

Minor League Manager of the Year, followed by a well-deserved promotion for the 1990 season. As the New York Yankees called him up to "the Show," Buck became a member of their coaching staff.

After two years as a staff coach, Showalter succeeded Stump Merrill as New York's manager in 1992. Back in Pensacola during the off-season, Buck had made a commitment to Pensacola Junior College to referee its basketball games. At the time he made the offer, he felt he would have the additional time to officiate. Even though Buck was now the manager of the New York Yankees, he kept his promise to PJC and dressed out in black-and-white stripes with a referee whistle.

While with the Yankees, Buck was named American League Manager of the Year during the strike-shortened 1994 season, as well as the American League manager for the 1995 All-Star Game. Although New York made the postseason playoffs for the first time since 1981, Showalter left the Yankees after the end of the year. The Arizona Diamondbacks became a National League expansion team for the 1998 season, hiring Buck as the manager two years before the team began official Major League play. Buck spent 1996 and 1997 helping to build the new team through franchise structuring and player acquisition. He managed the Diamondbacks for three official years thereafter.

Showalter became an on-air analyst for ESPN after his departure from Arizona, which lasted until the Rangers hired him to replace Jerry Narron as their manager in 2003. Buck was named the 2004 American League Manager of the Year, but after Texas failed to reach the playoffs for four straight seasons, Showalter was let go at the end of 2006. Later, Buck became the senior advisor to baseball operations with Cleveland and returned to ESPN as a baseball analyst. Just after the all-star break of 2010, Buck was signed as the manager of the Baltimore Orioles, with a contract through the 2013 season. Buck took the 2010 Baltimore Orioles by storm, leading the worst club in the majors toward winning more games. Although Showalter could easily boast of his managerial accomplishments, the self-proclaimed country boy keeps things simple and direct. When questioned by taunting teammates about why he pours ketchup on his steak—even in high-end New York restaurants—his reply is, "Because I like it that way, and that's enough."

HOSKEN

Tate High School's first baseman Bob Hicks became a first-round selection for the St. Louis Cardinals during the June 1978 draft. Cardinals scouting supervisor Chase Riddle stated that Hicks was an "above average runner with power [at the plate]." Riddle sensed that Hicks would grow in ability after he overcame his lack of experience. Although Bob did not go beyond Double-A ball, his speed and skill gave him a seven-year run as a farmhand with the Cardinals and Rangers.

Before trying out for his high school team, Hosken Powell began playing baseball in Pensacola's local summer leagues. Powell contends that it was the Woodham High School baseball coach who worked with him to develop his fundamentals. Coach Sam Fletcher instructed Hosken during the three years in which Powell was a first-string member of the Woodham Titans. During his senior year, Hosken batted .337, striking out only twice during the season. His talent secured him a position on the roster of the All-City and All-Big Five Conference teams.

After high school, Powell was given a baseball scholarship to Chipola Junior College, where he played alongside Buck Showalter and started in centerfield for the Indians. At the end of his first season at Chipola, Hosken's stats showed twenty-four RBIs, thirty-nine hits and one home run. The Indians made it into the state tournament in 1974, and Hosken was named to the Division I Conference first team and secured a position on the all-state team. Early in 1975, the Pittsburgh Pirates took notice of the Chipola outfielder and picked him during the first round of the first phase in the January draft. Powell did not sign with Pittsburgh, opting instead to continue his college experience.

Fred Waters utilized his influence with Minnesota and had Powell placed on their draft list. Although scouts from Boston and Cleveland talked to Hosken, he eventually signed with the Twins as a first-round draft pick in June 1975. Prior to answering to his professional assignment in Elizabethton, Tennessee, Powell finished out a commitment to the semiprofessional Pensacola Lyon's Braves, who were set to compete in the Fiesta of Five Flags Baseball Tournament. The tournament took place at the home field of the Clowns on West Fairfield Drive.

The 1975 Elizabethton Twins of the Appalachian League, under the management of Fred Waters, was the perfect launching pad for Hosken. During his first year as a professional, Powell hit .340 at the plate and led the league with twenty doubles. Waters's Twins finished second in their league, having the added advantage of Powell's "rifle arm" in the outfield. Minnesota advanced Hosken to Reno, Nevada, of the California League, in 1976 and up to Triple-A Tacoma, Washington, in 1977. Powell was invited to the Twins spring training camp at historic Tinker Field in Orlando, Florida, during the March 1978 preseason workout.

Hosken's first official game as a Minnesota Twin came on April 5, 1978, at age twenty-three. He played in 121 games, achieving a slugging percentage of .333 and a fielding percentage of .983 during his first season in the majors. Powell's batting average climbed from .247 in 1978 to .293 in 1979, but he was not able reach the elusive .300 average. Unfairly, the Twins added unneeded pressure to his developing career

After a career as a professional ballplayer, Hosken Powell returned to his hometown and began a new calling as a mentor and coach. Seeing a need and an opportunity to use baseball as a vehicle in which to inspire Pensacola's inner-city youth, Powell enlisted his experiences as a platform. Hosken found that as a veteran player he had a voice into the lives of those facing social and situational difficulties. *Courtesy of the author.*

by hyping Hosken as the next Rod Carew. The parallel was just not to be, although Hosken held up his share of the defensive load for the Twins. His presence at the plate did not suit the Twins expectations, resulting in a trade to the Toronto Blue Jays in December 1981.

Powell was released by Toronto halfway through the 1983 season and was picked up by the Brewers in July. After a season with Milwaukee's Triple-A club, Hosken moved toward retirement. Although retired from professional play, Hosken's life in baseball continued far into the future. Like so many of the men mentored by Fred Waters, Hosken emulated his old instructor by devoting himself to the lives of those just beginning their journey into the game. Powell used his Major League experience for the benefit of the Boys and Girls Club of Escambia County and the Pensacola High School baseball team. Hosken states that one of his goals is to coach a love for the game back into the hearts of Pensacola's inner-city young people.

Hot Sauce

Kevin Andrew Saucier grew up in a middle-class home close to Pensacola's Naval Air Station, where his father worked as a civilian government employee. "We did not have a lot for extras," says Saucier, "but we never knew if things were tight because Dad always found a way to get through." At age nine, Kevin Saucier was on the roof with his father helping to fix the family's aerial antenna when he looked down and saw his older brother Michael coming across the backyard decked out in a baseball uniform. When Kevin asked his father why his brother had on the jersey and pants, he was told that the elder Saucier had just been signed up to play in the Warrington Dixie Youth League. Kevin begged to play as well and was soon suiting up in his own uniform.

Kevin was an outfielder for Warrington at first, but Coach Henderson saw Saucier's potential as a pitcher. The coach's interest in Saucier, coupled with a baseball glove given as a Christmas gift from his parents, encouraged the young left-hander to continue with the team the following season. Playing on Pensacola's Westside through his high school years, Saucier encountered boys whose lives in the game would parallel his own.

Saucier did well at Escambia High School under the direction of Waters, but Kevin states that it was something that Coach Waters said that spurred him toward the goal of a life as a big leaguer. Kevin recalls joining the Escambia team and Waters watching him throw for the first time. "Your playing days in the field are over," charged Waters, "You will be strictly a pitcher from here on out." Kevin says that he did not actually hear his coach make the next statement, but several of his teammates on the sideline attested to hearing Fred Waters say, "Saucier will make a Major League pitcher one day."

Once again, Fred Waters's player assessment was correct. Opting to sign with the Phillies right out of high school, Saucier was picked up during

From the pitching mound at Escambia High School to throwing for a World Series Championship team to owning a restaurant, Kevin Saucier's life has been one full of diversified opportunity. After twelve years as a Minor and Major League pitcher, Kevin continued to use his abilities for the perpetuation of the game and its future. After working as a scout for Team USA Baseball and almost three decades with the Major League Scouting Bureau, Saucier says, "Success breeds success," and his life passion has been to give back to the sport that has given him so much. *Courtesy of Kevin Saucier.*

the June 1974 Amateur Draft and was sent to Philadelphia's Appalachian League affiliate. Kevin posted a 3.34 ERA, winning twelve games and losing nine for Class-A Spartanburg in 1975. By October 1978, Saucier had assembled enough tools for the Phillies to call him up as they finished their run at the National League pennant. Philadelphia won the National League East in 1978 but lost the league title to Don Sutton's Dodgers three games to one.

Kevin appeared in twenty-nine games in relief for the Phillies during the 1979 season, endearing himself to the Philadelphia fans. Saucier's antics in the bullpen are legendary, full of emotion and full of big-hearted camaraderie. The intensity of Kevin's personality shown in the clubhouse is secondary only to his persona on the mound. "To be successful in baseball, it has to burn in your heart," proclaims Kevin. He picked up the nickname "Hot Sauce," which was a direct reflection of Kevin's approach to the game. Saucier's credo in the bullpen became "Gimme the ball," as he was always ready for a challenge and his attitude was infectious to teammates, rallying them to push harder.

Along with teammates Pete Rose, Tug McGraw, Bob Boone, Larry Bowa and Mike Schmidt, Saucier and the 1980 Phillies finished their season with a 91–71 record. After clinching the National League Championship over the Astros, Philadelphia captured the World Series title by beating the Royals four games to two. Kevin says that to date, winning the World Series is the greatest memory of his baseball career, and this is further reflected by Saucier being chosen by the fans as the "Most Popular Phillie" in 1980.

In order to acquire pitcher Sparky Lyle from the Rangers at the end of the season, Saucier was dealt to Texas. Three weeks later, Kevin was traded to the Detroit Tigers under manager Sparky Anderson. Kevin responded by having his best year in the Major Leagues and throwing a 1.65 ERA. Saucier and Anderson did not always see eye-to-eye, and although Sparky was more than used to managing eccentric personalities, his understanding of pitchers left something to be desired. By 1982, Kevin began having trouble with his control on the mound. Saucier explains that he simply "lost touch with things" and struggled in to get the ball across the plate. Detroit released him to Triple-A Evansville for the remainder of the season.

After working with a pitching coach, voluntarily playing through winter instructional leagues and practicing with first the Tigers and then the Richmond Braves during the 1983 spring training exercises, Kevin knew it was time to look at what was next after baseball. Back in Pensacola, Kevin Saucier and business partner David Del Gallo opened Saucier's Dugout, a sports-themed pizza restaurant. Local fans loved the food and enjoyed Kevin's wall-to-wall memorabilia on display.

The long hours at the restaurant and Kevin's unchanging love for the game kept calling him back to baseball. Nowadays, Kevin serves as a regional scouting director for the Major League Baseball Scouting Bureau. Working also as a scout for Team USA Baseball in the World Baseball League, Saucier has been given countless opportunities to be instrumental in the development of players. "I want to be remembered for my love of the game. Baseball has taken good care of me, and I want to take care of the game and its future," states Saucier.

When asked about his personal insight into the reason Pensacola continues to be a hotbed for Major League prospects, Kevin's quick reply is, "Success breeds success." He goes on to explain that so many former players like him have been interested in the success of area youth and because of this were willing to give back to the town that ignited their careers. "I remember being in high school at Escambia and being inspired by hometown professionals like Kenny Wright and Jimmy Hutto," Saucier recalls. Just like other former Major Leaguers from Pensacola, Kevin Saucier is always ready to inspire the next generation of players or have a lively conversation with fans.

SQUEAKY PARKER AND PENSACOLA'S DRAFTEES

Pensacola's pros remain tied to their roots by utilizing area high school fields for winter exercises, hosting regional clinics and offering availability for personal instruction. "I am always interested in advancing the local guys if I can," Kevin Saucier states emphatically. A word from a seasoned scout or tenured college coach can go a long way for a young man with Major League aspirations. During the 1980s and early 1990s, the Fred Waters Baseball Clinics afforded Escambia County young people the opportunity to learn from active players of the time such as Jeff Brantley, Will Clark and Travis Fryman. The clinic had been championed by professional scout Squeaky Parker, who made the event a success through his passion to see players excel and his endless connections in the world of pro ball.

During Parker's forty-three years in scouting and instruction, he worked for the Pirates, Phillies, Giants and Orioles, moving to Pensacola with his wife, Carolyn, for the city's strategic location in regard to baseball. After his eventual retirement, the Cincinnati Reds coaxed Parker back into the world he loved to become the senior assistant to the general manager. His 2006 appointment lasted all too briefly, as he returned to attend to Carolyn full-time while she battled cancer. Many Pensacola players who signed professional contracts passed under the watchful eye of Squeaky Parker as he made his rounds to area high school and college games.

In 1978, the Rangers selected Escambia High's William Gregory Eason, assigning the left-handed pitcher to their Gulf Coast League Rookie club. The Royals picked up Steven Patterson from Pensacola Junior College in 1979, sending Patterson to the Gulf Coast Royals and then, the next season, Fort Myers. Picks for the St. Louis Cardinals from Pensacola Junior College in 1980 were pitchers Donald Hughes and Dave Droschak, with Hughes reporting to the Johnson City, Tennessee affiliate in 1980 and Droschak to Springfield, Illinois, in 1982. The Phillies selected Henry "Lebo" Powell from Pine Forest High School during the first round of the June Amateur Draft. And Tate High's Mark Cooper went to Toronto during the 1980 draft, beginning his play for the Blue Jays organization in 1984.

The University of West Florida (UWF) began its college baseball program in 1981, the same year that the Major League players went on strike. For its first year in the Southern Division, the UWF team, under head coach Chuck Goldfarb, brought home the NAIA Southern States Conference championship trophy. Jim Spooner took over the position as the Argos' coach in 1983, a job that he held for twenty-three seasons.

During the Major League Baseball Amateur Drafts of 1981, Pensacola Junior College players were selected by two specific clubs. Right-handed pitcher Boyce Bailey and catcher Johnny Hawkins were chosen by the Yankees, while third baseman Thomas Fetting was picked by the Expos. Three additional Pensacola Junior College Pirates signed with professional franchises during the following two years. Blaze Katich inked to play outfield with the Expos in 1982, and in 1983, Joe Law contracted for the Oakland Athletics. Also in 1983, right-handed pitcher Bill Fulton turned away a bid from the Baltimore Orioles, eventually signing with the Yankees.

Tate High School placed second in the 4A Florida State Divisional Playoffs during the 1982 competition after an 8–7 loss to Miami Carol City. Although Tate's team lost the cup by one run, the players did not drop any observation by regional scouts. The Atlanta Braves selected David Miller, the Kansas City Royals decided on Deric Ladiner and the Montreal Expos opted for Joe Sims as part of their 1982 organizational acquisition. The Expos dipped into the Tate High pool again in 1983 with their signing of Robbie Mason. Playing for the University of West Florida, third baseman

Thomas Czuk became the first-ever Argo drafted by a professional club in being selected by the Athletics during the 1982 draft.

USA Today posted Tate High School as second in the nation for its 1984 team rankings. On Thursday, May 10, 1984, the Tate Aggies faced off against Sarasota during the Florida State 4A Championship semi-finals. The *Sarasota Herald-Tribune* reported that over 3,500 fans packed into Payne Park to see who would be awarded best in state. The score was tied at one apiece in the sixth inning when shortstop Jay Bell stepped into the batter's box with two outs and Ben DeArmon in scoring position on second. Bell sent a routine fly ball into left field, but to Sarasota's dismay, it was misjudged by their fielder. DeArmon scored, and under heighted tension, a bench-clearing confrontation ensued, with Bell right in the middle.

The Aggies, defending their 37–1 season record, stood confident with left-handed pitcher Mac Seibert. Seibert, who would later manage the Pensacola Pelicans, got himself out of a one-out bases-loaded jam in the bottom of the seventh inning. Aggies coach Randy Putman said of Seibert, "He's got a lot of guts. And when we need a big pitch, he's always got it." Putman had earlier served as the University of Alabama at Birmingham graduate assistant coach under head coach and former 1938 Pensacola Pilots outfielder Harry Walker.

The final score on the board was 3–1 in favor of the Tate Aggies. Bell, Seibert and company pitted against Miami Southridge during the finals and took a 4–2 win to secure the state championship. After returning home with the pennant, Coach Putman and the Tate baseball team were selected as National Champions by *Collegiate Baseball Newspaper*, and Randy was voted Southeastern Region Coach of the Year.

As the Major League Draft began in June 1984, Tate High School was once again in the spotlight. With a nod from Fred Waters, Jay Bell was drafted in the first round by Minnesota, later playing under Waters in Elizabethton. The Blue Jays selected catcher Mark Cooper, while the Athletics picked a trio of Aggies. Oakland chose infielder Tony Johnson, outfielder Kevin Russ and pitcher Mac Seibert, although Seibert did not sign, opting instead to throw for Jacksonville State University. He later signed with Detroit during the 1989 June Amateur Draft.

St. Louis selected Woodham High senior Tim Sossamon, but like Seibert, Sossamon desired to play college ball before making his way into the professional arena. Tim began at Pensacola Junior College, transferred to Louisiana State University and then contracted with the Phillies organization in 1986. Pensacola Junior College produced two 1984 draft choices. Right-handed pitcher David Miller, earlier selected by Atlanta, went with Kansas City, while Squeaky Parker, scouting for San Francisco, saw good potential in Greg Litton.

HOUND DOG

Jimmy Presley began his life in the game on the neighborhood fields throughout southern Escambia County. Jimmy played Dixie Youth Baseball for both the Brent and Myrtle Grove teams. His 1974 team won the Dixie Youth World Series, eliminating Columbus, North Carolina, in a 3–2 final. Under the direction of Escambia High School's diligent coaching staff, Presley received instruction that far exceeded baseball alone.

At Escambia, the "Waters Way" encompassed life skills, good decision-making ability, how to be a man of integrity and the ability to stay true to your convictions. Former Pensacola Senators owner Joe Panaccione said of Waters, "Even the opposing teams listened to Fred's instruction. They followed after him like a bunch of little ducks." Fred Waters's influence in Jimmy's life would serve him as a player and afterward in the jobs that would be open for him in the greater world of baseball.

The Seattle Mariners drafted Presley during the June 1979 selection with scout S.E. "Rip" Tutor serving as the signing ambassador for the franchise. Jim's first assignment took him to the other end of the country, dropping him into service as a shortstop with Seattle's Northwest League affiliate in Bellingham, Washington. During the following season, Presley covered second base, third base and shortstop for the Wausau (Wisconsin) Timbers, belting twelve home runs in 126 plate appearances. Jim stayed with the Timbers for half of the 1981 season, putting twelve more over the fence before moving up to Double-A Lynn, Massachusetts. While with the Lynn Sailors, Jim homered eight times in 1981 and twenty-two times in 1982.

Climbing successfully through the Mariners farm system, Presley debuted with the Seattle club mid-season 1984. Prior to suiting up for Seattle on June 24, Jimmy carried a .317 batting average while covering third base in sixty-nine games for Triple-A Salt Lake City. The rookie fared well against American League pitchers, collecting his first Major League hit off future Hall of Famer Bert Blyleven. He participated in seventy games to complete the season with the Mariners, taking ten balls deep over the wall and posting thirty-six RBIs.

Pensacola's Dixie Youth Baseball program has seeded early developmental skills into the lives of young people participating throughout the city's league parks. Jim Presley was no exception to that gift, as he utilized the early fundamental training and crafted it into a Major League career. After delivering quality outings for three franchises during eight seasons in the majors, the All-Star made the transition to coach in 1996. Taking a cue from the mentorship he received as a Pensacola youth league player, Jimmy began a new venture in molding the future of young athletes on a professional level. *Courtesy of Mike McCormick.*

Jimmy dropped in twenty-eight home runs in 1985 and drove in eighty-four base runners, and by the 1986 season, Presley had become a Seattle fan favorite. The Mariner faithful cheered on the "Hound Dog," and adding to the delight of Seattle's baseball community, Jimmy represented them during the 1986 All-Star Game held in the Astrodome. Wrapping up the 1986 season, Jim sent a total of twenty-seven beyond the fence. Three of his 1986 home runs came in one game on September 1 against the Detroit Tigers and pitcher Jack Morris. Presley was ranked twenty-first during the 1986 vote for American League MVP.

Presley stayed with the Mariners through 1989 but saw reduced playing time during his last season with the arrival of Edgar Martinez. With third base secured by Martinez, Seattle traded Jimmy to the Atlanta Braves on January 24, 1990. Predominantly stationed at third base, Jim did cover both corners for Atlanta, giving the Braves some infield flexibility. Atlanta granted Presley free agency in November, making way for San Diego to sign him three months later. The Padres third bag was a mixed platoon during 1991, and Jimmy got in just twenty games for the year before being released in June. The Rangers acquired Presley but sent him to Triple-A Oklahoma City.

Jim Presley's abilities as a hitter coupled with the ethics and tenacity ingrained by his Pensacola upbringing made him a valuable asset for training developing players. The Arizona Diamondback organization began its player refinement process toward its first Major League season in 1998 by building out its farm system two years in advance. Jimmy contracted as the hitting coach for the Lethbridge club in 1986, joining fellow Escambia High School alumnus Dennis Lewallyn.

Jimmy filled his same position for the 1997 South Bend affiliate and then became the hitting coach for the new Arizona Diamondbacks under the management of Buck Showalter. Northwest Florida secured a quorum in the Diamondbacks organization with Presley, Lewallyn, Showalter and shortstop Jay Bell. Jim continued as Arizona's hitting instructor through 2000, leaving along with Showalter at the end of the year. Arizona secured Presley's services once again in 2004 and 2005 as its Pioneer League manager with the Missoula, Montana club.

The Florida Marlins hired Jimmy as their hitting instructor in 2006, a position he held through 2010 before being fired along with manager Fredi Gonzales and bench coach Carlos Tosca. Jimmy Presley partnered again with Buck Showalter in 2011, as Showalter had taken the helm of the Baltimore Orioles as their third manager during the previous season.

Working as Baltimore's hitting coach, Presley brought a grand example of Pensacola grit and moxie. After Jimmy ended his playing career, he completed his education through the University of West Florida, earning a master's degree in educational leadership. He was inducted into the Escambia High School Hall of Fame in 2010 along with Dallas Cowboys running back Emmitt Smith.

SCOTTI MADISON

During the fall of 1985, over twenty professional scouts assembled in Pensacola to watch the Junior College Baseball Tournament, where several specific players were under the watchful eyes of the Major League representatives. Jerome Walton, fielding for Enterprise State, all but sealed his value for the Cubs during the competition, signing with Chicago that following January. Over the course of the summer, Pace High School secured the 2A state championship, and Pensacola Junior College was proudly represented during the 1985 draft. The Pirates selected PJC right-handed pitcher Tom Hoffman, and the Red Sox signed lefty Gregg Magistri.

Three area high schools saw players appropriated to professional clubs in the 1985 draft. Pine Forest High School's Jerome Nelson went to the Angels, Walter Watford from Washington High enlisted with the Blue Jays and Tate's Ben Webb and Deric Lanier signed for the Pirates and Royals, respectfully. Another Tate High graduate graced the newspapers with his first appearance as a Major Leaguer on July 6, 1985. Pensacola-born Scotti Madison donned a Detroit Tigers uniform as a designated hitter under manager Sparky Anderson.

Madison was drafted by the Cincinnati Reds in 1976 but did not sign. He was selected in 1979 by the San Francisco Giants but again did not sign, opting instead for college play at Vanderbilt University. Vanderbilt had been one of three choices the two-sport athlete considered for his place of higher education. Playing both baseball and football, Scotti spoke with coach Bear Bryant about Alabama and also with Charlie McClendon about the possibility of Louisiana State. Vanderbilt won out with a promise to allow Madison to participate in both sports while still keeping his scholarship.

The 1980 Vanderbilt baseball team won the SEC Championship during Madison's senior season. Before the championship, however, Scotti was making a name for himself defensively and offensively at the plate. Catching for Vanderbilt in 1980, Scotti led the team in batting with a .399 average and was tops with eighty-one hits, along with fifty-six RBIs and fifteen home runs. For his efforts, Madison was awarded First Team All-SEC, First Team All-American and All-South Region honors. The Minnesota Twins drafted Madison in the third round of the June Amateur Draft, assigning him to the Orlando Twins, headquartered at Tinker Field.

As the Orlando Twins broke their 1981 spring training camp in Melbourne, Florida, Madison and fellow teammate Kent Hrbek were assigned to Minnesota's California League affiliate in Visalia. Madison and Hrbek decided to take Kent's pickup truck and drive to their appointed job with the Visalia Oaks. Scotti regaled the adventure to Vanderbilt sports historian Bill Traughber during a 2007 interview:

> *We got in Herbie's pickup truck and drove from Melbourne, Florida, all the way to Visalia, California. We stayed at my family's house in Pensacola. I knew a Vanderbilt girl in New Orleans, so we stopped there. I knew a girl in Houston, and we stopped there. I knew a girl from Vanderbilt in Phoenix, so we stopped there also. Then I said, "We're pretty close to Las Vegas, and I've never been there before—do you want to go?" He said, "Yeah, let's go to Las Vegas." Here I am in a pickup truck, blue jeans, and a t-shirt, and we pull up in front of Caesars Palace. We showed up two days late, and our coach was so mad. He couldn't say a lot because we were the two best players on the team. That year, Herbie made it to the Major Leagues in Minnesota. It was an exciting time.*

As Hrbek was cutting his teeth in the Twin Cities, Madison made his mark in the California League by posting a .342 batting average and popping twenty-six home runs and over one hundred RBIs. He was voted on to the league all-star squad for the year.

Six days into January 1982, the Twins dealt Madison to the Dodgers in a trade for Bobby Castillo. Although Scotti never played off the Dodgers bench in Chavez Ravine, he was invited to the Los Angeles training camp, where he hobnobbed with Hollywood entertainers Cyndi Lauper, Danny Kaye and Frank Sinatra at after-game functions. The Tigers purchased Madison from the Dodgers on March 19, 1984, giving him his first real taste of Major League competition the following season. Scotti contends that Kirk Gibson and Darrell Evens took him "under their wing," although his two years with the Tigers were somewhat of a nightmare.

Both the 1985 and 1986 seasons found Scotti Madison between the Tigers Minor League clubs and the Detroit dugout. Scotti had just twenty-two plate appearances with Detroit during the two-year span. In the midst of his big-league time at the plate, Madison went without getting a single hit. Detroit granted him free agency midway through October. One month later, Kansas City picked up the Tate High catcher as a free agent, culminating in Madison's first Major League hit in 1987 as the Royals played the Minnesota Twins. Frank Viola, who had won the Cy Young Award the previous season, stood on the mound for the Twins that day.

Facing Viola, Scotti Madison hit a fastball, sending it into left center field for a double. In his next at-bat, Madison hit Viola's changeup for another double. Yet an additional two-bagger came with a connection to a curveball. Madison went three for four for his first-ever Major League hits. The Royals gave Scotti his free agency at the end of the 1988 season, and the Cincinnati Reds offered him a contract during the first week of the 1989 season. Madison enjoyed playing under manager Pete Rose but experienced grief along with the rest of the team as Rose became embroiled in a betting scandal.

Scotti Madison retired after the 1989 season and pursued a career in insurance and sales of proprietary products. During a ten-year period while working for AFLAC, Madison was responsible for securing Wal-Mart as a customer for the company. He was also listed as AFLAC's top sales associate six years in a row. For several years, Scotti has been actively involved with humanitarian efforts in the Dominican Republic and Haiti, including a focused work for the cure of HIV.

JAY BELL: A LIFE IN THE GAME

The University of West Florida's Bret Simmermacher drafted with the Seattle Mariners organization in 1986. Right-handed Pensacola Junior College pitcher Steve Newton signed with the Mets during the 1986 draft, while college teammate and Pensacola High School graduate Mark Whiten contracted with the Blue Jays. The Jays also picked PJC outfielder Paul Rodgers as an amateur choice. That summer, Tate High School topped Lake Mary 9–3 to win the 4A Florida State High School Championship. Tate's Chris Cassels gained selection by the Brewers during the Amateur Entry Draft and began playing for their Pioneer League club the following season.

"Baseball is a game that is meant to be enjoyed," declares Jay Bell. While this statement is taken for granted by some, Bell is one who has lived it. During his earliest summers playing in Pensacola's Babe Ruth League and his seasons on Tate High School's championship squad, Bell has entered the game with the idea of enjoying it first. Jay's eighteen years in the Major Leagues culminated in a desire to keep the fun and enjoyment going, as he launched out into coaching for Team USA and the Arizona Diamondbacks franchise. *Courtesy of the author.*

As the Tate High baseball team was positioning for another state champion cup, one of its former members was beginning his career in the majors.

Jay Stuart Bell was born on Eglin Air Force Base, just east of Pensacola. Growing up in the City of Five Flags, Bell played Bill Bond Baseball and secured a place on Tate coach Randy Putman's squad. Bell's position at shortstop was backed up by underclassman Travis Fryman. Jay states that Putman was one of the most influential coaches of his career, speaking volumes toward personal and athletic development. One thing that

Randy ingrained into Jay was the understanding that fear of failure had absolutely no place on the ball field. "If you live your life from at-bat to at-bat, you are always living with fear of failure," Bell relayed at a 2008 dinner honoring Putman.

Fear of failure did not haunt Jay like it did with others, as demonstrated from his days as a Pensacola youth leaguer. He was successful in having fun all along the way. "Baseball is a game that is meant to be enjoyed. There are a lot of Major League players who don't enjoy the game, but they play it because that's what they do best," declared Bell.

The Minnesota Twins drafted Bell in the first round of the 1984 Major League Amateur Draft, sending him to Fred Waters's Elizabethton Twins. Jay poked six home runs for Waters while covering his familiar shortstop position defensively. In 1985, Bell was made a member of the Visalia Oaks, but after 106 games into the season, he became one of four players traded to Cleveland in a deal that brought Bert Blyleven to the Twins. Bell spent the remainder of the year with Double-A Waterbury, Connecticut, of the Eastern League.

The following season with Waterbury, Jay buried seven over the wall, successfully slugged 137 hits and played in 138 games before being called up with Cleveland. Bell's first game as a Major League player came on September 29, 1986, with the Indians facing the Twins. Bert Blyleven stood on the mound for Minnesota as Jay came to the plate for his inaugural Major League at-bat. Looking at his old organization and the player that he had been traded for, Bell took the first pitch Blyleven served to him and drove in a home run.

Cleveland utilized Jay's talents in a limited fashion, working him between the home franchise and its Triple-A club. Not until the Indians traded Bell during 1989 preseason to the Pittsburgh Pirates did he have the opportunity to prove himself as an everyday player. Jay became the Pirates full-time shortstop in 1990, and he held that post for seven seasons. During his tenure in the Bucs' number-six position, Bell experienced three consecutive National League East titles from 1990 to 1992. The 1993 season became Jay's shining backdrop to showcase his talents, as he was honored with Silver Slugger and Rawlings Gold Glove Awards. That same year, Jay experienced the honor of playing in the All-Star game in Baltimore, as did his old Tate teammate Travis Fryman.

Pittsburgh went through a salary purge at the end of the 1996 season, with many players, including Jay, falling victim to the streamlining action. The Pirates sent Bell to the Kansas City Royals, where Jay enjoyed a decent year at the plate, batting .292 and hitting twenty-one home runs. On November 4, 1997, the Royals granted Bell free agency. Thirteen days later, he signed as one of the first players with the expansion Arizona Diamondbacks organization, bringing him together with his friend from Pensacola, Buck Showalter.

Bell's leadership on the field and in the clubhouse was noted by Arizona ownership, coaches and players. Jay moved to second base beginning in 1998, and by 1999 he had made the position his. Bell went to the All-Star game for Arizona in 1999 and belted thirty-eight home runs for the team during the season. One of those dingers came during a contest in which a raffle-winning fan chose the inning in which a grand slam would be hit and the player who would hit it. The prize for the correct guess was $1 million.

In the bottom of the sixth inning, Jay Bell stepped to the plate with the bases loaded. Bell did not disappoint. Fan Glyene Hoyle left the park that evening with great memories and a check that changed her life. Jay continued as a Diamondback through 2002, helping the team to a World Series win in 2001. After a season with the Mets in 2003, he returned to the Arizona franchise as a bench coach until 2006, leaving only to spend more quality time as a husband and father. Jay Bell later served as an advisory board member for the Baseball Assistance Team, accepted a job as Team USA's first base coach in 2010 and was set in as the Double-A Mobile Bay Bears hitting coach in 2012. On October 31, 2012, the Pittsburgh Pirates announced that Jay Bell would become their hitting coach, once again giving Bell the opportunity to share his Major League–caliber talent.

A SAD FAREWELL

The 1987 draft produced seven players originating from Pensacola schools. From the University of West Florida, the Yankees took outfielder Paul Ramos, and the Braves selected left-handed pitcher Randy Ward. Pensacola Junior College's right-hander Charles Guetter went to the Twins, while Benjamin Franklin Pierce signed to pitch for the Royals organization. Jason Townley from Escambia High benefited from the Jays' scouting report, penning with Toronto. Tate High School had two of its own picked up in 1987: pitcher Ben Webb enlisted with Pittsburgh, while infielder Travis Fryman was chosen by Detroit.

Washington High outfielder Derrick Warren was chosen by the Mets in 1988 but signed with the Mariners four years later. Michael Brown of Catholic High pressed the attention of the Tigers, while Charlie White out of Woodham signed for St. Louis. Ben Howze from rival Washington was picked by Montreal during the 1988 selection. J.M. Tate again sent a duo to the professionals, as outfielder Tony Tucker made good with Minnesota and Dave Partrick signed with the California Angels. Pensacola Junior College was acknowledged with two selections in 1988 in right-handed pitcher Michael Emmons under the Dodgers and shortstop Brian Noack for the White Sox.

With the 1989 mid-season draft underway, Pittsburgh signed Jon Rocca from Tate, and Jason McFarland went with San Francisco after graduating from Pensacola High. Pensacola Junior College saw the Yankees opt for Tim Garland, while the Blue Jays chose Jeff Cheek, who would begin playing for the Toronto Gulf Coast League affiliate in 1992. Jeff Cheek, son of legendary Blue Jay's announcer Tom Cheek, played under the direction of Pensacola's J.J. Cannon for his last two seasons in the minors. The University of West Florida's baseball program produced two draft selections in 1989, with the Brewers taking Patrick Rehwinkel and the Tigers choosing Australian-born right-hander Mark Ettles.

The Pensacola Men's Baseball League began its first season of operation in 1988, giving Pensacola-area men over the age of twenty-seven the opportunity to play competitive, organized baseball. After more than thirty years of helping countless young men achieve their personal potential as athletes and citizens, Fred Waters died in Pensacola on August 28, 1989. No words could describe the emotion felt throughout the world of baseball, as one of the greatest legacies in Pensacola sports history passed into immortality.

GREG LITTON: PENSACOLA'S BASEBALL AMBASSADOR

Although born in New Orleans, Louisiana, Jon Gregory Litton grew up in the Republic of Panama after his father's job dictated a move to Central America. Greg experienced some of his earliest ties to baseball on the streets of Coco Solo. Greg says that while playing with his school chums he tended to be one of the top athletes, a position he would have to regain when the family moved to Pensacola. Greg's father had been an All-SEC ballplayer at

Mississippi State and, in later years, coached both baseball and football with passion at Christobal High School. It was expected that Greg would be his leading disciple, picking up where the senior Litton left off.

Upon trying out for the baseball team at Woodham High School, Litton quickly found that the skill level he had enjoyed in Panama was challenged by what was being produced in Pensacola. During his freshman year, Greg went out for the squad only to be cut during the first round of evaluations. "We lived right across the street from the school, and I had to leave the tryouts and go tell my dad," says Greg. Even with concern about disappointing his father, Greg walked straight into the house to report his shortcoming. "My dad has always been one of my greatest influences and encouragers," Litton admits with a smile. As Greg relayed the afternoon's events of not making the team, his dad's reply took him by surprise. Litton's father simply said, "We'll do better next year." Greg did do better the following year, and with hard work and continued support from his family, he made the Woodham team and positioned himself for a career in the game.

Litton attended Pensacola Junior College after graduation, playing in front of his hometown crowd as a PJC Pirate. Among the scouts watching Greg's developing abilities was Pensacola-based Ken "Squeaky" Parker. Parker had signed Will Clark to a contract with San Francisco in 1985, a year after Clark played on the USA Olympic Baseball team. When asked if he took notice of the professional scouts in the stands at PJC, Greg Litton said, "Not really. I tried to stay pretty focused on my game. But when I did know that a particular scout or two was at the game, I seemed to overcompensate and play lousy." Litton's ability on the field was not all that Squeaky Parker saw when he watched Greg play at PJC. He saw Greg's passion and heart for the sport. Along with fundamentals, he saw a passion that cannot be taught—a passion that Kevin Saucier says "burns in your heart like a fire."

Greg was signed as an infielder with the San Francisco Giants organization in the January 1984 Amateur Draft. Nineteen-year-old Litton's first assignment was to the Everett Giants of the Northwest League, where he posted a .235 batting average and smacked four home runs in sixty-two games. The following season, he popped twelve over the wall for Fresno and played as an outfielder. From 1986 to 1988, Greg moved up effectively through the Giants' farm system but never pushed past a .278 batting average in his pre-Major League experience. Greg's strength, whether in the outfield, at second base or as a shortstop, was his everyday determination to make the right play and exude leadership as a team player.

As with many young boys, Greg Litton held an ambition to become a Major League baseball player, and on May 2, 1989, all of Greg's hard work and determination paid off. Manager Roger Craig utilized Greg as a utility player for the Giants in 1989, positioning him in various spots around the infield and outfield—Litton even caught in two games. Unbeknownst to Greg as he became a member of the 1989 Giants, his rookie year would take him to the postseason. Along with teammates Will Clark, Jeff Brantley and Brett Butler, Litton's Giants beat the Cubs four games to one, winning the National League pennant. The win would take San Francisco into the World Series to face the cross-bay Oakland Athletics in what would become the longest delayed series in baseball history.

Game 1 of the "Battle of the Bay" began on October 14, 1989, in Oakland, with the Athletics topping the Giants 5–0. Game 2 at Oakland went the way of the first, as the Athletics outhit the Giants in a 5–1 final score. Game 3 had been scheduled to start at 5:35 p.m. on October 17 across the bay in Candlestick Park. With the stands filled to capacity and the players making final preparations, a devastating earthquake struck the bay area thirty-one minutes before the start of the game. Due to the aftermath and destruction, Game 3 was postponed until October 27. It has been proposed that the third outing of the series actually saved countless lives, as fans were already at the ballpark and not on the highways during the quake.

Back in Candlestick Park for the third game of the series, down two games to none, the Giants were feeling not only the shakeup of the quake but also the effects of Oakland's bats. The outcome of the game was not as they had desired, with the Athletics administering thirteen runs over the Giants seven. Game 4, at Candlestick, found the Giants down 8–2 going into the bottom of the seventh inning. Reliever Gene Nelson came to the mound for Oakland and walked the first batter, catcher Terry Kennedy. Terry is the son of former Major Leaguer and Bronson Bomber Bob Kennedy.

With Kennedy on first, Greg Litton stepped into the batter's box. Gene Nelson served Greg the perfect pitch, and Litton took him deep for a two-run homer over the left field wall. The Giants scored two more in the inning, but that would be all. The final score of Game 4 of the 1989 World Series was 9–6 favoring the Athletics. Although Oakland swept its National League opponents, Greg considers his World Series home run as one of his greatest career memories. Among Greg's other cherished memories is one that places him securely in baseball history. Greg Litton became one of a small list of Major League players on to successfully work all nine field positions during a single game.

On July 22, 1991, Greg Litton and the San Francisco Giants faced the Minnesota Twins in an exhibition Hall of Fame game hosted in Cooperstown, New York. For the occasion, Litton's manager, Roger Craig, decided to put Litton's diverse fielding abilities to the ultimate test. During the course of the competition, Greg was moved through the lineup, playing all nine positions on the field before the game's end. The Woodham High graduate would later continue to prove his adaptability as he transitioned from ballplayer to gemologist to Minor League broadcaster. *Courtesy of Greg Litton.*

On July 22, 1991, the San Francisco Giants played the Minnesota Twins in a Hall of Fame game at Doubleday Field in Cooperstown, New York. Before the game began, Giants manager Roger Craig spoke to Greg about an idea he had in which Greg would be implemented as the ultimate utility man. Litton said that Craig had earlier spoken about the stunt in regard to a regular season game, but it would have in fact "showed up" the other team in an unsportsmanlike manner. However, the exhibition against the Twins was the perfect setting to enter Greg into the record books. During the course of the match, amid the festivities and fans surrounding the Baseball Hall of Fame celebratory game, Greg Litton moved from position to position, playing each effectively and entering into the annals of baseball history.

After retirement from baseball, Greg attained a postgraduate degree in diamond grading and appraisal from the Gemological Institute of America. Litton has also used his oratory abilities to inspire others toward achieving excellence in their own lives by playing a significant role as motivational speaker. Working with such programs as Just Say No, Greg brings to his audiences a wealth of personal examples directed at perseverance, teamwork and dedication. In pursuit of making a difference and changing lives, Greg has partnered with Pensacola baseball owner Quint Studer and the Studer Group Speaking Bureau. One of Litton's greatest enjoyments in life has been the ability to coach his daughter's softball team. And as professional affiliated baseball returned to Pensacola in 2012 with the Blue Wahoos, Greg partnered with tenured sportscaster Dan Shugart in calling televised games from the press box.

THE RETURN OF U.S. NAVY BASEBALL

While in Pensacola for a 1990 dedication event at the National Museum of Naval Aviation, President George H.W. Bush requested the reestablishment of a military baseball program. Well familiar with baseball being used as a morale booster during his days as a World War II naval aviator, President Bush spoke about the importance of the sport for the men in service. When President Bush asked how the base team was doing, Pensacola Naval Air Station flight student Ensign Terry Allvord responded, "Mr. President, I believe [navy] baseball was another casualty of Vietnam." The president said that something should be done about that issue and urged the reinstatement of an organized league to benefit the welfare of military personnel.

Allvord took it upon himself to pursue the president's challenge, and the following afternoon, he placed a notice on the bulletin board at the base gym announcing tryouts. The result of Allvord's effort was the turnout of over 150 players and a league fielding ten teams. The Pensacola-based U.S. Navy Baseball Club, dubbed the Southwestern Baseball League, quickly grew with men from all branches of the military as well as several civilians. Halfway through the season, the league held an annual all-star game featuring sailors against marines, which sparked the idea for the U.S. Military All-Stars.

Allvord says that Pensacola was historically and geographically ideal to begin the worthy endeavor and formulate the vision that has now become a worldwide venue:

> *The support was amazing, and the community immediately got behind our annual Navy vs. Marine Corps Baseball Challenge. I can't think of a better place to have restarted military baseball in the modern era. The level of talent that has come through our organization has been superb. I have always been amazed at the players who may have went on to significant professional careers but decided to serve their country. I also remember hearing these types of statements about the greats of World War II, so I'm hopeful we have continued the tradition of the heroes who came before us.*

During the years that followed, Allvord created over forty military teams, the U.S. Military All-Stars and the Heroes of the Diamond "Red, White and Blue Tour." Now retired, Lieutenant Commander Allvord has taken the non-government-funded goodwill baseball program to forty-five states and over twelve countries, generating support and awareness for U.S. troops. Participating in MLB Legends Games and mixed-squad exhibition venues, the Heroes of the Diamond military personnel mingle with former professional players such as Pensacola's Mark Whiten.

In speaking about the significance of the "Red, White and Blue Tour" and the legacy of their work, Terry Allvord told *Baseball America*,

> *The goal of the program is to promote the awareness of the folks overseas. Really, the main focus here is to connect with communities and charities and that every minute people are putting their lives on the line. We don't want them to forget that people are over there. We know it—all of us have taken turns—people are over there on duty and people are carrying the rod for us*

right now. To honor the players that have played with us and have died in action, we hang their jerseys in our dugout before every game. And there's a lot of numbers, there's more than a dozen jerseys that we hang—it's tough, but it's why we're there.

IF ONLY A STADIUM

The Southwestern Baseball League drew fans in Pensacola as their player numbers increased during the early 1990s. Followers of Allvord's league, along with those of PJC and UWF, continued to prove that the city wanted organized baseball within its limits. Democratic senator Gwen Margolis reported to the *Miami Herald* on May 9, 1990, that the Florida Senate Appropriations Committee had earmarked a sum of money to go to Pensacola in the event it would build a Minor League baseball stadium. Margolis, as the appropriations chairperson, stated, "Although it is a lean budget, there is $500,000 to help Pensacola build a stadium."

Pensacola has long been a standout as a prime location for generating revenue and a dedicated fan base in the eyes of Minor League Baseball. Prior to the 1990 season, the Toronto Blue Jays were considering moving their Knoxville, Tennessee Double-A affiliate, and Pensacola was in the running as a possible landing spot. The cost to Pensacola to be the recipient of the Southern League franchise was the price of building a park to house them, but the city council could not agree on the $8–$10 million expenditure.

Major League Baseball expanded the National League by two teams in the beginning of the 1993 season. As the Colorado Rockies and Florida Marlins built their franchises and farm systems, the league shifted its Minor League clubs in various areas, replacing Triple-A affiliates in cities where Double-A parks already existed. The Chicago Cubs' Charlotte Knights Double-A affiliate were one such club. A new Triple-A baseball team was designated for their city, and talks ensued among club owners and Minor League Baseball's front office about where to relocate them. Again Pensacola was written in as a desirable location, along with New Orleans, Mobile and Baton Rouge. Another scenario in the city realignment dilemma was to move the Cincinnati Reds Triple-A Nashville Sounds to Pensacola. In both situations, Pensacola missed the opportunity just shy of a stadium.

Although professional baseball had yet to make its way back to Pensacola by the 1990s, the city kept pace with municipalities larger in size by turning out its share of professional players. After two years at Pensacola Junior College, outfielder Mark Steffens was drafted by the Phillies in 1988 and began playing for their Princeton, West Virginia club in 1990. The California Angels selected outfielder Steve Morgan and catcher Earl Partrick from Tate High during the 1990 draft.

Escambia High School won the 1991 Florida State 3A Championship by shutting down Barron Collier High from Naples 7–5 in the final game at Baseball City. Escambia High pitcher Evan Bailey was selected by the Astros during the June Amateur Draft. The Yankees chose Jon Boddy from Woodham and William Lawrence from Pensacola Junior College. Right-handed pitcher Chris Coulter, also of PJC, was drafted by the Indians. Patrick Underhill from the University of West Florida went to the Rangers, while Tate's Troy Fryman signed with the White Sox and became the second of the Fryman brothers to play professionally.

Pensacola Junior College and the University of West Florida experienced activity during the 1993 Amateur Draft. PJC Pitcher Brian Boeth was selected by the Angels, while fellow pitcher Jon Updike was drafted by the Mariners. Jason Smith contracted to the expansion Rockies out of UWF, as teammate Chris Schmitt signed with the Brewers. Four 1993 area high school seniors took the attention of regional scouts, with Escambia catcher Lloyd Wade making a selection by the Tigers and Woodham pitcher Victor Rodriguez penning his name with Toronto. The Florida Marlins organization drafted Tate High's Scott Southard, while an earlier Aggie graduate, Jarod Fryman, signed with the Milwaukee Brewers. After attending Jefferson Davis Community College, Jarod became the third in the Fryman household to sign a Minor League contract.

TRAVIS FRYMAN: PENSACOLA'S QUINTESSENTIAL PLAYER

David Travis Fryman could be regarded as the quintessential Pensacola baseball player and a prime example of the standard of determination grown on the Gulf Coast. Fryman's ability to play competitive baseball was complemented by the work ethic taught to him by his father and his community. As with many of the boys coming off Pensacola's high school diamonds, Travis had not been given the proverbial "silver spoon" but rather what Dennis Lewallyn calls the "wooden spoon." "We had enough and didn't lack, but we had to work for everything we got," says Lewallyn.

This was precisely Travis Fryman; he had the goods but had to work for his success.

Fryman was a standout at Tate High School, but he had large spikes to fill in regard to the accomplishments of the Aggies who had gone before him. The Detroit Tigers drafted Travis during the first round of the 1987 Amateur Draft, sending the Tate infielder to their Appalachian League club, where he played sixty-seven games at shortstop. He batted .234 for the Bristol Tigers and dropped in two home runs. While Travis's defensive abilities kept runners on their toes, his appearances at the plate were not what he wanted from himself.

Returning to Pensacola over the winter, Travis found an ally and hitting instructor in the form of an old friend. Baseball scout Squeaky Parker cared greatly about development of players and did as much as he could to inspire and instruct those that he had access to. Squeaky was all business, and if one was looking for a coach who would be his buddy, he had better look elsewhere. However, in the trenches, an aspiring, hardworking player could not have anyone greater at his back. Parker took Fryman on as a project that lasted for Travis's three seasons in the Minor Leagues. Squeaky trained with each of the Fryman brothers, but he and Travis had a special agreement.

To overcome his struggles at the plate, Parker threw Travis batting practice during each off-season until Fryman received his call to Detroit. Travis grew in ability and confidence, all the while confirming his promise to Parker. The commitment that Travis had made to his hometown hitting instructor was that upon the signing of Fryman's first big-league contract, he would buy Squeaky a new car. Parker kept his end of the bargain by making Travis a better hitter, and Travis delivered on his oath to the old scout by parking a new vehicle in Squeaky's garage.

Travis idolized the Big Red Machine's David Concepcion as he was growing up. Watching the Cincinnati infielder's grit and excellence had inspired Fryman to improve his own abilities. The Tigers called Fryman up mid-season 1990 for a July 7 game against the Royals at Tiger Stadium. Manager Sparky Anderson used Fryman at shortstop, third base and as a designated hitter during his first sixty-six games with Detroit that year. Travis split his time between short and third in 1991 and experienced a good year at the plate, driving twenty-one over the fence and hitting in ninety-one runs. Travis was ranked sixth in voting for the American League Rookie of the Year in 1991.

The Tigers were confident in Travis's abilities and handed him the everyday shortstop job in 1992 when an injured Alan Trammell was

Tenured professional scout Squeaky Parker took special interest in Travis Fryman, seeing more than just a little potential in his future as a big leaguer. Fryman had been a standout infielder at Tate High School and had provided good offensive capabilities at the plate. However, Travis's leap into the world of professional baseball came at the price of additional hard work and focused development under the direction of Parker. All the extra effort paid off, as Fryman debuted with the Detroit Tigers in 1990 and continued to play in the majors for thirteen seasons. *Courtesy of Mike McCormick.*

taken out of the lineup. Travis did not disappoint his team; he covered short with finesse, earning him an American League All-Star selection. He also continued to show the effects from Squeaky Parker's batting practice by belting twenty homers and logging a .266 batting average, which was enough to win him a Silver Slugger Award.

Sparky Anderson started Travis at shortstop in 1993 but moved him over to what was to be his position at third base for the remainder of Fryman's time in Detroit. Travis finished the 1993 season with twenty-two home runs, a .300 batting average and a second All-Star Game roster spot. He was also voted the American League's All-Star Third Baseman by *Baseball America*. Travis was chosen again for the 1994 and 1996 American League All-Star squads.

On November 18, 1997, Travis was traded to the Arizona Diamondbacks. The Tigers acquired three players, including one Minor Leaguer, in the swap for Fryman. Less than two weeks later, Arizona sent Travis to Cleveland for Matt Williams. Travis's leadership in Detroit was quickly missed in the Tigers clubhouse. Longtime Detroit broadcaster Ernie Harwell summed up the feelings of both fans and players in the loss of Fryman: "Travis was a great leader and a great talent. The Tigers should have never let him go. He's one of those true team players."

Detroit's loss was Cleveland's gain as Travis picked right back up with the Indians where he had left off with the Tigers. He worked hard every day, led by example and offered his insight and experience to younger players. Jim Thome, the Indians third baseman, shifted over to first in 1998 to make room for Travis. Thome had covered the third bag for Cleveland since his rookie year in 1991, but rather than seeing Fryman as a usurper, Jim embraced him as a role model. Just before Travis Fryman's last game in 2002, Thome reflected on his and the team's regard for the All-Star third baseman. "We've loved him since the day he got here. He's been like a dad to us," said Jim.

Fryman and the Indians won the American League Division Series in 1998, and Travis was voted eighteenth for the season's league MVP. In 2000, Travis was ranked seventeenth in the MVP polls, played in his fifth All-Star Game and won the Rawlings American League Gold Glove Award for third base. That same season, the Indians reacquired fellow Pensacolan Mark Whiten. During the 2000 season, Travis set career highs with a .321 batting average, thirty-one doubles and 106 RBIs. Unfortunately, the hard-playing thirty-one-year-old began to experience discomfort from injuries, which contributed to his retirement in 2002. Fryman's last professional game took place on September 29 at age thirty-three.

Far from walking away from baseball altogether, Travis was a natural as a coach and mentor. Just as Squeaky Parker had done for him, Travis worked out with Minor Leaguers from the Pensacola area when they were home during the off-season. Travis's base of operation was his old high school and the Tate ball field, where players like John Webb and Seth Taylor benefited from the "in-house" instruction. Webb emphatically stated of Fryman's one-on-one workouts, "I can't get help like this anywhere else." By 2008, Travis was back with the Cleveland organization as the manager of the Mahoning Valley Scrappers in the New York-Penn League. He held the position for three years before moving back up to Cleveland in 2011 as their defensive coordinator.

HARD HITTIN' WHITEN

Pensacola High School football coach Leo Carvalis saw potential in Mark Whiten's athletic ability while recruiting for the PHS team during Mark's junior year. Mark was uncertain of his own talents, but Carvalis anticipated more for Whiten than Mark did for himself. Carvalis pursued Mark in the hallways of Pensacola High, convincing the junior to try out for the football team. Leo Carvalis knew that Whiten had what it took to acquire a college athletic scholarship; however, he was not absolute in what sport Mark would be most likely to secure his "ride." Leo encouraged Whiten to also try out for the baseball team at Pensacola High. "We used the 'more eggs you have in the basket the better chance you have' philosophy," says Carvalis.

Whiten's "eggs" began to hatch in 1984 as he had proved himself on both the gridiron and the diamond for Pensacola High. Although Mark became an NFL prospect prior to entering college, it was Pensacola Junior College's baseball coach Buddy Kinser who foresaw Whiten's future when he signed Mark before the 1984 season. Kinser's baseball program developed Mark's fundamentals and his self-confidence. Kinser commented on Mark after he signed his first professional contact, "Mark was not certain that he would play pro ball, but I was when I first brought him to PJC."

The Toronto Blue Jays perceived Mark in the same light as Kinser, drafting Whiten during the fifth round of the January 1986 Regular Phase Major League Draft. In Medicine Hat, Alberta, Whiten spent seventy games in the outfield for the Blue Jays. The Pioneer League offered the nineteen-year-old roughly the same level of competition that he had known at PJC, and in response, Mark parked ten behind the fence and delivered a .300 average at the plate. Closer to home for the 1987 season, Toronto sent Whiten to Myrtle Beach, South Carolina, and then to Dunedin, Florida, for the following year. Mark's 1988 work schedule was split between Class-A Dunedin and Double-A Knoxville. As Whiten began to face pitchers closer to the Major League ranks, the hard-hitting outfielder struggled some with his ability to get his timing down. But when Whiten did connect, the repercussions for the man on the mound were devastating.

Even if Mark's bat fell asleep during a few plate appearances, his defensive arm was a completely different matter. He had become known as one of the strongest fielding arms in the minors and was supremely accurate. In 1990, the Jays positioned Mark with their Triple-A club in Syracuse, New York,

Confidence in his own playing abilities was not Mark Whiten's strength during his initial years at Pensacola High School. However, after encouragement from coaches—both at PHS and Pensacola Junior College—Whiten's inner voice kicked in. Mark gained the nickname "Hard Hittin'" Whiten for his explosive power at the plate and relentless pursuit of the outfield fence. *Courtesy of the author.*

with the intention of having him ready to move up at a moment's notice. During the first half of the season, Mark homered fourteen times, brought his batting average up to .290 and hit nineteen doubles. On July 12, 1990, Toronto listed Whiten on their twenty-five-man Major League roster. The boy from Pensacola High who never thought he would play professional ball sat in the dugout next to teammates Fred McGriff, John Olerud, Pat Borders and manager Cito Gaston.

In his first thirty-three games for the Blue Jays, Mark registered a .273 batting average and a 1.00 fielding average. He retained his rookie status for 1991 and was ranked sixth in American League Rookie of the Year voting. Mark earned the nickname "Hard-Hittin'" Whiten for his launch pad–like contact at the plate. Unfortunately, Mark suffered from sporadic lapses of concentration, and ultimately, so did the consistency of his hitting. The Blue Jays did not have the patience to develop Whiten's adjustment to Major League pitchers, thus ensued a trade to Cleveland Indians at the end of June.

After two seasons in Cleveland, Mark was dealt to the St. Louis Cardinals, where he adjusted to National League bullpens with somewhat of a vengeance. Of the twenty-five home runs Hard-Hittin' Whiten registered during the 1993 season, five of them became record-book material. On August 11, during a game against the Pirates at Three Rivers Stadium, Mark drove a 464-foot home run into the right field upper deck, becoming the first visiting player to ever achieve the feat. Then, on a warm September 7 evening in Cincinnati, the Cardinals were facing the Reds for the second game of a double-header when Whiten's bat came alive.

During the course of the game, Mark batted in twelve runners and hit four home runs, including a grand slam. Only eleven other players in the history of the game had hit four homers in a single game—a list that includes Gehrig, Mays and Hodges. But none of the eleven had ever batted in as many runs during a nine-inning stretch. The only other man to knock in twelve for a single game was Hall of Famer "Sunny Jim" Bottomley in 1924. Additionally, with Mark's RBIs from the first game, he tied Nate Colbert's 1972 record for runs batted in during a double-header. Teammate Todd Zeile made the comment about Mark's missile shots from the plate, "You can't even do what he does in batting practice."

Mark finished the year with a .253 batting average, twenty-five home runs and ninety-nine runs batted in, but regularity of contact continued to elude Mark. He was determined to have the missing component of his arsenal rectified and enrolled himself into a St. Petersburg, Florida instructional league during the off-season. Back with St. Louis in 1994, Whiten suffered pulled rib cage muscles early in the season, which kept him to participating in just ninety-two games that year and eventually led to a trade to the Red Sox the following April. Mark spent as much time with Triple-A Pawtucket in 1995 as he did with the Boston club. Unable to completely overcome his physical difficulty, the Red Sox traded Mark to the Phillies in July.

Over the course of the next five years, Mark would dress out in the uniforms of five Major League organizations and their Minor League affiliates. Whiten's numbers at the plate were decent, and his arm in the field was always welcome. Philadelphia, Atlanta, Seattle, the New York Yankees and Cleveland all enlisted Mark from 1996 to 2000. Back in Cleveland in May 1998, the Indians rotated Mark to Triple-A Buffalo for a good portion of the season. One of the many benefits of Mark's flexibility to produce in part-time duty for the home club was that he was a natural at helping to train young hitters on their way up. While with Cleveland, on July 31, 1998, Whiten pitched his one and only inning in a Major League uniform. Against the Oakland Athletics, Mark walked two and gave up one hit and an earned run but struck out three.

Mark Whiten played for the Veracruz Rojos of the Mexican League in 2001 in an eight-game comeback effort. In 2002, he fielded for the Dodgers' Las Vegas 51s along with secondary first baseman Phil Hiatt from Pensacola's Catholic High. The Independent Long Island Mallards put Mark to work for a few games in 2003, but Whiten had already made the decision to use his talents in a new and equally productive way. Although Whiten had never played within the Rangers system, Texas gave Mark an opportunity to duplicate himself in the development of Minor League players. Mark became the hitting coach for the league champion Spokane Indians in 2005 and the Arizona League Rangers in 2006.

Never laying down his bat, Mark became involved with the Major League Baseball Players Alumni Association, supporting the preservation of baseball's history by becoming an active roster member for their Legends of the Game circuit. The event fields former Major and Minor League players along with honorary teammates such as Terry Allvord's Heroes of the Diamond. Mark has also participated in the Father's Day Hall of Fame Classic held in Cooperstown, New York. In every instance, Whiten reveals his old form in winning home run derby exhibitions and throwing out runners at the plate. When asked to what he attributes to his sudden bursts of power, Mark replies with a laughing smile, "A couple of extra slices of pizza."

HOMER HIATT

Fourteen-year-old Phil Hiatt and teammate Travis Fryman helped the 1983 Brent All-Stars to reach the league World Series. After graduating

Pensacola Catholic High School head baseball coach Richard LaBounty worked on perfecting the defensive capabilities of his infielder Phil Hiatt. What LaBounty saw in Hiatt caused him to practice with Phil long after most other coaches would have called it a day. Hiatt's CHS teammate Jeff English says that the school's field did not yet have lights when they played there. "As the sun started to set, Coach LaBounty would instruct all the players to pull up their vehicles to the diamond's edge and turn their headlights on," says English. The innovation worked, and it gave Phil an edge toward getting a call from the Kansas City Royals. *Courtesy of Phil Hiatt.*

from Pensacola's Catholic High School in 1987, Phil developed some of his early fielding skills while first playing for Jefferson Community College and then Louisiana Tech University. However, his aggressiveness at the plate and defensive tenacity were garnered under the direction of Catholic coach

Richard LaBounty. The Kansas City Royals drafted Hiatt during the eighth round of the 1990 Amateur Draft, sending him to Eugene, Oregon, of the Northwest League. Phil's seventy-three games with the Eugene Emeralds were the beginning of a career that would span fifteen seasons and cover eight Major League organizations and two continents.

Phil was an average hitter for the Emeralds, posting .294 for the season, but was at the top of his game at shortstop. Davenport's (Florida) Baseball City Royals would be Hiatt's team for the first half of the 1991 season, and he would play with the Memphis Chicks during the second half. The Class-A Baseball City Royals were the Minor League tenants of the short-lived Boardwalk and Baseball theme park. Double-A Memphis carried with it a long history dating back to 1901, with some of that history crossing paths with Pensacola's teams of the early 1900s. Phil stayed with Memphis into 1992 but was moved out to Triple-A Omaha at the end of the season.

The Royals were viewing Hiatt as the heir apparent to the versatile Kevin Seitzer, who had been released by Kansas City in 1992. Phil had pitched and covered the middle infield while at Catholic High, but during the past three years in the minors, his portfolio had expanded to third, first and the outfield. Kansas City was in need of an adaptable and resourceful defensive utility man on its bench, and while Hiatt's bat had not yet made great strides, the Royals took the chance that Phil would find his groove in Kansas City.

Hiatt was invited to the Royals' 1993 spring training camp at Baseball City Stadium as part of their forty-man roster. Phil's debut with Kansas City followed immediately after spring training on April 7 at twenty-three years of age. As regular infielder Keith Miller was on the disabled list, Phil came into the Royals' dugout under manager Hal McRae as a platoon mate for third baseman Gary Gaetti. Hiatt also participated in nine games as the Royals' designated hitter, giving a few innings of rest to regular DH George Brett. "I had no business in big-league ball," Hiatt later said. "Mentally and physically, I was not ready to be there. But like most young players, I did well for the first couple of months, then I struggled, but stayed up all year."

After eighty-one games, Kansas City just did not see what it had hoped to in Phil's plate appearances. His .218 batting average ushered him back to Omaha to finish out the last twelve games of the season. Phil spent 1994 with Omaha and Memphis, collecting a combined batting average of .294 between the two teams. During Phil's last year with the Royals organization, he played twenty games in Omaha before returning to Kansas City. Hiatt had a little over one hundred plate appearances for the Royals in 1995. And just prior to a trade in September for Detroit's Juan Samuel, Phil discovered that he had been playing for two solid weeks with a collapsed lung.

Detroit placed Phil with Triple-A Toledo for the beginning of 1996, where he popped forty-two home runs and batted in 119 runs for the Mud Hens. Detroit called him up to cover third base near the end of the season, giving Phil the opportunity to play once again alongside his friend from Pensacola, shortstop Travis Fryman. Phil Nevin ended up playing third every day that September, and the Tigers released Hiatt in November. "I was a little upset I had been pushed [into the majors] when I was young. I wondered what would have happened had I been a little older," reflected Hiatt. Determined to excel in the game at all costs, Phil made it known that he would play in Japan.

Phil joined the 1997 Hanshin Tigers, a sister team to Detroit in the Nippon Professional Baseball League. Based in Koshien, Japan, the Hanshin Tigers have been compared to the Boston Red Sox due to their die-hard fan base. Hiatt's batting average reached .291 with Hanshin, and beyond that he was having fun. Phil says that he was the only American on the team besides Mike Greenwell, who was injured sometime into the season and had to return to the States. The New York Yankees signed Phil as a free agent in January 1998 only to release him in April. Five days after his release from the Yankees, Cleveland signed Hiatt to a single-season contract.

The Indians placed Phil on their Triple-A Buffalo roster, where he played first, third and outfield and belted thirty-one homers in 119 at-bats—but there was no call up to Cleveland. By the time Hiatt landed in Cincinnati's Indianapolis affiliate after a trade to the Reds in 1999 and then another shift into Colorado's system in 2000, he had become comfortable with the notion that he was going to be a career Minor Leaguer. With true Pensacola style, Hiatt was determined to make his mark in the arena he was given. In Colorado Springs, he drove in 109 runs and cracked thirty-six home runs. And in 2001, he won the Pacific Coast League MVP, hitting .330 and dropping forty-four over the wall for the Dodgers' Las Vegas club.

Comparisons had begun to surface among the media and teammates to Kevin Costner's character from the movie *Bull Durham*. Some had started calling Phil "Crash," but after an Indianapolis newspaper headlined a story with "Homer Hiatt Does it Again," teammates bestowed Phil with the honoring moniker. "Homer" Hiatt found personal pleasure in the fact that he had become a Minor League career man, as it gave him opportunity to give young hitters advice and share experiences with impressionable minds.

Phil Hiatt reached his final season in 2005 with the Washington Nationals franchise. During his career, he had played for thirteen different Major and Minor League clubs, combining for a batting average of .272, dumped 317 homers behind the fence and won Most Valuable Player in two different leagues. Although Phil Hiatt saw just a few actual games as a Major Leaguer, his career was one of distinction and achievement. Phil has continued his passion to see players excel in the game through private instruction and personal mentoring. Hiatt is also a frequent guest coach at Pensacola-area youth baseball clinics.

CHAPTER 7
THE LONG-BALL ERA: 1994–FORWARD

PENSACOLA PRODUCES PROFESSIONALS

Pensacola's entrance into the age of the long ball set in motion events that would mark a brand-new awakening for the city's legacy within the game. The national sport was evolving once again, and the faster pace of the game, along with heightened offensive and defensive competition, made even the most muted fans rise out of their seats in vibrant team support. Hitter-friendly ballparks began to take the place of the old "cookie cutter" stadiums, with seats purposely built close to the field and the players. The new parks were reminiscent of the intimate Crosley Field, Wrigley Field and Shibe Park. And although the multimillion-dollar player was somewhat of a different breed than those from the days of Russ Scarritt and Babe Ruth, the proximity to the action both in person and via the media enlisted a whole new generation of support.

As the Long-Ball Era opened its gates to Major League Baseball, the pieces were falling into place on Northwest Florida's Gulf Coast for Pensacola to regain its position in the world of the professional game. Among the many of Pensacola's homegrown players who would see big-league competition during their careers, several would return to help rebuild the future legacy of the game in the City of Five Flags. Talmadge Nunnari, John Webb and Billy Sadler are but a few from the list of Pensacola players of the Long-Ball Era who made the decision to extend the history of baseball in the city of their childhoods.

Illinois-born entrepreneur Quint Studer adopted Pensacola as his southern home. Not long after his arrival in the Port City, Quint and his wife, Rishy, invested in the Pensacola community (and in a personal dream) by purchasing the Pensacola Pelicans. Ever the developer, Studer immediately began refining the infrastructure of his new independent club and playing facilities. As the team's needs and fan seating first outgrew the confines of Pensacola Junior College and later the University of West Florida, Studer proposed a brand-new stadium on an unused portion of Pensacola's waterfront. Behind the scenes, Quint was exploring the vision of bringing affiliated baseball back to town for the first time since 1962. *Courtesy of the Pensacola Blue Wahoos.*

The draw of Pensacola's pristine environment and economic opportunities evoked vision in transplanted entrepreneurs such as Quint Studer. Studer, who understood the relevance of baseball's historical significance in Pensacola, was willing to gamble on the reorganization of a baseball experience on a scale larger than ever before. As in the days of Wally Dashiell and Joe Panaccione, Pensacola made room for growth and prosperity through the vehicle of baseball in the era of the long ball. The Pensacola Pelicans landed in town for a brief stay, but it was long enough to re-infuse a passion and an understanding of the importance of baseball in Pensacola.

The Pensacola Gulf Coast experienced back-to-back hurricanes in 1995, with one right in the midst of the summer baseball leagues. Outdoor sports and activities were suspended in late July as an impending storm approached the Florida Panhandle. Hurricane Erin made landfall in central Florida first as a Category 1 storm and then turned toward the Gulf Coast, making a second landfall as a Category 2. Just as repairs to businesses and homes were underway, Hurricane Opal, a Category 4 storm, caused havoc for Pensacola and the surrounding region. Although many normal activities along the Emerald Coast took some time to climb back to full strength after the devastation of the 1995 hurricane season, youth league, high school and college baseball came back swinging for the fences.

During the season prior to the two storms, University of West Florida right-handed pitcher Steve Gay signed with the independent Ogden Raptors of the Pioneer League, and fellow righty Steve Beck was enlisted by the Brewers. Pensacola Junior College sent catcher Fred Anson off to the Mariners organization in 1994, while two Pensacola-area high school pitchers, Pine Forest High's Bennie Robbins and Escambia's Kendall Hill, drafted with Atlanta that same year. Bryan Wright from Escambia High School was drafted as a second baseman by the Red Sox in 1995 and later played for the Pensacola Pelicans during their 2002 inaugural season.

Four Pensacola Junior College players were drafted during the 1995 mid-season recruiting campaign, including outfielders Brandon Black, who headed to the Mets, and Matt Abernathy with the Padres. PJC pitcher Francis Scott Key and second baseman Doug Franklin had also played together at Tate High. Key was selected by the Royals and Franklin the Blue Jays. PJC sent three more to the selection rounds in 1996: right-handed pitcher Kenny Avera was selected by the Angels, left-handed pitcher Mark Curtis penned with the Blue Jays and righty Jason McBride caught the attention of the New York Yankees.

Gulf Breeze High School, just across Pensacola Bay, was honored with two players being selected in the 1996 draft. Pitcher Pete Della Ratta signed with Oakland, but his first real experience in the game came with the University of South Alabama. The Angels took interest in Gulf Breeze hurler William Robbins, while the Cleveland Indians picked two from Woodham High in outfielder Miles Bryant and first baseman Alfred Leatherwood. Catholic, Escambia and Pine Forest High Schools each offered a single player for Major League Baseball's 1996 Amateur Draft. Pine Forest right-hander Jake Jacobs went to Minnesota, Catholic's Jeff Farnsworth signed with Seattle and would see Major League play in 2002 and Escambia's Bryan Houston was drafted by the Tigers as an outfielder.

The University of West Florida's pitching development program positioned right-hander Ron Ricks for a contract with the Angels during the 1997 draft, while area high schools were heavily scouted for prospect picks. David Wigley graduated from Pensacola High and headed to Wallace

Community College after being picked by the Rangers. Tampa Bay chose pitcher Josh Davis of Catholic High in 1997, but Davis took the collegiate path with Tallahassee Community College. The Reds made a prospective advance toward Chad Rodgers from Pine Forest, and Tate also had two players at the signing table—Finley Woodward threw in the Cardinals' farm system after playing for Auburn University, and catcher Ryan Satterwhite was picked by the Indians, later catching for the Pelicans in 2002.

Washington High's David Justice made the 1997 selection by Minnesota, while teammates Dave Elder and Talmadge Nunnari headed to the Rangers and the Expos respectively. Elder went first to Georgia Tech University before beginning play in a Texas affiliate uniform, and "T" Nunnari headed east across Florida to Jacksonville University. Washington High's senior baseball squad proudly boasted another pair of draftees during the 1998 selection process, as infielder Nate Espy contracted with the Phillies and pitcher Eric Bush with the Indians.

Toronto scouts chose Ryan Houston from Escambia, the Angels picked Darren Blakely out of Pensacola High and the Braves began the professional career of Tim Spooneybarger from Pine Forest. After Tate High School's 1998 baseball team won the state championship, its draft picks consisted of pitcher Frankie McGill with the Rangers, shortstop Bryce Pelfrey with the Pirates and pitcher Heath Kelly with the Marlins. Erik Smallwood prompted a selection by Milwaukee but did not sign. After playing college ball, Erik was drafted with the Orioles in 2002 and fielded for the Pelicans in 2004.

Pensacola Junior College shortstops Kyle Hawthorne and Ivan Reyes drafted in 1998. Hawthorne went with the Twins and Reyes with the Yankees. The Mets selected PJC outfielder Cory Harris in 1999, while the Diamondbacks picked first baseman Jim Kavourias. Kavourias later contracted with the Marlins in 2000. Ellis Debrow was selected by the Red Sox from Woodham, Seth Taylor from Tate by the Yankees and Kyle Middleton of Escambia by the Kansas City Royals. Pitchers John Webb from Pensacola High and Brad Salmon from Tate signed their very first contracts toward the Major Leagues. Webb contracted with Chicago and Salmon with Cincinnati.

"T"

Talmadge Raphael Nunnari, known to most simply as "T," grew up in Pensacola knowing the joy of hard work and a job well done. The Nunnaris,

Talmadge "T" Nunnari (left) spent six seasons in the Expos organization, reaching the Major Leagues in 2002. The former Washington High School All-Star and Bill Bond League alumnus dedicated himself to the development of other players on the same level that he had gained in his own career. *Courtesy of the Pensacola Pelicans (Amarillo Sox).*

originally from Sicily, made their home in Florida's first settlement in the late 1800s. T's family quickly ingratiated themselves into the Pensacola community as merchants and shopkeepers. One side of his family later owned Mama Nunnari's Italian Restaurant, while Talmadge's grandfather was the proprietor of Johnny's Barber Shop. T began playing baseball in Pensacola's youth leagues, including Bill Bond Baseball, where he was radically influenced by the legacy of Coach Bill Bond.

As a member of the Washington High School baseball team, Nunnari excelled on the diamond and caught the attention of regional scouts. T's good nature further endeared him to those interested in his playing abilities. T was granted a scholarship to Wallace Community College, where he played for two seasons before being awarded a scholarship to Jacksonville University. The Montreal Expos signed Talmadge in the ninth round of the 1997 amateur draft under the direction of scout Doug Carpenter. After college, Nunnari began fulfilling his contract with Montreal and headed to Short Season A-Ball in Vermont as his first assignment. The twenty-two-year-old batted .318 in sixty-two games and scored a fielding percentage of .989 for the Vermont Expos. Talmadge was awarded a position on the 1997 Sun Belt Conference All-Star squad and was voted Player of the Year.

At the end of Vermont's season, the Expos moved Nunnari to the Cape Fear Crocs for an additional nine games. Cape Fear's 1998 roster included Talmadge for the first half of the year, during which he batted in fifty-one runs and eighteen doubles. His batting average climbed to .304, with two home runs in the mix. The Class-A Jupiter, Florida, Hammerheads enlisted Nunnari for the last half of 1998 and the beginning of the 1999 season. Nunnari moved from Class-A Jupiter to Double-A Harrisburg, Pennsylvania, during the course of the year, but not before he claimed his right at the plate with forty-four RBIs, seventeen doubles, five home runs and a .356 batting average. Upon arriving with the Harrisburg Senators, T found a team running toward an Eastern League pennant and helped them claim their trophy in the postseason.

During the 2000 regular season, Nunnari moved from Harrisburg to Triple-A Ottawa, and then on September 7, the Washington High all-star dressed out for the Montreal Expos. Talmadge Nunnari's Major League career spanned the course of just eighteen games and five at-bats, but the Pensacola first baseman had achieved what many only muse over. Nunnari's first hit came off Marlins pitcher A.J. Burnett in front of the Montreal fans.

After another brief stint in the minors in 2002, Nunnari returned home to join the inaugural Pensacola Pelicans and help them win the Southeastern

League pennant. Although the Pelicans were an independent, unaffiliated team, the move became one of the most important in T's life, as well as the lives of Pensacola fans. Talmadge was called back to the Harrisburg Senators for twelve games in 2003, and because he was under contract, T could not don a Pelicans uniform for that year. Although not able to play for the Pels in 2003, T still availed himself to the needs of the new Pensacola team, splitting his time between the front office and as the hitting instructor.

Beginning with the 2004 season, Nunnari's role with the club started its ascent, as he was one of the best public relations features that owners Quint and Rishy Studer could have hoped for in the community. The homegrown player became the locally trusted face of the team. Nunnari knew Pensacola, and the people of Pensacola knew him. Talmadge took the field again for the Pelicans in 2004 and filled a much-needed position as assistant general manager. Talmadge viewed his responsibilities in the front office extremely seriously, using his sports management degree to its fullest. Public appearances on behalf of the team in area schools and youth groups were an everyday affair for Talmadge.

Nunnari's influence and mentorship among the Pelicans players was easily noted, and the Studers had no reservations about placing more of the day-to-day operations in his hands. In the middle of the 2006 season, the Pelicans were without a GM, and Quint Studer had but to glance across the office to find a more than qualified replacement. Under Nunnari's leadership, Pensacola set attendance records and excelled in fan support along the Emerald Coast. Going into the 2009 season, the Pelicans were now short a field manager, and in true Nunnari style, T took the bull by the horns and split his time between the office and the dugout. Nunnari filled the position as Pensacola's manager through the team's final season in 2010.

As Pensacola progressed toward its rejuvenated status as a professionally affiliated town, Talmadge Nunnari set his focus on further building the mentoring skills he had developed with the Pelicans. In January 2012, the official announcement was given that Nunnari would return to his alma mater and join the coaching staff of Jacksonville University. T's proficiency for bringing out the best in a player's development found a new platform to showcase his abilities.

SPOONEY

Pitcher Derell McCall drafted with the Oakland Athletics in 2000 after throwing for Tate High. McCall's teammate and second baseman Tim Merritt signed with the Mariners during the 2001 draft. Pensacola Junior College hurler Billy Sadler also gained interest from the Mariners in 2001 but did not take their offer, deciding instead to play for Louisiana State College and later accepting a position with San Francisco. Vincent Cerni and Greg Kisch from the University of West Florida both signed with the Chillicothe Paints of the independent Frontier League. Escambia's Warren Hanna drafted into the Cubs organization, and Pine Forest's Cliff Dancy interested the Marlins.

Dancy was traded to the Phillies, and while making his preparations to play for Philadelphia's Batavia Muckdogs, fellow Pine Forest graduate Tim Spooneybarger was heading toward his Major League debut. Tim was a devout Braves fan as he was growing up in the youth leagues of Pensacola. On a family trip to Atlanta when Tim was just a boy, the Spooneybargers dropped into Fulton County Stadium to catch a Braves game. Standing outside the ballpark, Tim told his father what so many young boys contemplate, "Dad, I want to play here one day." Although multitudes of boys muse over the anticipation of playing professional baseball, few ever attain it. Tim Spooneybarger would become one of the few.

Tim's last name presented a problem for the local sporting goods companies servicing the leagues around Pensacola. The Bellview Dixie Youth organization usually contracted uniform and equipment services from Browning's, Dixon Brothers or Penny's Sporting Goods. All had the task of wrapping Tim's thirteen-letter last name onto a boy's slim-size jersey. Those who performed the duty never forgot it and benevolently sighed with compassion for Tim's Major League equipment managers. Former Catholic High pitcher/outfielder Jeff English worked for Penny's Sporting Goods during Tim's younger years. "You try getting 'Spooneybarger' to fit on the back of a t-shirt shoulder to shoulder. It's not easy, and hyphenating it wasn't a realistic option. There's no telling how many shirts we went through before it actually looked right and even," reminisced English.

Spooneybarger underwent shoulder surgery during his senior year at Pine Forest, resulting in Tim pitching in only three games for his final year of high school. The Braves still liked what they saw, understanding that this pitcher with a quirky sense of humor had the attitude and determination to overcome the difficulties. Atlanta selected Spooney in the twenty-ninth round of the June 1998 Amateur Draft, with Tim first enrolling at Okaloosa-Walton Community College in Niceville, Florida. Atlanta officials desired to see the progress of Tim's shoulder surgery and whether or not it was affecting his delivery. Almost every time a scout from the Braves stopped in to see the Pensacola hurler throw in a college game, Tim did not pitch. After a bit of frustration on the part of the scout, "Spooney" took the mound for three innings, which was enough to convince the Braves bird dog. A package contract followed, including a four-year college scholarship.

Tim was sent to the Danville (Virginia) Braves in the Appalachian League, where he posted a 2.22 ERA under manager J.J. Cannon. Whether or not the camaraderie of Cannon and Spooneybarger—both hailing from Pensacola—had much influence on Tim's pitching, he did settle into the Rookie League well enough to capture a 3–0 record and thirty-six strikeouts in relief. The remainder of the 1999 season took Tim over to Class-A Macon, Georgia, where he threw ten innings. At Myrtle Beach in 2000, Tim again had a 3–0 record to go with fifty-seven strikeouts during forty-nine innings of work. His shoulder began troubling him once more; however, the discomfort could not stop his overpowering presence on the mound or his eccentric antics in the clubhouse.

In a *USA Today* interview, Tim Spooneybarger described himself in this way:

> *I dance to a different drummer. My idea of a good time is just being able to talk and laugh with somebody. I can make a joke about most anything. I certainly don't want to offend anyone. I think I do things a bit differently. I'm a different guy. I'm different in a good way, and I'm having as much fun as I can because this is something I have wanted for so long. I'm going to make the best of it.*

Tim comes from a very conservative family, and Spooney's tattooed arms and off-the-cuff remarks don't necessarily reflect his traditional upbringing. The Braves brought Tim up to Double-A Greenville for fifteen games at the beginning of 2001 and then on to Triple-A Richmond. On September 5, 2001, Tim Spooneybarger's childhood dream came true.

The Braves called Tim up to "The Show," giving him the opportunity to play for his favorite team—thus achieving a fan's ultimate fantasy. On his first day with the team, sitting next to his childhood idol John Smoltz, Tim revealed that he was in the sixth grade when he saw John pitch against the Minnesota Twins during the 1991 World Series. Smoltz responded that the information was kind of odd and that it was the first time that had ever happened with a teammate. Spooney threw in four games for Atlanta during 2001, delivering a 2.25 ERA. Manager Bobby Cox believed the twenty-one-year-old could easily have a future in Atlanta.

Cox told reporters that Spooneybarger had more movement on his ball than he had ever seen before and that Tim immediately endeared himself to the Atlanta fans. Being outspoken and innocent all at the same time made Tim likeable—even to those who did not understand him. Back with the club in 2002, Tim pitched in fifty-one innings and struck out thirty-three batters. His 2.63 ERA in middle relief all but assured him a place in the Atlanta bullpen for years to come. Youthful zealousness being what it is, Spooney entered into a heated argument with Atlanta pitching coach Leo Mazzone. The verbal altercation between the two men placed the rookie in a poor light and ultimately contributed to Tim being traded to the Florida Marlins.

While the Marlins may not have been Tim's first choice in clubs, it certainly wasn't a bad place to land. He played the entire 2003 season with the Major League squad, as Florida found itself in postseason games. Winning first the division series and then overcoming the Chicago Cubs for the National League Championship, the Marlins went on to take the World Series title, beating the Yankees four games to two. Tim underwent two Tommy John surgeries in 2004 and 2005, restricting him to limited playing time. After he threw in only four games in 2005 for the Marlins' Jupiter, Florida affiliate, Tim hung up the spikes for a while. The Baltimore Orioles signed Spooney to the Aberdeen Ironbirds in 2008, but after six games, that was it.

Tim Spooneybarger continued his quest to come back to the diamond, and although his shoulder did not return to the form he once knew, his determination and finesse inspired countless numbers of Gulf Coast boys to follow their own dreams of playing in the big leagues. Tim made a decision that many former Pensacola players have made over the decades. That decision was to give back to the community that had given him the opportunity to reach his own aspirations. Spooneybarger became the pitching coach for Washington High School and enlisted as a personal instructor at the Pelicans' training academy.

THE ELDER

The Anaheim Angels selected Catholic High's Anthony Mandel during the 2002 draft. Pensacola Junior College put two forward in the draft with Chris Maher getting the nod from Atlanta and former Pine Forest pitcher Erik Thompson going with Texas. Rodney Story gained interest from Minnesota, while Spencer Grogan received an offer from the San Diego Padres. Grogan chose not to sign with the Padres, heading to college before contracting with the San Francisco Giants in 2004.

Booker T. Washington pitcher David Elder was drafted by the Texas Rangers during the fourth round of the 1997 June Amateur Draft. Elder's first season in the Texas farm system was played with the Rookie Class Pulaski Rangers. In twenty games and thirty-two innings pitched, Dave had fifty-seven strikeouts and boasted a 1.95 ERA in relief. Arm issues kept him off the roster in 1998, but he moved up from Class-A to Double-A in 1999. After gaining his strength back in 2000, he was again posting good numbers by the end of 2001 with the Triple-A Oklahoma Red Hawks. On December 18, 2001, the Rangers traded Elder to the Cleveland Indians for the verbally controversial pitcher John Rocker.

Cleveland put Elder right to work in the minors in 2002, first with Akron, then on to Buffalo through mid-season. Dave put on his first official Major League uniform in the Indians clubhouse for a July 24, 2002 game, dressing out alongside crosstown Pensacola baseball rival Travis Fryman. Dave pitched relief in fifteen games before season's end. But Elder's elbow made him less than effective on the mound and inhibited him from pitching more than two and a third innings in 2003. Elder, facing his old team at The Ballpark in Arlington on May 11, 2003, squared off against Rangers first baseman Rafael Palmeiro. Palmeiro stepped to the plate in search of a career milestone, and Dave surrendered Rafael's five hundredth career home run.

Elder was released by the Indians in October 2003, contracting with Atlanta the following February. Over the next three seasons, Dave Elder signed his name to contracts involving four different clubs. Along with Atlanta, Dave's name graced the front office desks of the New York Yankees, Cincinnati Reds and Kansas City Royals. The Royals officially released Elder midway through 2006, and although still hampered with soreness, Dave was not done yet.

In 2007, Elder signed on with the Somerset Patriots in the independent Atlantic League and later the Laguna Vaqueros in the Mexican League before retiring. Dave Elder's passion for the game outweighed the adversity he faced in his arm. Joining with friend Matt Clark, Elder co-founded Foundation Sports in Lovejoy, Georgia, a hands-on baseball and softball training facility designed to bring the most potential out of players and coaches.

PENSACOLA'S MIRACLE LEAGUE

During a 1997 summer youth baseball practice in Rockdale County, Georgia, coach Eddie Bagwell invited a seven-year-old wheelchair-bound child to join the team. The gesture became the impetus for the creation of the Miracle League, which provides disabled children the opportunity to participate in organized baseball games. The children participating in the Miracle League dress in team uniforms, make on-field plays and round the bases—just as their peers do on traditional diamonds. The Miracle League players are given a specialized playing field to accommodate walkers, wheelchairs and limb braces. After the inaugural season in Georgia, the league quickly grew and gained widespread attention across the nation.

In 2002, the Miracle League of Pensacola was organized by Larry and Donna Thompson, who had experienced the tragic loss of their own child and desired to see other children excel beyond any physical limitation. With great support from community businesses and individuals, funds were raised to break ground for Mitchell Homes Miracle League Park on Nine Mile Road in Pensacola. The Miracle League of Pensacola fills a void left by traditional youth baseball programs and provides athletic opportunities that might not otherwise be attained.

The first full season for the Miracle League of Pensacola took place in 2005 using a playing surface composed of rubber tire crumbs formed into soft and forgivable tiles. Just steps away from the youth fields of the Northeast Pensacola Baseball complex, Miracle League Park projects an all-star presence. The mission statement for Pensacola's Miracle League reflects the ability of the game of baseball to make anyone feel like an instant hero with but one at-bat: "To provide a safe organized baseball league and facilities for Gulf Coast children with mental and/or physical challenges where every player plays, every player hits, every player gets on base, every player scores, and every player wins—every inning."

FARNSWORTH TRAVELS THE GLOBE

Jeff Farnsworth attended Pensacola Catholic High School before pitching for the University of West Florida in 1995. As the June 1996 MLB Amateur Draft rolled around, the Seattle Mariners reined in the right-hander, sending him to their Everett, Washington affiliate. Farnsworth transitioned into a relief position for the Class-A Lancaster, California, Jet Hawks for 1998 and 1999. After a 9–3 record with the New Haven Ravens in 2000, Jeff made the starting rotation on the San Antonio Missions pitching staff in 2001. He delivered eleven wins and ten losses amidst 113 strikeouts in twenty-seven games.

The Detroit Tigers acquired Farnsworth on December 13, 2001, in the Rule 5 Draft and lost no time in getting their new pitcher into the bullpen. Jeff reported early for spring training with the Tigers pitchers and catchers at their facility in Lakeland, Florida. On April 3, 2002, Farnsworth began his single-season career in the Major Leagues. In the forty-four appearances Jeff threw in relief, he posted a 5.79 ERA and registered a 2-3 record in seventy innings of work. During the off-season, Farnsworth worked on developing himself in Winter League ball, where he was a member of the All-Star team. Jeff spent 2003 with the Tigers' Eastern League club, the Erie SeaWolves, and was then granted free agency in October.

Over the course of five seasons, Jeff took the mound as a farmhand for the Brewers, White Sox, Red Sox and three independents. During the qualifying games for the 2008 Olympics, Jeff went 1–0 with only a single run allowed in four relief situations as a member of Team USA. Farnsworth worked in the Venezuelan Winter League, and in 2009, he signed with Nettuno, Italy, of the Italian Baseball League. In the Final Four of the European Cup, Jeff struck out fourteen and allowed only five hits in a 1–0 victory over Bologna. For his efforts, Farnsworth won Most Valuable Player for the series.

THE PELICANS FLY IN

The independent All-American Association baseball league closed up shop after only one season of activity. Of the six teams that comprised the defunct 2001 league, Baton Rouge and Montgomery (Alabama) joined the newly reformed Southeastern League for the 2002 season. Taking the name of the former Deep South Class-B circuit, the league harkened back to its historical foundations. Pensacola joined the new independent Southeastern League along with Montgomery, Baton Rouge, Ozark and Selma (Alabama) and Americus (Georgia).

The 2002 Pensacola Pelicans began their inaugural season in June playing at Pensacola Junior College's Pirate Field. As the Pelicans did not have a physical office during the first months of existence, the Pensacola Sports Association (PSA) stepped in from its downtown headquarters to help. PSA volunteers assisted in selling tickets, working concessions, interacting with fans, providing Pelicans merchandise and extending hospitality in the stands.

Kenny Huth became the Pelicans' first field manager, overseeing Pensacola's only professional team since the 1962 Senators. Huth, a former Minor Leaguer, had worked as a manager and coach in the Tigers and Red Sox organizations and had been a scout for the Tampa Bay Devil Rays. Kenny's managerial oversight for the Pelicans was reminiscent of his days as a developmental instructor for the Angels in their Queensland, Australia international camp. Pensacola's players in 2002 consisted of mostly individuals with little Minor League or college experience. Only two players on Pensacola's first-year roster had known the feel of Major League play. First baseman/outfielder Talmadge Nunnari and pitcher Steve Rain were considered veterans.

Midway through the season, the Ozark and Americus franchises folded, and the Pensacola Pelicans were bought out by Quint Studer. Studer, a native of Illinois, grew up following baseball on Chicago's South Side. Quint had overcome the adversities of partial deafness and a slight speech impediment and had become a noted leader in hospital management and a motivational trainer for business excellence. Quint's love of the game birthed a dream of team ownership. An earlier move to the Gulf Coast from Chicago gave him the perfect backdrop in which to achieve his vision. Little did anyone imagine at the time—including Quint—just how large his dream would grow. Studer was immediately rewarded for his team acquisition, as the Pelicans delivered the league championship.

Along with the change in ownership also came a new Pelicans field manager. Pete Della Ratta, a resident of Gulf Breeze, became the Pelicans' player/manager midway through the season. Della Ratta had pitched through the Oakland farm system after graduating from Gulf Breeze High School. He returned to the Gulf Coast after seven seasons in the minors. Della Ratta spent time with the Florida Marlins after leaving the Pelicans but returned as Pensacola's pitching coach in 2007.

The Pelicans' new owner understood the challenges of overcoming adversity and was well positioned for the task of reinstituting professional-level baseball in Pensacola. Quint Studer's hearing difficulty caused him to struggle in school, so he attempted entry into the military as an alternative for further education. Although the Vietnam War was in full swing at the time and the military was signing most all who were of age for service, Studer was turned away due to his disability.

Assuming that it was a waste of time, Studer took a shot in the dark and attempted the entrance exam for the University of Wisconsin. He passed. College study came with its own set of difficulties, and Quint's initial grades reflected it. Above the wrinkles of life, Studer was determined to move forward in bettering himself. He graduated with a bachelor's degree in special education. In applying his degree, Studer took a position at a Janesville, Wisconsin high school that prepared the mentally challenged for the outside workforce.

Over the course of the next few years, Studer's personal obstacles took him through addiction, debt and depression and left him without a vision for his future. Quint marks Christmas Day 1982 as the turning point in his life, when he decided to step out of mediocrity and follow the passion inside of him. His personal recovery from addiction took him directly into the path of helping others. Studer became a community relations manager for a substance abuse hospital, and his dedicated and developmental work gained the attention of Chicago's Mercy Hospital executives. Studer joined Mercy's business development team at their request and quickly climbed to a leadership position in the organization.

After six years at Mercy Hospital, Quint took on an overwhelming challenge in helping to turn around Chicago's Holy Cross Hospital from certain demise. In a little over a year, the facility was turning a profit, and Studer was being sought after as a consultant on business management. Pensacola's Baptist Health Care invited Studer to the City of Five Flags, and in just under six months, he was named president of Baptist Hospital. Studer made notable advancements for Baptist Hospital and was listed among the top one hundred most powerful individuals in modern healthcare. In 2000, Quint stepped out on his own to form the Studer Group, a private healthcare consulting firm. In 2002, Studer furthered his vision of personal accomplishment by acquiring the Pensacola Pelicans and pointed the organization toward the same bright horizon that he enjoyed in hospital management.

COLLEGIATE EXCELLENCE:
JIM SPOONER AND BILL HAMILTON

Pitcher D'Antonio Warren from Woodham High School was selected by the Kansas City Royals in the thirty-first round of the June 2003 Amateur Draft. University of West Florida right-hander Jeremy Noegal attracted interest from Toronto's regional scout, and outfielder Josey Shannon signed with Baton Rouge in the independent Southeastern League. Shannon later fielded for the Pelicans in 2004. From Pensacola Junior College, Minnesota selected catcher Nicholas Anderson, while Atlanta signed Devin Anderson, sending him to the Gulf Coast League Braves in Orlando.

Head baseball coaches Bill Hamilton from Pensacola Junior College and Jim Spooner from the University of West Florida had become regional legends over the course of their tenures. Each was known for turning out not only quality players but also for truly developing the skill sets that were needed in professional baseball.

Bill Hamilton took the position of head baseball coach for Pensacola Junior College in 1990 after four years as an assistant coach in Marianna, Florida, and Columbus, Georgia. Hamilton grew up in Marianna and became the assistant coach at Chipola Junior College prior to joining the coaching staff at Columbus State College. At Columbus, Hamilton helped lead the team to two College World Series appearances. As PJC's head baseball coach, Bill Hamilton was an almost immediate Pensacola favorite.

In 1999, Bill coached his team to an incredible 35–14 season, breaking numerous school records and sending five PJC players to the ranks of professional baseball. During the 2000 season, Hamilton took on a dual role as head baseball coach and athletic director for the college, and under Hamilton, the PJC Pirates took the state title and finished sixth in the national tournament. By 2008, Hamilton's Pirates had earned the number-one position in the national rankings for junior colleges.

Bill was nearing a personal career milestone as the 2010 season began, and by April, he had attained it. Bill Hamilton earned seven hundred wins as a college coach, further ensuring his induction into the National Junior College Athletic Hall of Fame. Hamilton retired as PJC's head baseball coach at the end of his historic 2010 season and immediately signed on as the school's full-time athletic director. Beyond impressive player development and team leadership, Bill scouted professionally for the Cleveland Indians, Texas Rangers and Arizona Diamondbacks.

Jim Spooner became the head baseball coach for the University of West Florida just prior to the 1983 season. Spooner had coached at Edison Community College in his hometown of Fort Meyers, Florida, before coming to UWF. Jim's playing career had also begun at Edison before continuing at Florida State University under the coaching direction of former Major Leaguer Fred Hatfield. As head coach for UWF, Spooner became only the third man to hold that position during the history of the school's baseball program.

Spooner had the ability to see a player's inner potential beyond any outward limitations. Players who worked under Jim's tutelage often commented on how Coach Spooner brought more strength and talent out of them than they ever knew they personally possessed. Twenty UWF players from Spooner's twenty-three seasons as head coach went on to sign professional contracts, and Jim was twice named the National Association of Intercollegiate Athletics District 27 Coach of the Year. Spooner's Argonauts won three Southern States titles and two Gulf South Conference East Division championships. And in 1989, Jim managed the Argos to a sixth-place finish in the NAIA World Series. The *Collegiate Baseball Newspaper* poll ranked UWF's baseball team as #19 in 2003 and #12 in 2005. Jim announced his retirement from UWF in 2005 and was inducted into the Pensacola Sports Association Hall of Fame the very next year.

In 1995, Spooner, along with partner Wayne Stephenson, opened the Jim Spooner Baseball School in Pensacola. After retirement from the university, Jim joined the Baseball Factory as assistant personnel recruiting director for underclass exclusive players. Just after joining the baseball development company, Jim Spooner was diagnosed with acute myelogenous leukemia in September 2007. Although the disease kept Jim from actively working at the game he so loved, he still continued to watch university squad practices and encourage players. On August 22, 2008, the University of West Florida renamed the college field in honor of the former coach, but Spooner was unable to attend the dedication due to the advanced state of his illness.

Jim Spooner died on September 13, 2008, at age sixty-two. The University of West Florida forever enshrined Jim in school legacy during its 2008–09 Hall of Fame induction ceremony. Bill Hamilton says that there are few men in college baseball who have been as revered as Jim Spooner. "I have never respected any coach more than I did Jim," says Hamilton.

CARBO

In order to meet the league requirements for independent Minor League play, the ballpark at the University of West Florida underwent renovations beginning in May 2003. The reason for the renovation was that Quint Studer intended to move the Pelicans to the university's field, as they were quickly outgrowing the facilities afforded by PJC. Studer contributed $500,000 to the project, which included added lawn seating to accommodate an additional five hundred spectators, a premium seating section, a new public address system, a new backstop and accessible viewing areas for the physically disabled. The upgrades certainly benefited the university team, although they had to share a Pelicans-branded environment.

The Pelicans won their 2003 season opener against the Houma (Louisiana) Hawks. On June 13, 2003, the Selma Cloverleafs came into town to face the Pelicans during their last season at PJC. On Selma's roster was a thirty-four-year-old first baseman by the name of John Henry Williams. John Henry was the son of legendary baseball great Ted Williams, and while the younger Williams had a head for business, he did not necessarily have his father's eye at the plate. He had made seven unfruitful plate appearances for the Gulf Coast League Red Sox in his short time with the team during the prior season. In the top of the ninth inning, the Cloverleafs sent Williams to bat, and he hoped to execute his first professional hit. Taking a fastball served up by the Pelicans pitcher, John Henry dropped a soft pop-up into short left field just behind shortstop Heath Kelly. A few months after experiencing the thrill that his father had enjoyed as hitter, John Henry Williams died of acute myelogenous leukemia. Midway through the Pelicans' season, Heath Kelly signed a contract with the Tampa Bay Devil Rays.

Pensacola welcomed Bernie Carbo as its field manager in 2003. Studer gave Carbo the ability to build his own coaching staff, and Bernie's first move was securing the services of Pedro Borbon as the Pelicans pitching coach. Bernie knew Pedro from their time together with the Reds. Bernie states that Borbon was an effective pitching coach for the Pelicans but had the reputation of being a bit quirky. Carbo gives an example of Borbon sitting in the dugout during the last game of a home stand: "We were in the top of the ninth and down by a couple of runs. I asked Pedro what he thought we should do about our pitcher. Pedro says, 'I'll get a righty and a lefty warming up. Let's leave this guy in for another inning or so.' So I say, 'Man, we are in the ninth inning—get your head in the game!'"

During the first-ever Major League Baseball Free Agent Amateur Draft, seventeen-year-old Carbo was the first-round draft pick for the Cincinnati Reds, ahead of Johnny Bench. Predominantly an outfielder, Carbo started with the Reds in what would be later viewed as the building years of Cincinnati's "Big Red Machine."

In 1970, Bernie came under the tutelage of Reds manager George "Sparky" Anderson, who platooned Carbo with Hal McRae in left field. Bernie's first Major League hit happened at Cincinnati's Crosley Field. Carbo belted a far-reaching home run off Expos pitcher Joe Sparma. Bernie claims that his hit became the longest home run in baseball history: "I hit it out of the park onto Route I-75. It landed in a truck and they found it in Florida 1,300 miles away."

Beyond Anderson, Carbo enjoyed the dedication of Cincinnati legend Joe Nuxhall. "One of the highlights of coming up with the Reds was getting to take batting practice from Nuxie. It was an honor just to be on the field with that guy," reflects Carbo. In 1970, Bernie batted .310, scored an on-base percentage of .454, drove in sixty-three runs and belted twenty-one home runs. *The Sporting News* named Carbo Rookie of the Year, and he came in second for the Baseball Writers' Association ballot for the same. The Reds won the 1970 National League pennant but lost to the Baltimore Orioles in the World Series.

The Reds traded Carbo to St. Louis on May 19, 1972, for first baseman/outfielder Joe Hague, and Bernie's batting average with the Cardinals topped out at .286 in 1973 with eight home runs. St. Louis sent Carbo to Boston at the end of the 1973 season, where he found new friends and new fans with the Red Sox. Boston platooned Carbo in all three outfield positions, as well as using him as a designated hitter. His bat did not stand out as an offensive masterpiece for Boston in 1974, although Bernie's fielding ability passed most scrutiny. By 1975, Carbo had nestled into the Red Sox culture, and in the sixth game of the '75 World Series, Bernie Carbo became a hero in the hearts of the Red Sox Nation.

Boston reached the Fall Classic by sweeping the Athletics in the American League Championship Series, and the Red Sox then faced Carbo's old team, the Cincinnati Reds, for the world title. As Game 6 began, Boston was looking at sudden death, down two games to three for the series. Going into the bottom of the eighth inning in certain elimination, Boston trailed 6–3. With Boston's Fred Lynn on second and Rico Petrocelli on first, Carbo took an ugly swing on a Rawly Eastwick fastball and connected to send it over the center field wall.

The game stayed tied until the bottom of the twelfth inning, when Red Sox catcher Carlton Fisk hit one of the most memorable home runs in World Series history—a home run that would have not been possible without Carbo's game-tying homer in the eighth. The Red Sox could not stay alive in Game 7 and lost the series to the Reds. But Carbo's home run in Game 6 became legendary, and it was later honored at the 2004 Boston Red Sox Hall of Fame induction ceremony as one of the most unforgettable moments in Red Sox history.

Bernie says that his three seasons with Pensacola were very enjoyable. "I loved the Pensacola fans," he reminisces. "They always got into my on-field performance of the 'YMCA' on the third base line. The Channel 3 sportscasters were really good to me, and Quint Studer was great to work with. I thought very strongly about moving to Pensacola permanently—just because of the hospitality I felt here." Bernie Carbo left the Pelicans after

Quint Studer brought in veteran Major Leaguer Bernie Carbo (right) to manage the Pelicans in 2003. Studer gave Bernie a lot of flexibility in running the team. In return, Bernie shaped the Pelicans and endeared himself to the Pensacola fans. "I really loved being in Pensacola," says Bernie. "Everyone was so warm and friendly—they just took me right in as family." Bernie Carbo, known for his on- and off-the-field personality, never disappointed the Pelican faithful during his three seasons with the club. *Courtesy of the Pensacola Pelicans (Amarillo Sox).*

the 2005 season to pursue ministry full-time, offering youth baseball clinics and personal instruction based on his baseball experience and faith. Carbo holds an annual fantasy baseball camp in February at Hank Aaron Stadium in Mobile, Alabama.

Carbo and the Pelicans topped the league as the 2003 regular season champions. After the victorious year, Pensacola swept Macon during the playoffs but lost the championship to the Baton Rouge Riverbats.

THE PELICANS CHANGE LEAGUES

Listed as an "expert" in the all-time hit-by-pitch roster, Escambia High's Cory Middleton reached first base by "taking one for the team" on an average of about one in every forty pitches thrown to him. Cory signed with Detroit in 2004, achieving his unique title over the course of his next five seasons in the minors. Fellow Escambian Rhett James enrolled at Pensacola Junior College to play under Bill Hamilton and then headed on to Florida State University before being drafted by the Marlins in 2004. Tate graduate Bo Brown also played for Hamilton at PJC and signed as an undrafted free agent that same season. Brown later played for the Pensacola Pelicans in 2006.

The Twins' scout picked right-hander Patrick Bryant out of Catholic High, while the Blue Jays and the White Sox selected two additional players produced by the Catholic coaches. Both Catholic graduates, Tim Land with the Blue Jays and Logan Williamson with the White Sox, also had PJC's baseball program in common prior to their 2004 draft selections. Williamson later pitched for the Pelicans in 2007. Right-handed pitcher Chad Blackwell drafted under the Royals organization and threw for Coach Hamilton at PJC and for the University of South Carolina before filling his contract with Kansas City. University of West Florida catcher Matt Bacon inked with the Mets as an undrafted free agent in the 2004 draft, while UWF infielder Patrick Cottrell got the call from the Devil Rays. Hunter Vick played middle infield for the university and did not have to go far after his 2004 contract was signed. Vick drafted with the Pensacola Pelicans just as the team was moving its home field operations to UWF.

Former Pelicans assistant general manager and UWF player Jason Libbert recalls the season Pensacola began its shared relationship on the Argonauts field:

It was my senior year. We left for the conference tournament knowing they were going to come in and do some renovations. When we got back, fences were down, trees were down and concrete and new bleachers were going up. It was neat seeing it transform to a more fan-friendly ballpark. Before, it had this 8-foot or 10-foot-high fence all down the line, and [it] felt like we were in a cage. I was surprised how much the lower fences opened it up. I think I went to work for the Pelicans that next day. We had a preseason party at the park where fans could walk around the construction and see where their seats were going to be. So I went from playing on the field at UWF to giving tours in less than a week. I always joke that I helped build the park. I did put together all the picnic tables that are still out there. I think my back still hurts from that.

The Southeastern League began to implode at the end of the 2003 season. Macon returned its franchise to the league due to a disastrous financial year; the Houma Hawks developed legal issues with their parish, creating an inability for the Hawks to play their home games at their normal location; and Quint Studer removed Pensacola from the mix, seeing the writing on the wall for certain organizational failure. Studer said that Pensacola should be involved in a league that had proven stability and longevity. Quint purchased the Ozark-Springfield Mountain Ducks of the independent Central League, relocating them to the Gulf Coast and placing the Pelicans moniker on his new acquisition.

The independent Central Baseball League (CBL) held fast to its history and standards as the former Texas-Louisiana League, which began in 1994. Pensacola joined seven other cities to round out the gritty league's new 2004 circuit. The Coastal Bend Aviators, San Angelo Colts, El Paso Diablos, Edinburg Roadrunners, Fort Worth Cats, Shreveport Sports and Jackson Senators became the Pelicans' fresh opponents. Pensacola started its 2004 season a bit on the rough side but recovered with a nineteen-game winning streak. The Pelicans finished in second place for the first half of the year and then won the CBL East Division Second-Half Championship. Pensacola was eliminated in the first round of the postseason playoffs by the Shreveport Sports but not before fans of the league had begun to take notice of the new formidable rivals.

During the course of the Pelicans inaugural representation in the CBL, four Pensacola players were scouted and purchased by Major League organizations. Five Pelicans had been named either CBL Pitcher or Batter of the Week, and centerfielder Rafael Alvarez was named the 2004 CBL Player of the Year. Alvarez was presented with his award by league commissioner Miles Wolff on August 27 during a Pelicans home stand.

Along with the Pelicans, baseball had once again taken its place as a citywide focal point in Pensacola. The team was an anchor for the community to rally around, and other local venues reaped the rewards of the energy created by Studer's club. In 2004, Pensacola was chosen as the site for the Homeschool World Series Association's annual tournament. The HWSA continued to host the yearly event in Pensacola through 2009, diverting only in 2005 due to field damage by Hurricane Ivan.

On January 14, 2004, local baseball legend Don Sutton was honored with an induction into the Pensacola Sports Association's Wall of Fame, featured in a display at the Pensacola Regional Airport. On May 11, 2004, the PJC Pirates won the Florida Community College Activities Association State Championship in Kissimmee. Bill Hamilton's Pirates took a 2–1 victory over Central Florida Community College for the pennant.

JOHN WEBB

John Floyd Webb Jr. became the second player born in Pensacola to debut in Major League Baseball during the 2004 regular season. Webb's family was intensely active within the Pensacola community, with John and his brother James playing youth baseball and his twin sister Janet developing into an accomplished gymnast. Webb's parents, John Sr. and Jody, were involved with their children and served faithfully in their local church. The Webb boys came to love the diamond through their father's passion for the game. John Sr., a much-loved and venerated music educator in the Escambia County school system, played Senior League baseball and coached his boys in the finer points of the sport.

Right-handed pitcher John Jr. graduated from Pensacola High School and began building the tools required for a professional bullpen position. Manatee Community College in Sarasota was the perfect arena for Webb to experience more rigorous competition than he had known at Pensacola High. John spent two seasons at Manatee and was selected by the Chicago Cubs in the nineteenth round of the 1999 Major League Baseball Amateur Draft. Scout Harry Suskil signed Webb for Chicago during the June draft, with John immediately reporting to the Cubs' Arizona Rookie League affiliate in Mesa. Webb threw in eighteen games for Mesa before he was transitioned to the Cubs Class-A club in Eugene, Oregon, for two games. In his entry year into Minor League pitching, John posted a 3.19 ERA in relief.

The next three years would be Webb's building seasons, as the Cubs routed the young righty through their farm system and placed him on the roster of six different teams. His best year in Chicago's Minor Leagues was with the 2000 Lansing Lugnuts of the Class-A Midwest League, where Webb's ERA was recorded at 2.47 in twenty-one mound appearances. In February 2004, the Tampa Bay Devil Rays selected John off waivers from the Cubs, sending him first to Double-A Montgomery, Alabama, and then to the Triple-A Durham Bulls.

Tampa Bay brought Webb up as a reliever for the Devil Rays pitching staff on August 2, 2004, with Webb getting nine innings of work prior to the end of the season. The following year, Webb put in an additional few innings for the Devil Rays and finished out the regular season in Durham. Tampa Bay granted John free agency on October 3, 2005, and twenty-five days later, he signed with the Cardinals. The 2006 Triple-A Memphis Redbirds used Webb in a more dominant role than he had previously known in the minors, and a rejuvenated Major League career may have presented itself with St. Louis had it not been for an oblique injury. St. Louis granted John free agency in October.

One month after his release from St. Louis, the Chicago Cubs picked John up again for another go. His old club had not forgotten about its original assay of Webb's abilities, trusting that his injury was mended for service. Triple-A Iowa sent John to the mound thirty-one times in 2007, but his strength was just not up to where the Cubs needed him to be. John gave Chicago all that he had, and in return the Cubs gave his arm as much faith as possible, even extending an invitation and pitching time during the parent club's spring training exercises. John Webb returned to Pensacola in 2008, joining the Pelicans to the delight of the home crowd.

John's arm injury was not the only personal trauma he dealt with while pitching professionally. In December 2001, much to the shock of Webb's family and the Pensacola community at large, John's father passed away due to a heart attack. John's brother James had been a cancer survivor during his early teenage years but eventually succumbed to the disease at the age of seventeen. Originally begun as a response to cover his brother's mounting medical expenses, the Pensacola-based John Webb Winter Golf Tournament grew into an organization benefiting Sacred Heart Hospital's Child Life program. Founded in 2002, the John Webb Foundation hosts an annual golf tournament that helps raise funds and awareness for the needs of children facing life-threatening illnesses. John has continued feeding his love for the game after retirement by coaching high school baseball in Arizona.

A NEW DIAMOND ON THE BAYFRONT

"If you believe in the impossible, the incredible can come true," touted Pensacola's *Independent News* in its November 10, 2005 edition. The quote came from the film adaptation of W.P. Kinsella's magic realist baseball novel *Shoeless Joe*, better known for its screen name, *Field of Dreams*. *Independent News* writer Duwayne Escobedo amusingly chose one of the film's lesser-verbalized script lines to represent Quint Studer's vision for a waterfront stadium in downtown Pensacola. Studer had already proven that if a team was given a place to play in southern Escambia County that the community would turn out in support.

Earlier in the year, design mock-ups were presented for the Vince Whibbs Sr. Community Maritime Park. The proposed project surrounded a 3,500-seat multi-use baseball stadium and included an exterior maritime history museum, shopping venues, restaurants and classrooms for use by the University of West Florida. The plans for the ball field were centered on its multipurpose use for hosting concerts and other sporting events. Populous, the architectural group chosen to design Pensacola's stadium, was the firm responsible for the New York Yankees new park that opened in 2009.

Pensacola citizens became divided over the Maritime Park project, listing reasons for and against ranging from sentimental emotion to financial statistics. Naysayers contended that the private-public cost sharing would place undue burden on the city and would leave an unused albatross on the Pensacola Bay shoreline if the baseball "fad" were to wane. The park's proposed location was a 27.5-acre tract of land known locally as the Trillium property. The prime real estate, which had once been a dumping area for the ballast material deposited from the holds of tall ships sailing into Pensacola Bay, had become overgrown, impassable and the bedroom of numerous homeless transients. Supporters of the project cited Minor League park and city development success stories from Montgomery, Alabama; Charleston, South Carolina; Dayton, Ohio; and Winnipeg, Manitoba, Canada. The Dayton Dragons had experienced similar opposition in the development of Fifth Third Field in an urban blight area of their city. As a testimony to what a professional baseball team can bring to the economical development of its host town, the Class-A Dragons set Minor League records in attendance by selling out every game for eleven straight seasons.

Community leaders Mike Wiggins and Mort O'Sullivan praised Studer for his plan in a hopes of reviving downtown Pensacola with a new breed of tourists and a place for citizens to gather in a collective identity—just as they did watching the Pilots, Fliers, Dons and Senators. Pensacola native Bob Bishop reminisced about sitting in the stands at Admiral Mason Park:

> *We were right there on the water. You got to be with all of your friends, watching your team, eating a hotdog underneath the open sky. I got to see a lot of great players come through here. It was like a slice of heaven. The day's worries just dropped off, and you felt like Pensacola was the center of the world. I sure wish we had that again.*

Regardless of the banter in the newspapers and town meetings focused on the new park proposal, the Pelicans were settling into their new digs at the university. Bernie Carbo was again at the helm as their field manager, amusing the crowd as much as directing the team. "I liked to work the fans as the 'Man in the Stands' like old Bill Veeck used to do," says Carbo. "I would go up and sit with folks before the game and sometimes even between innings. They loved it, and it got everybody involved." In what would be the last year of organization for the Central Baseball League, the Pels enjoyed another successful season both in CBL standings and fan attendance.

The Pelicans ended their 2005 season with the second-best record in the CBL and faced the Fort Worth Cats in the championship. Fort Worth upset the Pelicans in a best-of-five series. The contest went down to the wire, with the Cats taking three games over Pensacola's two. Gate receipts for the Pelicans rose almost 65 percent from the previous year, and the Pelicans faithful snapped up t-shirts, caps, foam fingers and anything with the bird-at-bat logo they could find. Quint Studer's wife, Rishy, had been instrumental in providing Pelican merchandise to a demanding market. As with any Minor League operation, it is oftentimes "all hands on deck" to make the machine operate to its potential. Rishy Studer opened her garage as a t-shirt production facility, screen printing "Pelican Wear" by hand.

Pensacola first baseman Mario Valdez played for the Chicago White Sox in 1997 and the Oakland Athletics in 2000 and 2001. At the beginning of the 2005 season, Valdez left Pensacola to join the Mexican League to play for Mexico City. Pitcher Edwar Ramirez signed a professional contract with the Angels organization mid-season and later threw for the Yankees and Athletics. At the end of the year, the CBL ceased operation. Pensacola, Fort Worth, Shreveport, Coastal Bend and El Paso joined Sioux City, Sioux Falls, St. Paul and Lincoln from the Northern League to form the American Association, a new mega independent league organization. The St. Joseph Blacksnakes also came on board for an even ten-team league.

The 2005 Amateur Draft dipped into Pensacola Junior College once again, drawing right-handed pitchers William Jostock to the Mets and Clayton Caulfield to the Braves. Darren Byrd, another righty from Pine Forest High School, took a bid from the Phillies. Various independent league scouts found Pensacola a profitable resource and monitored local high schools for credible prospects. The Frontier League, with its headquarters based in the Midwest, drafted first baseman Donnie Burkhalter out of Pensacola High School. As the 2005 Pensacola baseball season came to a close, Tate High School won the state championship for the seventh time since 1962.

PENSACOLA—WHERE EVERYONE PLAYS

The most current incarnation of the American Association began its foundational roots in October 2005, when it was dubbed the American Association of Independent Professional Baseball. The revered American Association name boasts a history dating back to 1882. As a professional organization, it fielded such teams as the Cincinnati Red Stockings, New York Metropolitans and Brooklyn Bridegrooms. The twenty-first-century embodiment linked itself to no Major League club and functioned as an independent organization in cities not served by Major or Minor League franchises.

The American Association playing level is often referenced as somewhere between Class-A and Double-A, and its players are not generally scouted by Major League teams in any large degree. However, the independent American Association provides a chance for many players to prove their value and often provides an opportunity to make a return to affiliated ball or acquire a first-time run at the pros. While independent baseball is not categorized as developmental in regard to the careers of its players, it is extremely grand entertainment for baseball fans. Additional benefits include a rallying point for the community, a place for added jobs, an advertising opportunity for merchants and a sense of pride for the local fan.

The Pelicans became a great fit for the newest embodiment of the American Association. Team ownership throughout the league included New York Yankees minority owner Marvin Goldklang, comedian Bill Murray, singer Jimmy Buffett and Mike Veeck, son of legendary baseball owner and entrepreneur Bill Veeck. Mike Veeck's "Fun is Good" business model personified the approach to the league's mentality for day-to-day operations. Pensacola, taking their lead from Veeck, advertised that a fan's experience at a Pelicans game was one "Where Everyone Plays." Every fan, every day, was a part of the Pelican family, and if anyone doubted that statement, they had but to stay a little longer after the end of any game. Quint Studer instituted early on in the life of the club that every player, coach and front office executive would be on the field to receive fans, encourage support, sign autographs and pose for pictures. Budding T-ballers in Pensacola knew that they could speak with the players and get a tip or two on any given game night.

Fan participation rose drastically again in 2006, with an average attendance calculated at over 1,600 per game, proving once more that Pensacola would support the game of baseball consistently. On July 4, 2006, 3,326 participants joined their city team to watch the game and stay for the fireworks display afterward. The first-ever "Pack the Track Night" rolled out in 2006, allowing fans to sit on the warning track during the game. Over 4,200 Pensacola faithful surrounded their team for the event. Additionally, watching Pelicans games was no longer limited to those coming through the gates of the university's field, as the historic first televised professional Pensacola baseball game aired in July.

In the midst of a yearly record attendance of almost eighty thousand fans, the Pelicans experienced their first losing season since their inception. But Pensacola players and coaches made a stir among their affiliated counterparts, as four Pelican roster players and two coaches signed contracts with Major League organizations during the course of the year. Pitcher Gerardo Casadiego went to the Yankees along with shortstop Carlos Mendoza, while pitchers Tony Pierce and Clint Sodowski signed with the Braves. Sodowski had spent five seasons in the majors earlier in his career. Coach Craig Bjornson took a position with the Mariners and Coach George Hernandez with the Marlins. Former Pelican Joe Espada also became a coach in the Florida Marlins organization.

As a throwback to the Dodgers' training facility at Ellyson Field, Pensacola became a haven for baseball instruction in 2006. Bernie Carbo launched his fantasy camp in May at UWF, featuring instructional and recreational play alongside former Major Leaguers. Former Detroit Tiger and Pensacola transplant Jake Wood held free clinics for inner-city youth through the Boys and Girls Club. The Pelicans offered a fall instructional league to area high school players in September and October and introduced a winter program through the Pelicans Training Academy.

Pensacola Junior College contributed five men to MLB selections in June. Jared Grace opted for further education and college-level play at Florida A&M after being tapped by the Royals, while teammate Nicholas Francis took Kansas City's offer. Dwight Delgado became an independent for the Sioux Falls Canaries, D'Marcus Ingram drafted with the Cardinals and pitcher Kevin Thompson enlisted with the Diamondbacks. UWF's Todd Androsko also became an independent with the Pensacola Pelicans. Tate High graduates Ian Paxton and Brandon Brown gained the interest of Tampa Bay, with Paxton accepting and Brown electing for college play. During the draft, the Diamondbacks included Catholic High infielder Clayton Conner on their list of new recruits.

James Kash Beauchamp was hired as the Pelicans field manager in 2006, just one season after leaving his position as hitting coach with the all-Japanese Samurai Bears of the Golden Baseball League. Beauchamp played twelve seasons in the minors before becoming a venerated coach and manager among both affiliated and independent leagues. Kash grew up in the game as the son of Major League first baseman and outfielder Jim Beauchamp. The Atlanta Braves enlisted the elder Beauchamp as their bench coach from 1991 to 1998, following a decade and a half of Minor League managing experience. Kash mirrored his father's passion and intensity for the game.

Jason Libbert remembers Kash being an "all business" but fan-appreciated manager for the Pelicans. "He was very passionate about the game and coaching," Libbert recalls. "Sometimes his 'passion' could get the best of him during a game, and he would have a 'conversation' with the umpires. It really fired up the players and fans. Fans loved to watch him." While managing the Wichita Wingnuts in 2008, Beauchamp gave a prime example of one of his "conversations" with umpires. Kash took grand issue with a call made by one of the officials, which was followed by Beauchamp removing his shoe and attempting to make the umpire smell it in order to demonstrate that the call "stunk." The action was rewarded with a four-game suspension for Beauchamp and an overnight media sensation on television sports highlights and viral internet feeds.

Beyond the sometimes on-the-field outspokenness, Kash Beauchamp's personality and knowledge of baseball has continued to endear him to followers of the game. Fox Sports Radio hired Kash as their co-host for *The*

Drive in their Columbus, Georgia market. While listeners enjoy the insights and anecdotes of Beauchamp during their daily commute, players working toward their careers in the sport receive one-on-one instruction from Kash through the Chattahoochee Valley Baseball Academy.

SADLER BUILDS ON A LEGACY

William Henry Sadler IV was initiated into the game through the Bill Bond League. As a senior at Pensacola's Catholic High School in 2000, the right-handed pitcher also played shortstop for his squad. His senior year batting average reached .452, with eight home runs and forty-one runs batted in. From the mound, he collected a 4–1 record with three complete-game shutouts and was named Florida Class 3A 2000 Player of the Year. He was chosen by the Mariners during the 2000 and 2001 summer drafts but opted for college instead. Signing with Pensacola Junior College in 2001, Sadler threw a complete game no-hitter against Lyon College, collecting fourteen strikeouts for his effort. Billy hit twelve home runs for PJC in 2002, and his ERA stood at 3.68.

Louisiana State University was the next rung on Sadler's career ladder. Billy took part in the 2003 College World Series against Cal State Fullerton and the University of South Carolina, where he again gained the attention of Major League scouts. He was selected by the San Francisco Giants in the sixth round of the 2003 Amateur Draft and signed his contract with the Giants on June 28 under the guidance of San Francisco scout Tom Korenek.

From mid-2003 through September 2006, Billy threw with four San Francisco Minor League affiliates. The Hagerstown (Maryland) Suns became his first call of duty, as he made twelve appearances out of the bullpen and earned one save. Sadler pitched for San Jose of the California League for the first half of 2004 and the Norwich (Connecticut) Navigators for the second. He earned three saves in 2004, and his combined ERA was 2.90.

Sadler stayed with Norwich through the entire 2005 season, collecting a 6–5 record. The Connecticut team went through a name change in 2006 and became the Defenders. The new name was fitting for Sadler, as he defended his position and a 2.56 ERA. The Giants farm system moved him along to Triple-A Fresno and then onto the Giants roster under manager Felipe Alou. During his debut for San Francisco, Sadler allowed three runs in four innings of work, striking out six batters.

The Giants returned Billy to the farm in 2007, giving him the opportunity to further develop his skills. In 2008, his pitching duties were split between the Fresno Grizzlies and the Giants parent club. Sadler tossed in twenty-two games for Fresno, and he was activated for thirty-three games with the Giants, clearing an ERA of 4.06 and racking up forty-two strikeouts. During the 2009 spring training exercises, Billy split a fingernail on his pitching hand in a game against the Oakland Athletics, cutting short his time on the mound. Sadler pitched in just one regular season game for the Giants before the front office designated him for assignment to Fresno to make room on the roster for infielder Freddy Sanchez.

The reassignment to Fresno came at the end of July, with Sadler making the decision not to take the outright assignment. San Francisco optioned for his release. As a free agent, Sadler signed with the Houston Astros on August 18, 2009, and participated in nineteen games in the farm system before being called up to the Major League club at the beginning of September. After just a single game for Houston, Billy was placed on the sixty-day disabled list with right shoulder scapular dyskinesis. Sometimes referred to as "SICK scapula," Billy's condition was caused by the abnormal movement of his shoulder blade while pitching. After two months on the disabled list, Billy's injury had not improved, and the twenty-seven-year-old right-hander returned to Pensacola, invoking the professionals at the Andrews Institute in nearby Gulf Breeze for help.

As a leader in orthopedics and sports medicine, the Andrews Institute has brought healing and wholeness to an impressive list of professional athletes. Although the facility's client roster is confidential, appreciative testimonials abound for the consultation and successful medical procedures performed by Dr. Andrews and his staff. Gratitude for the Andrews Institute has been expressed by legendary quarterbacks Brett Favre and Tom Brady, first baseman Albert Pujols and outfielder Manny Ramirez. Sadler began his workouts at the institute alongside Ramirez, who Billy had once struck out at AT&T Park.

Although Sadler would have rather been working his craft out of a Major League bullpen, he did not allow the extra time on his hands go to waste. Remembering the importance of the special instruction he gained at Pensacola's Bill Bond Field and the Fred Waters Clinic, Sadler made the decision to give back to the community he loved so deeply. In 2009, Sadler and several supporters launched the Billy Sadler–Bill Bond Baseball Clinic, which is hosted by current and former professionals and designed to instruct young people in fundamentals and developmental exercises. Among the numerous local players who have participated in the clinic are Greg Litton,

After injury prevented Billy Sadler from returning to his occupation as a professional pitcher, Sadler made Pensacola his base of operations once again. The former Catholic High School graduate went right to work on helping area players advance their capabilities for a stake in the game. Billy established the annual Billy Sadler–Bill Bond Baseball Clinic, where young players are coupled with veteran and current Major Leaguers for a practice experience second to none. Sadler also partnered with the Andrews Institute in creating a training facility for Billy Sadler Baseball, a one-on-one developmental program. *Courtesy of the author.*

Phil Hiatt, Wes Mugarian and Tim Spooneybarger. Coaches from Pensacola State College and the University of West Florida have joined in making Sadler's efforts a success for regional baseball and softball players. In 2012, Sadler launched Billy Sadler Baseball LLC to ensure the longevity of quality baseball education on the Gulf Coast.

ADRON CHAMBERS

The Pensacola Pelicans selected PJC pitcher Jeff Rodriguez and UWF catcher Bo Williams in 2007. The Kansas City Royals selected Patrick Norris from Pensacola High School, while the Laredo Broncos of the independent United League snapped up Greg Kealy from PJC. Additionally, junior college outfielder Adron Chambers signed with the St. Louis Cardinals after a unique journey into baseball.

Chambers, born on October 8, 1986, in Pensacola, attended Pensacola High School and excelled in football. The gridiron became Adron's field of play early in life as an athlete, and as a senior at PHS, Chambers listed high in the scoring for many state-level player prospect publications. The *Orlando Sentinel* rated the quarterback/defensive back as the No. 49 prospect in the state of Florida. Adron was listed as the No. 62 top prospect in Florida by *SuperPrep Magazine* and was further named among the state's most talented candidates by the recruiting web site for Sun State Football. Primarily playing quarterback for Pensacola High, Chambers helped lead the team to the state semifinals.

Adron received college scholarship offers from Vanderbilt, Troy, University of Mississippi, Middle Tennessee State, Auburn University and Mississippi State. But it was MSU that gained his allegiance, athleticism and hard work. The scouts continued to rank him high as a draft choice, but a knee injury and an off-field incident that warranted suspension from the football team mandated Chambers to rethink his future. Chambers had shown some interest in baseball during his high school years. Adron possessed good speed on the bases and an above-average arm on the mound. His fastball averaged in the mid-eighties, and the same throwing strength also made him a quality outfielder. Baseball would now be his future, but Adron would have to prove himself to a new sports culture.

The Pensacola High graduate turned to Bill Hamilton at PJC for a shot at establishing himself on the diamond. Hamilton was recovering at home from hip replacement surgery and asked that Adron come see him at his house. "I had heard a great deal about his abilities, but I wanted to know if he was serious and could be trusted. I knew if I could look him in the eyes I would know for sure," says Hamilton. From his recliner, Bill Hamilton spoke with Chambers and then made the decision to sign Adron with the Pensacola Junior College baseball team.

After completing PJC, the ranked-football-prospect-turned-baseball-player tried out with the Cubs in Clearwater, a Pirates camp in his hometown, and talked to Braves and Reds scouts covering the Northwest Florida region. Chambers says that he heard about a St. Louis tryout camp in Memphis and purchased a bus ticket in order to perform before the Cardinals screeners. After seeing Chambers, St. Louis signed the versatile player as an outfielder and sent him to their Rookie League staff in Johnson City, Tennessee, in 2007.

St. Louis worked Adron through its farm system at a fairly steady pace over the course of four years. Chambers reached the Triple-A club at the end of the 2010 season. His batting average climbed from .238 with Class-A Quad City in 2008 to .290 with the Memphis Redbirds in 2010. Chambers began the 2010 season with an invitation to join St. Louis at its spring camp in Jupiter, Florida. Cardinals manager Tony La Russa commented on Chamber's good attitude and personal workout ethics, stating that, "He goes about it right."Adron Chambers began 2011 as a member of the Memphis Redbirds but continued to be listed on the Cardinals forty-man roster with much anticipation of his call-up.

Adron's debut with St. Louis came on September 6, 2011, in a game against the Brewers. He stayed with the Cardinals for eighteen games before returning to Memphis. As the Cardinals advanced toward the postseason, Chambers was placed on their expanded roster in September. Adron covered the outfield in portions of all five division series games against Philadelphia and in all five games of the league championship series against Milwaukee. Although activated for Game 7, Chambers did not take the field during the Cardinals' World Series victory over Texas, but he had served his team effectively in helping them to win their eleventh World Championship trophy. From Triple-A at the beginning of the season to dressing out with the Cardinals for the World Series, Adron Chambers's first year in the majors mirrored the experience of fellow Pensacolan Johnny Lewis.

BRAD SALMON

As a boy, Pensacola's Bradley Keith Salmon was a typical all-American kid who enjoyed the game of baseball as a fan and a youth leaguer. Salmon's father worked for United Parcel Service and his mother for BellSouth, both keeping employment hours that would make it possible to view their son's baseball games in the evening. Like many Pensacola-area youth, Brad's interest in baseball was just a notch above his passion for hunting and fishing. The bountiful waters and woods surrounding Pensacola gave Salmon ample opportunity to indulge in his endeavors afield.

Brad was another recipient of the quality baseball program offered by Tate High School, and Salmon excelled at his craft on the mound. Brad pitched for the Tate High team when they won the 1998 Florida State High School Championship. The New York Mets captured Salmon's fan patronage during his formative years, but it was the Cincinnati Reds in the 1998 Major League Amateur Draft that chose Brad in the thirty-first round. Salmon headed to Jefferson Davis Community College as his initial proving ground and was selected again by Cincinnati in the 1999 draft in the twenty-first round.

Salmon's first port of call for Cincinnati in 1999 was with the Billings Mustangs under the guidance of former player and veteran manager Russ Nixon. Out of the bullpen for the Mustangs, Brad posted a 2–2 record in sixteen games and forty-nine innings. Brad's Class-A career stretched over four and a half seasons, taking him to Clinton, Iowa; Stockton, California; Potomac, Virginia; and Dayton, Ohio. The Reds were certain of the potential in their rookie right-handed reliever but wanted to see his development through to completion.

Brad split 2005 between Double-A Chattanooga and Triple-A Louisville, pitching for a combined ERA of 3.34 in forty-seven games. The work between the two cities was the same in 2006; however, he lowered his ERA to 2.44 in fifty-five games. Reporting to the Reds 2007 spring training exercises, Brad prepared for what was certain to be his breakout season. Cincinnati gave Salmon his Major League opportunity on May 1, 2007, in Houston with one inning of work in the bottom of the ninth. Salmon ended the game for Cincinnati with eleven pitches, which included a pop fly out, a walked batter and a double play. The Reds beat the Astros 11–3.

The world of professional baseball is a boy's fantasy, a land of dead heroes, a classroom for life lessons, a cruel mistress and a torrid lover. Baseball is a national obsession, a reminder of what is pure and an iron-fisted business all rolled into one. No other sport will, in one moment, lift you into angelic ecstasy and crush your heart the very next second the way that baseball can. Former baseball commissioner A. Bartlett Giamatti spoke of baseball in the November 1977 *Yale Alumni Magazine* in this manner: "It breaks your heart. It is designed to break your heart. The game begins in spring, when everything else begins again, and it blossoms in the summer, filling the afternoons and evenings, and then as soon as the chill rains come, it stops and leaves you to face the fall alone." Brad Salmon was granted free agency by the Reds on December 12, 2007, signed again by Cincinnati two days later and traded to the Royals on March 19, 2008, in the middle of spring training.

Salmon spent 2008 with the Royals' Omaha, Nebraska affiliate, pitching just over one hundred innings and earning an 8–7 record in relief. By November, he was once again a free agent, and he signed a brief contract with the White Sox in December. Chicago released Brad on April 4, 2009, and he was picked up by the Los Angeles Angels of Anaheim on April 22. The Angels sent Salmon to Salt Lake in the Pacific Coast League in 2009, granting him free agency in November. Brad joined the 2010 Acereros de Monclova of the Mexican League for nine games of work before returning to Pensacola to raise his family and enjoy the Florida outdoors.

Salmon says that Ken Griffey Jr. was the player he most admired as a teammate, contending that it was incredibly gratifying to be "playing a kid's game out there—it's what I love to do." When asked how other young people could attain the dream he had by playing in the big leagues, Brad replied, "Work as hard as you can, but have fun doing it." While Brad Salmon's career as a Major League pitcher may not have been long in comparison to others, no one can surpass him in the fun he had while it lasted.

One of Salmon's fondest memories in the majors came during his rookie season while he was getting ready to warm up before a game in Cincinnati:

> *I had just set my stuff down and I hear*[d] *somebody call my name. I turned around and it was our GM Walt Jocketty. I thought, "Oh man, I must be in trouble for the big boss to come down and get me." He said, "Salmon, follow me. Someone wants to meet you." So I follow*[ed] *him up to the visitors' press box. We walked through the door and there was Don Sutton. Man that was cool. We talked about both of us being from Pensacola and going to Tate. That was a real highlight, I can tell you.*

BIG MAC

Pelicans general manager Talmadge Nunnari announced the new field manager for the 2006 season during a December press conference. Cantonment resident Malcolm Howard "Mac" Seibert became the Pelicans' fourth manager since the team's inception. Seibert filled the void left by the outgoing Beauchamp, who had been named the vice-president and director of baseball operations for the independent South Coast League. Seibert was a product of the Pensacola baseball machine, but his local ties were not the impetus for his being hired by the Pelicans. Mac's

Mac Seibert's appointment as the Pelicans' manager gave him a double opportunity in his hometown. His desire was to see playing excellence in both his own team and the youth teams dotting the Pensacola area. As a player with Tate High School's capable baseball program, Seibert had participated in regional developmental clinics that had supplemented his skill set, which inevitably seeded into his future as a player, scout and coach. To effectively see Pensacola young people receive the same level of instruction, Mac initiated the Pelican's Training Camp, which gave top-level lessons to all who attended. *Courtesy of the Pensacola Pelicans (Amarillo Sox).*

background in player development and organizational management were extensive and respected.

Seibert pitched for the Tate High School baseball program and was an active part of the team when it won the 1984 state and national titles. For his efforts on the mound, he was named the Florida Athlete of the Year. The Oakland Athletics selected Mac in the 1984 Amateur Draft, but the left-handed pitcher chose to continue his education and build his skills in college ball. Seibert began his college career at Jefferson Davis Community College in Brewton, Alabama, and then transferred to the University of Miami for one year of instruction under legendary coach Ron Fraser.

After Mac's season at Miami, he spent an additional year with Jacksonville State University, where he received NCAA All-American honors. The regional Major League scouts in the southeast had earmarked their notes on Seibert and pursued him at the end of his four-year education. It was the Detroit Tigers who captured his services, signing Mac in the 1989 draft during the thirty-sixth round. With Bristol, Detroit's Appalachian League affiliate, Seibert threw for a 2.66 ERA. The following season, with the Fayetteville Generals, Mac posted a 3.60 ERA in relief. As 1991 approached, Seibert began what was to be his true calling in the world of baseball—that of an instructor, leader and mentor. Leaving the game as a player, he returned to Jefferson Davis as a coach.

The Atlanta Braves called on Mac's abilities in 1996 as an organizational scout, as did the expansion Diamondbacks in 1998 and 1999. When the year 2000 rolled out on the calendar, the Tampa Bay Devil Rays sought Mac as their national scouting crosschecker. Shortly thereafter, the Baseball Factory enlisted Seibert as their vice-president and executive director of Team One Baseball. Joining the Pelicans in 2007, Mac brought a wealth of knowledge in player productivity. During his two years with Pensacola, Seibert lifted the team to a new level of competiveness and challenged the players to expect more from themselves on the field. Later, in 2008, Mac accepted a very alluring offer from the New York Mets to become their scouting supervisor and oversee their amateur developmental programs.

One of the first actions taken by Seibert as the Pelicans' manager was to announce a training camp for Pensacola-area youth. The camp was structured as a three-week affair in three separate locations: North Pensacola; Tiger Point, east of Gulf Breeze; and Spanish Fort, Alabama. Players third grade through sixth were given personal instruction in preparation for the upcoming season from coaches Seibert, Nunnari, Pete Della Ratta, Jim Spooner and Squeaky Parker.

The camp was part of the Pelicans' instructional activities supported by the new offices and training facility on Davis Highway. The building offered an indoor baseball and softball workout area and offered one-on-one lessons with Pelicans personnel and regional coaches. At the park, Pensacola was again setting league records in attendance, including an overflow crowd of 6,200 on June 24, 2007. By the end of the season, the Pelicans total attendance during the six years of their existence reached over 320,000 fans. The beginning of the 2007 season also saw the seventeenth Pelican signed to a Major League contract, as starter Kyle Middleton scripted with the Astros. Mac Siebert's personal goal for excellence became the standard for the Pelicans style of play and the team's relationship with the fans.

CHAMPIONS ALL THE SAME

Three Pensacola Junior College pitchers were listed as selections for the 2008 draft. Right-hander Eric Fornataro went to the Cardinals, left-hander Austin Garrett was chosen by the Nationals and Blaine Howell signed with the Reds. Two area high school players gained notice during the 2008 draft. Tate graduate David Doss saw an offer from the Cubs but opted to play for the University of South Alabama before accepting a 2009 call from the Phillies. Gulf Breeze outfielder Kameron Brunty turned away a selection by the Mets and signed with the University of Southern Mississippi. At the end of the 2008 season, Pelicans catcher David Golliner signed a Major League contract with the Angels.

Pelicans Brandon Sing and Rafael Alvarez received honors for their batting ability throughout 2008, and pitcher Donny Langdon was named to the American Association's South Division All-Star team. Pensacola finished the year 43–53, missing an opportunity for postseason play. Finding a replacement for the Pelicans field manager was an immediate concern after Mac Seibert accepted a position with the Mets.

Filling Seibert's spikes was no simple task, as Mac exemplified all the elements wanted by the Pelicans front office. Pelicans GM Nunnari took personal responsibility for the future success of the team and accepted a dual role in 2009 as both the general manager and field manager.

The first order of business for Talmadge was hiring former Royals and Pirates farmhand Justin Lord as the pitching coach, rehiring infield coordinator Lou Henry and bringing back James Gamble as the player procurement director. Lord had pitched for the St. Paul Saints and understood the special operations of independent baseball. Henry spent a year with the Pirates organization after playing for PJC and Troy State. He doubled as the Pelicans' first base coach, engaging fans and igniting the crowd. Gamble founded the independent Global Scouting Bureau and brought a depth of player development experience. Along with Nunnari, the three additions created a collective coaching arsenal.

Nunnari managed the Pelicans to a 53–43 record during the 2009 season, winning the second half of the year and solidifying their place in the playoffs. In the matchup for the American Association South Division title, Pensacola beat the Fort Worth Cats. The Cats first base coach and former Pensacola Senators manager, eighty-four-year-old Wayne Terwilliger, rarely traveled on road trips. He made the trek from Fort Worth to take part in the series to the delight of all in attendance at Jim Spooner Field. When approached for an interview after the end of the series, he was informed about a forthcoming project chronicling the history of baseball in Pensacola.

Under new field manager Talmadge Nunnari, the Pelicans secured the first-place position during the second half of the 2009 American Association season. Facing the Lincoln Saltdogs for the championship, Pensacola ultimately lost the pennant during a rainy final game at Jim Spooner Field. But fans were not sullen about the rain or the loss, as support for Pensacola baseball endured through all adversity. *Courtesy of Peter Ezra Murphy.*

In true "Twig" fashion, he threw up his arms in exuberance and proclaimed, "Oh good, I'm in that one."

The Pelicans faced the Lincoln Saltdogs in the championship series for a best-of-five challenge. The pennant race for the 2009 title went down to the wire in a fifth-game pitching duel in Pensacola. Rain had been predicted in the forecast and became a reality in the late innings. The storm drenched fans, but most refused to leave the park or even take shelter, cheering on their team to the very end. Although the Pelicans lost 2–1, the Pensacola baseball community's spirit was not dampened by the weather or the loss. The stands continued to hold onlookers as league president Miles Wolff presented the Saltdogs with the championship trophy. Amid the cheers of Pensacola's good sports, Lincoln's manager genuinely thanked their Gulf Coast hosts. As fans left the park, they literally stripped the team shop of anything and everything with a Pelicans logo. To the Pensacola faithful, the Pelicans were still winners.

During the year, Pensacola's ace pitcher Kyle Middleton signed his second Major League contract, this time with Oakland. The Mariners purchased infielder Jimmy Mojica after the playoffs, and the Boston Red Sox acquired Pensacola pitcher Tyler Wilson. Wilson returned to the Pelicans in 2010. Chase Burch, Pensacola's power-hitting designated hitter and infielder, was named league Rookie of the Year. Burch, Antoin Grey, Kyle Middleton and Hunter Davis had all been selected for the South Division 2009 All-Star team. In October, Kyle Middleton was named to *Baseball America*'s All-Independent First Team for 2009, a team composed of the best players from all the North American independent baseball leagues.

WINDS OF CHANGE

September 17, 2009, was the official day of the groundbreaking ceremony for what was to become the Pelicans' new home field and center of operations. After almost five years since its earliest conception, the first shovels dug into the future site of the Vince Wibbs Sr. Community Maritime Park. Joining Pelicans owner Quint Studer in turning over the initial lumps of pre-construction dirt was Pensacola mayor Mike Wiggins and an array of city dignitaries. Intermittent wind and rain greeted those attending the celebration, but the weather did not hold back the hundreds of supporters who gathered on the bayfront building site. The wind blowing in from the bay seemed to symbolize the anticipated manifestation of Pensacola's new ballpark. But behind the scenes, the city's future with the green diamond was expanding beyond what most of the citizens ever dared to imagine.

In the off-season, the Pelicans held their first-ever Hot Stove Banquet, featuring former Tampa Bay pitcher Jim Morris. Jim's life and short professional career on the mound was the subject of the popular 2002 Disney movie *The Rookie*. The Jim Morris story was one of determination, and it became the perfect backdrop for what was about to be realized by Pensacola baseball fans.

Earlier in the 2009 season, P.J. Walters debuted with the St. Louis Cardinals after five seasons in their Minor League system. Walters played his freshman year at Pace High School. Two right-handed pitchers out of the University of West Florida signed their first professional contracts: John Church with the Mets and Shane Greene with the Yankees. Former Pensacola Junior College righty Chris Sorce signed to Seattle during the mid-year draft, and Tate's David Boyd earned a selection from the Texas Rangers.

Two players with Pensacola-area ties participated in their first Major League games during the first month of the 2010 regular season. Pensacola-born Josh Donaldson dressed out for the Oakland Athletics, while Pace High pitcher Bobby Cassavah took the mound for the Los Angeles Angels. As the mid-season Amateur Draft ramped up operations, Gulf Breeze High right-hander Edward Lively earned a selection by the Indians, as did West Florida High School alumnus Brett Lee from the Angels. Kevin Johnson attended the University of West Florida after his graduation from West Florida High. Johnson contracted to Los Angeles, pitching in eighteen games for their Orem, Utah affiliate before finishing the season with the Pensacola Pelicans. Johnson rejoined the Angels organization in 2011.

Former Pine Forest outfielder Justin Fradejas pulled a pick by the Rockies in 2010 but chose college first. Paul Davis and Ryan Ditthardt, each a product of the Pensacola Junior College baseball program, earned selections from Major League clubs. Davis gained attention from the Red Sox and Ditthardt from the Astros. Tate infielders Brandon Brown, brother of Bo Brown, and Jet Butler took picks from the Mets during 2010. Brown played for Auburn University and Butler for Mississippi State before contracting with the Mets.

Wes Mugarian's fastball constantly registered ninety to ninety-two miles per hour for Cincinnati Reds scouts. Mugarian had already signed to play with the University of Alabama after his graduation from Pensacola's Catholic High when the Reds approached him with an offer. Wes was Cincinnati's fifth-round selection in the 2010 June Amateur Draft, and the club would not take no for an answer. The Reds met all of the requests made by Wes and his parents, seeing an incredible prospect for their organization in the young right-hander. Cincinnati's pitching coach Bryan Price worked out with Wes after the team flew the Mugarians to the Queen City for their first introduction into the franchise family. Wes's first pitching instruction as a member of the Goodyear (Arizona) Reds came from Cincinnati's legendary hurler Tom Browning. Wes's father, John, a scout and an accomplished ballplayer in his own right, first demonstrated the effectiveness of youth clinics on a large scale to Squeaky Parker, giving Parker the original idea for the Fred Waters Clinic.

Pensacola Junior College changed its name to Pensacola State College (PSC) in July 2010. The name change reflected the school's new four-year degree structure. After Bill Hamilton transitioned from his position as head baseball coach to PSC's athletic director, assistant coach Keith Little stepped up as the skipper in 2011. Keith built on the tradition of excellence in Pirates baseball and added to it his own style and strength. Little's experience as a player and coach at the collegiate level spanned over ten years.

As some Pensacola-area players were realizing their professional baseball aspirations and PSC was adjusting to a four-year program during July 2010, the Pelicans were in the wake of an eleven-game winning streak. Pensacola's top position in the standing for the second half of the season unfolded with two wins against Lincoln, a three-game sweep of the first-half champions, the Shreveport-Bossier Captains, a four-game sweep of the El Paso Diablos and two wins over the Fort Worth Cats.

Heading into August, the Pelicans enjoyed a four-and-a-half-game lead in the South Division, but Pensacola's winning streak was not the foremost headline story involving owner Quint Studer. A longtime goal of Studer's was to bring an affiliated baseball team back to Pensacola, and Quint was beginning the first steps toward achieving this desire by acquiring a Double-A club for the city. With the downtown stadium project underway, the pursuit of an affiliated baseball club was now possible in that the city would have a field large enough to house a team. Looking ahead to the future needs of the park and the business surrounding a professional Minor League team, Studer set appropriate measures in motion by hiring Bruce Baldwin as a technical consultant.

Baldwin served for almost twenty-eight seasons in the Atlanta Braves organization as the general manager for multiple Braves' Minor League teams. He was involved in team affiliation moves, stadium development and day-to-day business operations and won multiple awards for his excellence as a baseball executive. In 1984, the *Sporting News* named Bruce the Baseball Executive of the Year. Studer asked Baldwin to step in as the president of Pensacola Professional Baseball, ensuring the highest quality and attention to detail for the development of the city's crowning sports venue.

Pelicans outfielder Chase Porch was named 2010 American Association Rookie of the Year during the last week of August, just prior to the playoffs. Porch had played a crucial part in the Pelicans' ability to score runs by batting over .350 with runners in scoring position. Although securing a spot in postseason play, the Pelicans were not able to hold their season momentum and were eliminated during the first round of the playoffs. Pensacola's love for its team had held through from the first pitch of 2002 until the last out of 2010. The loss during the playoffs did not sway the exuberance of Emerald Coast baseball patrons, as the excitement for an affiliated team lay stirring in the minds of Pensacola fans.

Had Pensacola continued as an independent club with the American Association it would have taken part in the formation of a new mega league. The American Association of Independent Professional Baseball Clubs announced the expansion of the league to fourteen teams during an October 2010 press conference. Commissioner Miles Wolff released the names of the four former Northern League clubs, stating that those four clubs together drew almost 900,000 fans during the 2010 regular season. The regular season schedule would also be expanded to one hundred games in order to accommodate the fourteen team matchups.

Pelicans catcher Lou Palmisano was named to *Baseball America*'s First Team 2010 in the All-Independent League rankings. Palmisano's slugging percentage topped at .585, along with a .347 batting average. Lou's award was to be the last given to any Pensacola Pelican. To make room and allowances for the incoming Double-A team, Quint Studer was obligated to sell the Pelicans franchise to an ownership group in Amarillo, Texas. The Pensacola Pelicans flew west to become the Amarillo Sox.

PENSACOLA'S FIELD OF DREAMS

The acquisition of a Double-A team for Pensacola took an orchestrated and unique series of maneuvers on the part of Quint Studer and Bruce Baldwin. After the sale of the independent club to the Texas ownership cooperative, Northwest Florida Professional Baseball LLC made advancement toward what would become the occupying team of the Maritime Park. "To cause the full purchase to happen I had to acquire four signatures," says Studer. The four critical signatures required to make affiliated baseball a reality in Pensacola came from the owner of the team to be relocated to Pensacola; Minor League Baseball; the Southern League, which would be the regional circuit involving Pensacola's club; and the Mobile BayBears, who owned the territory franchise rights extending into Northwest Florida.

As if giving a red-wrapped Christmas present to the City of Five Flags, the Studers announced publicly in December 2010 the Major League affiliated club that would be represented in Pensacola. Beginning in 2012, the Cincinnati Reds organization added a new family member to its farm system. Florida's first settlement opened its doors to the oldest all-professional club in baseball.

Beyond receiving the needed signatures for purchasing the Reds affiliate and allowances to move them to Pensacola, Studer had a few additional hoops to jump through in seeing the venture to fruition. The Pelicans were to retain their name under the agreement of the sale to Amarillo, where the owners would then change it after the transaction was completed. Quint then purchased the Carolina Mudcats from Zebulon, North Carolina. The Mudcats had been associated with the Reds since the beginning of 2009. Under the agreement of the purchase, the Mudcats name would stay in Zebulon to be used with a new Class-A club.

Additionally, the Mobile BayBears required a sum to be paid by Studer for the realignment of their governing territory. However, a welcome Gulf Coast rivalry was ensured by the short drive down Interstate 10 for Pensacola and Mobile baseball advocates. Studer's personal payout for contractual purchase obligations was substantial, but Quint saw this as a minuscule price to pay in order to provide Pensacola with the level of professional play ushered in by a Double-A club. Quint announced via the Pensacola Professional Baseball web site, "Bringing affiliated baseball to Pensacola will continue to add to the rich sports history that already exists in the area. Seeing the future stars of Major League Baseball in a fun, family-friendly atmosphere will bring a new level of enthusiasm for the citizens of Pensacola and Northwest Florida."

The Southern League of Professional Baseball Clubs has organizational roots dating back to 1885, with names such as Luis Aparicio, Fergie Jenkins, Rollie Fingers, Harmon Killebrew and Casey Stengel listed among league alumni. As Pensacola finalized its agreement to become the next Southern League city in 2012, nine other teams made up the Double-A professional circuit. The Mobile BayBears (Arizona Diamondbacks), Chattanooga Lookouts (Los Angeles Dodgers), Birmingham Barons (Chicago White Sox), Mississippi Braves (Atlanta Braves), Huntsville Stars (Milwaukee Brewers), Jacksonville Suns (Florida Marlins), Montgomery Biscuits (Tampa Bay Rays), Jackson Generals (Seattle Mariners) and Tennessee Smokies (Chicago Cubs) filled out the league roster.

Pensacola police chief Chip Simmons remarked, "A team like this will create community excitement and involvement. It will be a rallying point where all of Pensacola can come together. Young and old, black and white, everyone will share."And community involvement was resting high at the top of Studer and Baldwin's list of importance for the new stadium. The original seating plans were designed for a three-thousand-fan capacity. To accommodate the regulations of Minor League Baseball and to assure adequate seating for patrons, the park blueprints were expanded to seat just over five thousand spectators.

NATIONAL CHAMPIONS

Pensacola State College athletic director Bill Hamilton and head baseball coach Keith Little hosted a press conference for the signing of three of their players to university squads on April 26, 2011. Third baseman and power hitter Blake Brown signed his contract with the University of Southern Mississippi; pitcher J.J. McLaughlin was welcomed onto the Cumberland University roster in Lebanon, Tennessee; and Josh Tanski, who pitched a 9–3 season for PSC, was assured a 2012 spot as an Argonaut with the University of West Florida.

Going into May 2011, the Argos carried a number-one national ranking among the National Collegiate Baseball Writers Association's Division II poll for five consecutive weeks. Head coach Mike Jeffcoat led the team to several school records and positioned the university's young baseball program to earn its ultimate prize. Jeffcoat, a product of Escambia High School and the University of West Florida under Jim Spooner, understood the dynamics of structuring a successful team on the Gulf Coast. Mike pitched in the Cardinals' farm system before beginning his coaching career in 1994 as the pitching instructor for Pensacola Junior College and as head coach with Alabama Southern Community College in 1995. Jeffcoat took over the UWF baseball program in 2005.

The University of West Florida team boarded their bus on May 4, 2011, bound for Millington, Tennessee, and the Gulf South Conference Baseball Tournament. The Argonauts won the tournament, making it the second straight GSC East Division regular season championship and the fourth in school's history. With a 17–3 conference record, the team set another high-water mark for conference wins during a single season. The Argos finished either first or second in the GSC East in five out of nine years beginning in 2002.

The momentum carried the Argos through their regional competition, securing a spot for a shot at the national pennant. Prior to the NCAA Division II National Championship, UWF had during the season carried a twenty-two-game winning streak. The tournament was held at the USA Baseball National Training Complex in Cary, North Carolina. All the hard work under the hot Florida sun paid off for UWF, as the university delivered the school's first National Championship in a 12–2 final game victory over Winona State.

Just off of their championship experience, five Argonauts gained further national attention as draft picks in Major League Baseball's 2011 amateur selection. Pitcher Ben Hawkins signed with the Nationals, shortstop Brandon Brewer and pitcher Daniel Vargas-Vila remained teammates after signing contracts with the Angels and outfielders Greg Pron and Dustin Lawley were selected by the Mets. Other area selections during the 2011 draft saw the Minnesota Twins pick Pace High graduate Adam Bryant and West Florida High's Brett Lee. Paul Davis, who had been a standout at Pensacola State College before playing at Florida Atlantic, signed his agreement with the Giants.

THE WAY FLORIDA AND BASEBALL SHOULD BE

Initial support for Pensacola's first affiliated team above the old Class-B level could not have been stronger, as over 9,600 citizens voted for the city referendum to make the new stadium a reality. Patrons began calling the team office as soon as the announcement of the franchise purchase was made. Fans clamored for the pre-purchase of tickets covering the seventy regular-season home games. As season tickets did become available, many of those individuals who had inhabited the bleachers at Jim Spooner Field were the first in line to secure their places at Maritime Park. Mark Downey, a lifelong Atlanta Braves fan and Pensacola real estate broker, was one of the first to purchase 2012 season tickets. "Man, I am not missing a single pitch in that first season," says Downey. "My dad would have loved this if he could have seen it, but I am making sure my boys do not miss it." Mark's dad was an advocate in Pensacola-area youth sports before his death and had very strong ties to Ohio and the Reds' home region.

Sean LaGasse, a former Pensacola pastor who recently relocated to the Orlando area, said that the new Reds farm club was so exciting for him that he would make a special trip back to Northwest Florida just to be a part of the inaugural season. "We have a lot of great baseball throughout Central Florida, but this is something I do not want to miss," declared LaGasse. Sean spent many enjoyable evenings with friends and family watching the Pelicans play while he ministered in Pensacola. Dave Stafford, a native of Liverpool, England, and a transplant to Escambia County, says that he has never had the privilege of watching a professional baseball game. Stafford vowed that his maiden voyage into the game would come in stands at the Maritime Park.

Home on leave from his duty aboard the USS *Abraham Lincoln*, Senior Medical Officer Michael Jacobs viewed the construction of the field from the vantage point of the restaurant parking lot next door. "I can't believe this is finally happening," Commander Jacobs stated with the smile of a Little Leaguer. "I cannot wait to come home and go to a game with this level of competition in my own backyard." Prior to leaving for assignment, Mike Jacobs was given a signed American Association baseball by his buddies in remembrance of the fun they shared while watching the Pensacola Pelicans. The ball sat on his desk aboard the ship. Jacobs, who was a valued member of the aerospace medical program at Pensacola NAS, represented his ship and his adopted Gulf Coast home as he threw out the ceremonial first pitch for the Seattle Mariners' 2011 Memorial Day festivities.

In anticipation of the arrival of the Reds farm club in 2012, Pensacola Professional Baseball set the bar high for fan participation and community involvement. With the Mudcats name staying in North Carolina, Pensacola's Double-A team was without a proper appellation. To remedy the untitled team, an open contest was enlisted to garner suggestions from the existing fan base. Six finalists were chosen out of over seventeen hundred entries. The final list was composed of the Redbones, Salty Dogs, Aviators, Loggerheads, Mullets and Blue Wahoos. A further vote in the "Name the Team" contest utilized the assistance of the *Pensacola News Journal*, and on May 24, 2011, the Pensacola Blue Wahoos were spoken into existence amid a throng of well-wishers.

Baseball and naval aviation have been synonymous with Pensacola for more than one hundred years. Pensacola's Naval Air Station has historically fielded teams able to compete with professional clubs such as the 1930 Boston Red Sox. The Southwest Men's League, founded at Pensacola NAS, was the early incarnation of the now revered Red, White and Blue Baseball Tour. Numerous airmen with big-league experience have trained and played on Pensacola's base recreation fields. Representing the naval aeronautics medical program and the City of Five Flags, Commander Mike Jacobs continued the tradition of Pensacola's military baseball when he threw out a ceremonial first pitch in Seattle. *Courtesy of the Seattle Mariners.*

Avid baseball fans were not the only Pensacolans to sing forth the benefits of having a hometown-affiliated team on their shores. Resident veteran players Greg Litton, Phil Hiatt, Dennis Lewallyn, Kevin Saucier, Hosken Powell and former Pensacola Senators owner Joe Panaccione agreed that the park and team would bring continued community advantages not realized since 1962. After the announcement of Cincinnati's Double-A team being relocated to the area, Buck Showalter reported to the *Pensacola News Journal,* "I doubt the people of Pensacola realize what a huge coup this is for them. If I had to pick a level of play and location, you couldn't ask for a better one. That's the way you would draw it up. It's a great level of play." Celebrated Minor League owner Mike Veeck proclaimed, "Pensacola will be a great market. It is a great town, just the way Florida and baseball should be."

Pensacola Bayfront Stadium was designed to withstand winds up to 150 miles per hour. In the event of a hurricane, the scoreboard pillars alone sit atop eighty-four feet of steel driven into the shoreline, assuring its lasting stability. The advantage to the park's placement was that every fan in every seat would have a view of Pensacola Bay. But due to the ever-present threat of tropical storms, measures were taken to ensure the park's integrity. The mix between practical construction and natural aesthetics created a very intimate, friendly venue. "We are going to provide the community with something they've never seen before," assured club president Bruce Baldwin.

After the announcement that veteran manager Jim Riggleman would fill the position as the Wahoos' skipper for 2012, season ticket sales reached toward the 2,300 mark. Riggleman managed in the Major Leagues for the Padres, Cubs, Mariners and the Nationals. Stepping back into the Double-A arena sparked Riggleman toward a new adventure. Just over one hundred cities thought the U.S. can boast of an affiliated Minor League team, and of that number, only thirty have a Double-A club. Riggleman and Pensacola native Dennis Lewallyn played together during their own Double-A experience. "This is a perfect town for Jim's personality," stated Lewallyn.

The Pensacola Blue Wahoos

April 5, 2012, became a historic day for the Port City, as the Cincinnati Reds' Minor League franchise took the field in the form of the Pensacola Blue Wahoos. Rain was forecasted, but under the rising full moon, the clouds parted amid the masses of well-wishers and newly converted fans. Quint Studer's dream had come to fruition, along with it the hopes and aspirations of a thankful community. A manicured diamond dazzled the onlookers as they found their seats and watched their home team fill the dugout.

Former Pelicans manager Bernie Carbo traveled in to be a part of the opening ceremonies and first pitch. "I never played in a Minor League stadium that looked this beautiful," Carbo said emphatically. "If you can't play well here, you can't play anywhere. This is top-notch." Reds vice-president of scouting and player development, Bill Bavasi, watched from atop the Hancock Bank Club Deck, commenting that Pensacola had put together one of the best parks he had ever seen in the Minor Leagues. "This is a really great town to be part of Cincinnati's farm system," contended Bavasi.

In the bottom of the first inning, Wahoos followers experienced their team's inaugural hit, as shortstop Didi Gregorious dropped one far enough to reach

As if apparitions stepping out of a magical cornfield onto the freshly groomed diamond, the inaugural members of the Pensacola Blue Wahoos took their positions on Opening Day, April 5, 2012. Many in the sellout crowd could not hold back the emotion of witnessing a professional baseball team once more on Pensacola's shoreline. Not since 1962 had the citizens of Pensacola gathered downtown as a community to watch a ball team that carried their name. *Courtesy of the Pensacola Blue Wahoos.*

first base. Center fielder Ryan LaMarre became the first to score a run in the new ballpark, and third baseman Henry Rodriguez slugged the Wahoos' first-ever home run during the bottom of the eighth inning. As the Pensacola Blue Wahoos overcame the Montgomery Biscuits 3–2 on opening night, the city knew that professional baseball was once again a reality on their shores.

During mid-May, Pensacola fans were given their first opportunity to experience one of the bittersweet facts of life in hosting a Minor League franchise—that fact being that a farm system is designed by nature to be a developmental tool for the parent club. Third baseman Mike Costanzo, who had just begun to endear himself to the inhabitants of Maritime's stands, was called up to Triple-A Louisville after participating in just eleven games for the Wahoos. On May 12, Costanzo received his nod onto the Major League bench, getting his first hit with the Reds on May 19 as a designated hitter. With runners on first and third in the top of the eighth inning, Mike hit a towering sacrifice fly to score Brandon Phillips. Just days earlier, Costanzo had played alongside Brandon's younger brother P.J. in Pensacola. Mike Costanzo helped the Reds beat the Yankees in New York in a 6–5 finish. Pensacola had now re-entered the world of baseball at full strength.

P.J. Phillips was asked about his feelings on playing for the same organization as his older brother Brandon. P.J. reflected that he and his brother, who has covered second base for the Reds since 2006, enjoy the opportunity to work for the same franchise. "It's really cool," states Phillips.

"The Reds truly appreciate you and preach good work ethic. They really care about you [and] stay on top of your development, like when they send in veteran guys such as Eric Davis to give you seasoned insights."

P.J. recounted not only his new experiences as a member of his brother's organization but also the powerful motivation for his career through the Blue Wahoos club and its fans:

> *Pensacola fans are the best, and they really have your back. They bring you real energy on and off the field. Even when I see some of them out on the street, they always greet me and tell me how much they enjoy seeing me play. Being here in Pensacola makes you feel as if you were already a big leaguer. Our field is one of the best I have ever played on, and the Wahoos staff and ownership have created an incredible atmosphere to play in.*

May and June were months of celebration within Pensacola's baseball community at large. The Blue Wahoos were turning the mildest spectators into devout followers, and area schools were again carving their place into the pillars of the game. On May 23, 2012, the Pensacola Catholic Crusaders captured their second 4A state baseball championship as the squad won 7–2 over Bishop Verot in Port St. Lucie. Catholic's championship title became the twenty-second such honor for Greater Pensacola. As the June Major League Draft began, area players gained widespread attention.

In a much anticipated selection, Pace High School shortstop Addison Russell was signed by the Oakland Athletics. "This guy is going to make it to the pros and fast," said scout Kevin Saucier as he watched Russell in 2009. Addison's teammate Patrick Irvine took a pick by the Mets. Tate's Mac Seibert, the son of the former Pelicans manager, was chosen by the Padres, while the Marlins spoke for UWF's Brian Ellington. Two incoming Pensacola State players were signed in the MLB First Year Player Draft, with Chase Patterson getting a selection by the Angels and Logan Sefrit going to the Mariners. Yet another pair of former area graduates gained preference in the First Year Player Draft. Tate's Jayce Boyd, most recently playing for Florida State, received a nod from the Mets, and while playing at the University of Alabama, Catholic High's Wade Wass vested interest from the Orioles.

During the remaining weeks of the Southern League's 2012 season, crowds turned out in grand style to watch their Pensacola Blue Wahoos in sold-out games, buying out the "Bait & Tackle" team store time after time. On July 24, the Cincinnati Reds signed a four-year affiliation extension with Pensacola, adding stability and excitement to the staying power of the Blue Wahoos. Then, less than a month later, newly promoted shortstop Billy Hamilton rewrote baseball history in August.

The 2012 Pensacola Blue Wahoos. *Front row, left to right*: Brodie Greene, Mark Fleury, Josh Fellhauer, Yordanys Perez, Rishy Studer (owner), Quint Studer (owner), Miguel Rojas, Daniel Corcino, Henry Rodriguez, Cody Puckett, Justin Freeman, Pedro Villarreal and Tony Jaramillo (hitting coach). *Back row, left to right*: Jonathan Griffith (executive vice-president), Jim Riggleman (manager), Tom Brown (pitching coach), Chris Manno, Ryan LaMarre, Didi Gregorius, J.C. Sulbaran, Tim Gustafson, Drew Hayes, Josh Ravin, Clayton Tanner, Joel Guzman, Mike Costanzo, Curtis Partch, Mark Serrano, Tim Crabbe, P.J. Phillips, Brian Peacock, Donnie Joseph, Dixie Davis, Jon Berdanier (strength and conditioning coach), Charles Leddon (athletic trainer) and Bruce Baldwin (president). *Courtesy of the Pensacola Blue Wahoos.*

Hamilton was sent in from the Reds' Bakersfield, California, club to take the place of Didi Gregorius, who had been sent up to Triple-A. Hamilton was already on his way to breaking the all-time Minor League base-stealing record upon his arrival in Pensacola. The former record was held by Vince Coleman, who stole 145 in 1983. Billy Hamilton's base-thieving ways brought Pensacola and the Wahoos to the attention of America's baseball nation, as he broke the record on August 21. Billy was crowned "The Man of Steal," and after the congratulatory accolades, the Baseball Hall of Fame affirmed Pensacola's resurgence into the national game by requesting the stolen bases, cleats and batting helmet from Hamilton's monumental achievement.

All throughout Pensacola's inaugural 2012 season, the affectionately dubbed "Wahooligans" rooted for their team with the same vigor as their predecessors had for the Fliers, Dons and Senators. Pensacola's enthusiasm for the game and abiding faith that one day professional baseball would return to them kept their dreams alive and brought reality to a vision. While the names Wally Dashiell, Bill McGhee, Neb Wilson and Fred Waters no longer appeared on the lineup card, the thrill of the game echoed across the bay just as strong as in the days of Legion Field and Admiral Mason Park—maybe even stronger. "There has always been a constant in Escambia County and the Pensacola area, and that is baseball," exclaimed Buck Showalter. And once again, Buck was completely right.

INDEX

A

Admiral Mason Park 10, 68, 101–104, 108, 109, 112, 125, 126, 130, 221, 248
Agee, George 93
Alabama-Florida League 55, 62, 99–104, 107, 110, 113, 117, 122, 126–131
Allvord, Terry 181–183, 191
Alston, Walter 81, 82, 86, 87, 136
American Association 32, 35, 42, 46, 54, 71, 222, 223, 234, 235, 239, 243
Andrews Institute 226, 227
Aparicio, Luis 109, 240
Arizona Diamondbacks 150, 159, 170, 174, 176, 187, 199, 211, 224, 233, 241
Armstrong, Louis 69, 70
Arthur Giants 90–94
Atlanta Braves 105, 137, 145, 146, 166, 170, 224, 233, 238, 241, 243

B

Babe Ruth League 95, 108–112, 125, 151, 174
Baird, Bob 127
Baker, Jake 72
Baldwin, Bruce 238–239, 245, 248
Baltimore Orioles 20, 40, 74, 106, 110, 115, 122, 159, 166, 170, 205, 214
Barberi, Bennie 116, 122

Barber, Steve 114–115, 123
Barrancas National Cemetery 49, 86
Bavasi, Bill 245
Bay City 10, 16
Bayfront Stadium 11, 245
    Vince Whibbs Sr. Community Maritime Park 220
Bayview Memorial Park 52, 61, 107
Beauchamp, James Kash 224, 232
Bebas, Gus 66
Belinsky, Bo 105, 106, 114
Bell, Jay 139, 144, 150, 167, 170, 173–176
Bell, William "Pit" 92
Birmingham, Joe 31, 32
Bisher, Furman 76
Blackwood, William 32
Blasingame, Don 110
Bloomer Girls 28
Blue Angels 9, 10, 140
Blue Wahoos 11, 136, 149, 181, 243, 245–248
Blyleven, Bert 119, 154, 168, 175
Bogan, William 143
Bond, Bill 52, 137–139, 174, 201
Bonner, Paul 55
Boone, Ray 109
Boston Braves 30, 57, 76, 77, 84, 87, 96
Boston Red Sox 52–55, 75, 76, 78, 121, 140, 141, 194, 215, 236, 244
Bouldin, Carl 123

Bowden, Earle 104, 107–108
Boyer, Ken 110
Boyle, John 20
Bragan, Bobby 58, 61–62
Brantley, Jeff 165, 179
Brinkman, Ed 123
Bronson Bombers 73, 74, 75, 77, 79, 80,
    121
Bronson Field 73–76, 79, 121
Brooklyn Dodgers 30, 42, 56, 57, 68, 73,
    75–77, 80, 81, 87, 127
Brooklyn Robins 40, 48, 49, 52
Brooks, Derrick 131
Browning, Tom 238
Bull Durham 115, 194
Burgess, Smoky 87
Burgo, Bill 87
Bush, George H.W. 181
Butler, Charity 124

C

Cannon, Joe "J.J." 147
Carbo, Bernie 105, 213–216, 221, 223, 245
Carolina Mudcats 240
Carvalis, Leo 188
Cassavah, Bobby 237
Central Baseball League 217, 221
Chalk, Wesley 87
Chambers, Adron 228–229
Chatham, Charles "Buster" 72
Cheek, Tom 13, 153, 154–156, 177
Chicago Cubs 35, 41, 77, 85, 109, 112,
    113, 127, 147, 150, 183, 205, 218,
    219, 241
Chicago White Sox 32, 48, 59, 75, 76, 78,
    93, 95, 109, 110, 116, 121, 124,
    221, 241
Chipola Junior College 149, 158, 160, 211
Cincinnati 15
Cincinnati Reds 11, 31, 32, 36, 47, 59, 133,
    134, 144, 151, 165, 171, 173, 183,
    206, 214, 230, 237, 240, 245, 247
City League 23, 24, 25, 26, 28, 29, 38, 68
Clark, Will 165, 178, 179
Cleveland Indians 48, 85, 107, 124, 129,
    139, 190, 198, 206, 211
Cleveland Naps 31, 32, 33, 34
Clowers, Bill 46
Cobb, Dr. E.S. 90
Cobb, Ty 23, 34, 36–37

Colman, David 92
Colorado Rockies 183
Combs, Earle 41, 51
Connatser, Bruce 46–48
Connors, Chuck 82
Corcino, Daniel 11, 248
Corry Field 73, 74
Costanzo, Mike 246, 248
Cotton States League 21, 30, 31, 47, 76, 98
Cowsar, Bob 78

D

Dashiell, Wally 46, 50, 57, 58, 59–61,
    63–66, 81, 86, 87, 93, 94, 96, 197
Davidson, Robert 112, 113
Davis, Fred 101, 103, 105, 113, 114
Deal, Ken 88
Dean, Dizzy 75, 134–136
Della Ratta, Pete 198, 209, 233
Denning, Otto 87
Detroit Tigers 11, 35, 36, 37, 48, 62, 72,
    84, 98, 131, 132, 133, 164, 170,
    171, 185, 186, 208, 233
Dickey, Bill 51
Dixon, Johnny 93
Dozier, George 95, 96
Dreisewerd, Clem "Steamboat" 57
Dudes 10, 18–19
Dunn, J.C. 117
Durocher, Leo 51, 72

E

Earnshaw, George 70
East Ends 25
Eddys 25
Ehlman, Charles 96
Elder, Dave 199, 206–207
Ellyson Field 73, 80, 81, 82, 86, 97, 223
English, Jeff 192, 203
Erickson, Blake 124
Erskine, Carl 81, 82, 87
Espada, Joe 223

F

Farnsworth, Jeff 198, 208
Fisher, Carl 86
Fitzgerald, Lou 105, 110, 111, 114, 115,
    116

Flood, Curt 110, 152
Florida Marlins 105, 170, 183, 184, 205, 209, 223, 241
Floyd, Bubba 62
Ford, Donald "Rex" 104, 105
Fort Barrancas 27, 37, 38, 43, 44, 49, 70, 71, 73
Fort Pickens 37, 38
Fox, Nellie 109
Franks, Herman 71, 72, 77, 82
Frazier, Vic 66
Fred Waters Baseball Clinic 119, 165
Fryman, Travis 139, 165, 174, 175, 176, 184–187, 191, 194, 206

G

Gamble, James 234, 235
Gassaway, Charlie "Sherriff" 58, 59
Gehrig, Lou 43, 44, 51
Gibbons, Walter "Dirk" 91
Gilks, Robert (Bob) 31, 35
Gill, George 85
Gittinger, Thomas Lewis 9
Goldfarb, Chuck 166
Gonzalez, Ney "Speedy" 117
Gordon, Earl 25–29
Graf, Kinner 66
Granada Park 69
Greenburg, Hank 84
Gregorious, Didi 245
Gremp, Buddy 76, 77
Griffith, Don 107–108, 110
Grimes, Burleigh 41
Gulf Breeze High School 198, 209, 237

H

Hamilton, Bill 211–212, 216, 218, 228, 229, 238, 241
Hamilton, Billy 11, 247
Hanna, Preston 119, 143, 144–147
Hardy, Frank 106
Harris, Vic 42
Harwells 18
Heffernan, Bert 88
Heinz, Leonard 78
Heiser, Roy 127
Henderson, Bill 52
Henencheck, Alvin 88
Henry, Lou 234

Herring, Bill 88
Hiatt, Phil 139, 191–195, 228, 244
Hicks, Fred 100
Hoerst, Lefty 63, 65
Holden, Bill 46, 47–50
Hope 10, 15, 16
Houston Astros 133, 142, 145, 153, 154, 226
Hoyt, Waite 42, 51
Hubbell, Carl 56
Huggins, Miller 42
Hutchings, Johnny 59, 62
Hutchinson, Fred 110
Hutchinson, Johnny 78
Huth, Kenny 209
Hutto, Jim 119, 139–143

I

Indianapolis Clowns 91, 92

J

Jackson, "Shoeless Joe" 23, 32, 33
Jackson, Travis 56
Jeffcoat, Mike 241
Jim Spooner Field 113, 235, 242
Jocketty, Walt 231
Johnson, Doc 32
Johnson, Kevin 237
Jones, Roy, Jr. 124

K

Kansas City Athletics 109, 127, 139
Kansas City Royals 140, 166, 175, 192, 199, 206, 211, 228
Kasko, Eddie 110
Keller, Hal 126
Kell, George 84
Kennedy, Bobby 67, 75, 76, 78
Kennedy, Forrest 96
Kennedy, John 123, 137
Kennedy, Ray 53
Kinser, Buddy 188
Kirby, LaRue 30, 31
Kirkland, Joe 88
Kitchens, Frank 56, 57
Kiwanis Park 69
Knowles, Otto 109, 116, 124
Kupfrian's Park 19, 20

Index

L

LaBounty, Richard 192
Lajoie, Napoleon "Nap" 32, 34
LaMarre, Ryan 246, 248
Lambert, Gene 63–65
Lazzeri, Tony 51, 52
Legion Field 9, 49, 50, 52, 53, 65, 66, 68, 82, 84–87, 92, 93, 102, 248
Lehew, Jim 110, 111, 114
Lewallyn, Dennis 119, 140, 146, 147–150, 154, 170, 184, 244, 245
Lewis, Johnny Joe 131–133
Lewis, Purvis 93, 145
Libbert, Jason 216, 224
Light Crust Dough Boys 36
Lions Park 69
Little, Keith 238, 241
Litton, Greg 95, 168, 177–181, 226, 244
Lopez, Al 75, 109
Lord, Justin 234, 235
Los Angeles Angels 106, 231, 237
Los Angeles Dodgers 133, 136, 241
Louisville Colonels 40, 41, 53, 77
Loun, Don 122, 127
Lybrand, Lefty 55, 109, 112
Lyons, Bobby 96

M

Macon, Max 56–57, 87
Madison, Scotti 151, 171–173
Magnolia Bluff Park 26, 28
Major League Baseball Players Alumni Association 191
Major League Baseball Scouting Bureau 165
Mallorys 16
Mann, Garth 62
Maritime Park 220, 236, 240, 242, 243
Martin, Pepper 82
Marvray, Charles 92, 93
Maxent Park 26, 40, 41, 42, 43, 44, 46, 49, 85
Maxwell, Bert 55
McCarthy, Joe 41
McCormick, Doc 116
McDaniel, Vernon 92
McGarry, Pete 70
McGhee, Bill 63–66, 72, 84, 88, 99–100, 101, 104, 105, 112, 248

McGraw, John 20, 23, 24
McIlwain, Stover "Smokey" 124
McMillin, Richard 96
Mendoza, Carlos 127, 223
Merritt, John 18, 19
Milwaukee Brewers 134, 184, 241
Minnesota Twins 119, 127, 129, 154, 172, 173, 175, 180, 181, 205, 242
Miracle League of Pensacola 207
Mobile Bay Bears 176
Mobley, Charles 93, 94
Montreal Expos 139, 155, 166, 201
Moore, Berry 127
Moore, Bill 122
Moore, Jackie 134
Morris, Jim 237
Mugarian, Wes 228, 237
Musial, Stan 110

N

Nee, Dan 55
Neill, Tommy 78, 84
Newark Bears 46
Newcombe, Don 82
Newhouser, Hal 84, 114, 115
New York Giants 20, 31, 55–56, 57, 71, 107, 127, 136
New York Mets 30, 53, 107, 131, 230, 233
New York Yankees 30, 35, 41–45, 47, 48, 50–52, 77, 103, 131, 141, 159, 191, 194, 198, 206, 220, 223
Nine Devils 36
Nunnari, Talmadge 139, 196, 199–202, 209, 232–235

O

Oakland Athletics 134, 166, 179, 191, 203, 221, 226, 233, 237, 247
O'Neil, Buck 91, 92, 112, 113
O'Neill, Steve 32
Onwards 20
Ott, Mel 56, 85
Ozark, Danny 82

P

Pace High School 171, 237, 247
Palmer, Harry 16, 18
Palmetto Park 21, 26, 27

Palmisano, Lou 239

Panaccione, Joe 96, 104, 106, 112, 113, 116, 117, 122, 123, 128, 130, 133, 168, 197, 244

Parker, Squeaky 119, 165–168, 178, 185–187, 233, 238

Partrick, Dave 109, 177

Pasek, Johnny 46, 48

Pastimes 18

Pelicans Training Academy 224

Pennock, Herb 51

Pensacola Angels 116, 119

Pensacola Baseball Park Association 16, 24, 25, 35

Pensacola Bay Brewery 10

Pensacola Catholic High School 90, 119, 191, 192, 208, 225, 227

Pensacola Christian High 143

Pensacola Dons 102, 103, 104, 107, 108, 111, 116, 127

Pensacola Fliers 50–52, 60, 68, 72, 78, 84, 87, 88, 105

Pensacola Flyers 28

Pensacola Giants 36, 42, 92

Pensacola High School 37, 38, 44, 49, 131, 141, 143, 162, 173, 188, 189, 218, 222, 228

Pensacola Junior College 98, 130, 153, 154, 159, 166, 167, 171, 173, 176, 177, 178, 184, 188, 189, 197, 198, 199, 203, 206, 209, 211, 216, 222, 224, 225, 229, 234, 237, 238, 241

Pensacola Little League 90, 94, 100

Pensacola Naval Air Station 52, 69, 70, 73, 76, 92, 108, 140, 181

Pensacola Pelicans 92, 139, 167, 197, 198, 201, 209, 210, 216, 224, 228, 237, 239, 243

Pensacola Pilots 45, 46, 49, 167

Pensacola Seagulls 92, 93, 113, 131, 132, 145

Pensacola Senators 11, 104, 107, 122, 123, 128, 168, 235, 244

Pensacola Sports Association 209, 212, 218

Pensacola State College 228, 238, 241, 242

Pepsi-Cola Stars 68, 90–94

Pericola, Frank 66

Perryman, Parson 46, 48, 50

Pete Caldwell's Field 69, 90

Petrich, Paul 78

Pets 18–21

Pfeiffer's Mill Cemetery 47

Philadelphia Phillies 11, 46, 48, 54, 59, 62, 63, 65, 70, 74, 75, 84, 85, 106, 141, 142, 144, 152, 153, 156, 162, 164, 164–167, 184, 190, 199, 203, 222, 234

Phillips, P.J. 246, 248

Pine Forest High School 166, 171, 198, 222

Pipgras, Ed 43, 46, 48

Pipgras, George 43

Pitko, Alex 62

Pittsburgh Pirates 48, 72, 127, 144, 160, 175, 176

Porch, Chase 239

Powell, Hosken 156, 158, 160–162, 244

Presley, Jimmy 150, 168–171

Pugh, Garfield 92

Putman, Randy 167, 174

R

Ramsey, Mendel 78

Ratenski, Ted 77

Red, White and Blue Tour 182

Renfroe, Dalton "Dabo" 109, 125, 127

Renfroe, Marshall 105–107, 127

Rickey, Branch 56, 68, 80–83, 86, 93, 97, 144

Riggleman, Jim 149, 245, 248

Ripken, Cal, Sr. 114–116

Rivera, Jim 95, 109

Robinson, Bobby 42

Robinson, Jackie 24, 42, 68, 83, 93

Robinson, Wilbert 40

Rochester Tribe 42

Rodriguez, Freddy 85

Rodriguez, Henry 246, 248

Rogovin, Saul 84

Roper, Henry 136

Rosa, Wilkin De La 11

Rose, Pete 117, 164, 173

Ross, Lou 98

Rounders 25

Ruark, Jim 78

Ruel, Muddy 53

Ruffing, Red 53

Russell, Addison 247

Ruth, Babe 32, 43, 51, 52, 54

Ryan, Jack 25, 54

S

Sadler, Billy 119, 139, 196, 203, 225–228
Sain, Johnny 76, 77, 78, 84
Salmon, Brad 199, 230–231
San Carlos Hotel 56, 62
San Diego Padres 206
San Francisco Giants 72, 119, 171, 178,
    180, 181, 206, 225
Saucier, Frank 98, 99
Saucier, Kevin 10, 95, 119, 140, 144, 147,
    153, 156, 162–165, 178, 244, 247
Saucier's Dugout 164
Saufley Field 73, 76, 99
Scarritt, Russ 52–55, 56, 112, 196
Schacht, Al 66
Schuda, Jim 117
Schulman, Howard 127
Scott, Minor 86, 88
Seattle Mariners 154, 168, 173, 208, 241,
    243
Seattle Pilots 123
Seibert, Mac 167, 232–234, 247
Sellergren, Willard 74
Seminoles 10, 99
Seville Square 10, 13–16
Shawkey, Bob 43
Showalter, Buck 102, 104, 150, 156–159,
    160, 170, 176, 244, 248
Shugart, Dan 181
Simmons, Chip 241
Sisler, George 48, 82
Smith, Emmitt 124, 171
Smith, Morton 96
Smith, P.J. 109
Snappers 30–31
Snow, Michelle 124
Southeastern League 45, 46, 49, 50, 53, 56,
    62, 66, 68, 72, 78, 84, 86, 88, 95,
    96, 102, 116, 201, 208, 211, 217
Southern Association 25, 28, 29, 35, 59,
    72, 87, 88, 96, 99, 133, 143
Southern Interstate League 24
Southern League 18, 20, 21, 26, 29, 70,
    133, 150, 183, 240, 247
Southwestern Baseball League 182, 183
Spahn, Warren 84, 141
Spalding, Albert 16
Speaker, Tris 25
Spearman Brewing Company 113

Spooner, Jim 166, 211–212, 233, 241
Spooneybarger, Tim 199, 203–205, 228
Spruell Memorial Cemetery 125
Stabler, Kenny 136
Staubach, Roger 108
Stengel, Casey 29, 30, 41, 75, 240
Stepanovich, George 114
St. John's Cemetery 9, 55
St. Louis Browns 18, 48, 57, 72, 80, 98,
    110, 111, 143
St. Louis Cardinals 20, 35, 57, 71, 80, 85,
    93, 107, 109, 116, 132, 160, 166,
    190, 228, 237
St. Michael's Cemetery 9
Stoviak, Ray 74, 75, 76
Studer, Quint 181, 197, 202, 210, 213, 215,
    217, 220, 221, 223, 236, 238, 239,
    240, 245
Sunday, Billy 16–18
Susko, Pete 46, 48
Sutton, Don 12, 95, 109, 125, 130, 133,
    135–137, 150, 156, 164, 218, 231

T

Tampa Bay Devil Rays 209, 213, 219, 233
Tate High School 99, 116, 124, 130, 133,
    135, 144, 160, 166, 167, 173, 174,
    176, 185, 186, 199, 222, 230, 232,
    233
Tebbetts, Birdie 84
Terry, Bill 55, 56
Terry Wayne East Park 69
Terwilliger, Wayne 126–130, 235
Texas Rangers 72, 127, 134, 151, 206, 211,
    237
Thompson, Charles 93
Thorpe, Bob 87, 88
Tincup, Ben 41
Toledo Mud Hens 32, 71, 77
Toronto Blue Jays 13, 155, 156, 161, 183,
    188
Townsend, Leo 30, 31
Tremark, Nick 67, 74–76
Tutwiler, Elmer 48, 49
Twilight League 49
Twogood, Forrest 71, 72

U

University of West Florida 113, 166, 171, 173, 176, 177, 184, 197, 198, 203, 208, 211, 212, 213, 216, 220, 228, 237, 241, 242
U.S. Navy Baseball Club 182

V

Vance, Dazzy 41, 75, 85
Vander Meer, Johnny 117
Veeck, Bill 76, 98–99, 221
Veeck, Mike 223, 244
Vickery, Bill 109
Vickery, Lou 109
Vostry, Bob 117

W

Walker, Frederick "Mysterious" 37, 38
Walker, Harry 62, 63, 99, 167
Walters, P.J. 237
Warringtons 23, 25
Washington High School 112, 200, 201, 205
Washington Senators 84, 107, 109, 117, 122, 123, 127, 128, 129, 130
Waters, Barney 99
Waters, Fred 116–119, 120, 122, 127, 128, 131, 141, 143, 144, 145, 147, 149, 150, 154, 160, 162, 167, 175, 177
Weathers, Arthur Lee 90
Weathers, Charles 95, 96
Weaver, Frank "Buck" 78, 85, 112
Webb, Earl 53
Webb, John 187, 196, 199, 218–220
Wells, Jake 18, 20, 21
Werley, George 114
West Florida High School 237
West, Lefty 72
Wheat, Zack 25, 41
Whiten, Mark 12, 173, 182, 187, 188–191
Whiting Field 73, 76, 78, 85
Williams, Davey 87, 88
Williams, Emory 92
Williams, Ray 96
Williams, Ted 67, 75, 76, 78, 79–80, 115, 120–121, 127, 213
Wilson, Archie 122, 126

Wilson, Neb 86–89, 95, 96, 102, 103, 110, 114, 248
Winkleman, Albert 31
Wolff, Miles 218, 236, 239
Woodham High School 160, 178, 211
Wood, Jake 224
Woodruff, Tommy 70
World Series 10, 20, 22, 30, 32, 33, 41, 48, 50, 59, 76, 80, 109, 120, 131, 132, 137, 141, 156, 163, 164, 176, 179, 205, 214, 215, 229
Wright, Ken 139–143
Wynn, Early 109, 156

ABOUT THE AUTHOR

S cott Brown, a transplanted native of Pensacola, Florida, is the president of the Mordecai Brown Legacy Foundation. He is also the co-author of *Three Finger: The Mordecai Brown Story* and has been featured in numerous articles surrounding the history of America's pastime. Scott serves as the international director of the Mordecai Brown School of Baseball, while also mentoring young athletes toward personal excellence and goal achievement. He is a member of the Society for American Baseball Research and the Major League Baseball Players Alumni Association, as well as a life member of the Old Timers Baseball Association of Chicago, Minor League Baseball Alumni Association and the Association of Professional Baseball Players of America.